Women: Models of Liberation

Marie Anne Mayeski

Sheed & Ward

Sheed & Ward™ is a service of National Catholic Reporter
Publishing Company, Inc.

Library of Congress Catalog Card Number: 87-62399

ISBN: 1-55612-086-9

Published by: Sheed & Ward
115 E. Armour Blvd. P.O. Box 419492
Kansas City, MO 64141-6492

To order, call: (800) 333-7373

282.082
Mary

Contents

Dedication:

To some of my own personal models,
Mary Friedman, Mary Cominski and Florence
Adamczyk—
mothers and teachers.

Acknowledgements

Though the finished work, with all its flaws, is my own responsibility, it would not have come to be without the help and support of many friends and colleagues.

I must thank, first of all, the staff of the Von der Ahe Library of Loyola Marymount University. Though the entire staff was unfailingly helpful, Tom Carter, Tony Amodeo, Doris Dunn and Christine Anderson earn particular thanks. Their willingness to utilize computer search capabilities and to exploit the Inter-library Loan facilities stretched the small boundaries of the Von der Ahe holdings and brought me many helpful resources.

The Research Committee of the University, our Academic Vice-President, Fr. Al Koppes and our Dean, Fr. Anthony Brzoska graciously allowed me summer research money to help in the initial stages of the work.

The Bennetts, Charlene and Dick, took me into their home in Paris; their hospitality and their enthusiasm for my work on Dhuoda made my weeks at the Bibliothèque Nationale an experience in christian friendship as well as scholarship. Thanks to them and to Josie Broehm whose letter was an alchemist's stone that transformed an introduction into an invitation.

Two LMU graduates, Trisha Crissman and Lorie Phelps, joined Maggi Lambert of our university staff in the tedious work of transcribing the original texts. Lorie's expertise with my computer saved my sanity on a number of occasions.

Various colleagues read the manuscript, in bits and pieces, at various stages of development. Sharon Locy, Michael Downey,

Tom Rausch, Mary Milligan, and Paul Ford, each gave helpful suggestions as well as encouragement. They and the rest of the faculty at Loyola Marymount University are a continuing challenge to me in their scholarly endeavors and their friendly courtesy. My thanks to them all.

Introduction

Women's experience of themselves in the church has been, for some time, both ambiguous and ambivalent. Many have continued to find themselves nourished by the abundance of grace and the richness of the tradition that they find within the community of faith. Others find themselves at serious odds with the community, cut off by a continued rejection of their own gifts, desires and experiences. Many women have formed bonds of kinship across denominational lines, the historical differences between the churches no longer as important to them as their common experience of oppression. Others find support for their spiritual hopes and development only outside all traditional institutions. Older women find themselves questioning positions they have accepted uncritically for most of their lives. Younger women search for an identity, steering an uneasy passage between the images of woman in their professional lives and those that are operative within the church. They consider the labels "feminist" and "christian" and wonder whether the two words together are oxymoronic.

There is no easy way out of the confusion and a resolution of the tensions is not likely to come soon. Among the resources which all christian women have, however, is the legacy of history, the experience of women who have struggled with some of these tensions in the past, though they may have labelled them differently. The women who have gone before us in the community of faith have had their own struggle for liberation. Like all christians, they knew the imprisonment of sin and sought to be free of it. As the community of faith began to work out the political and social implications of the gospel, many of these women sought also to secure their own liberation from the oppression of the social order by appeal to the spiritual freedom won for all by Christ. As the tradition developed, they continued to speak out, implicitly or explicitly, for total liberation—from sin and oppression—not just for themselves, but for all. Rarely were they fully heard, but their voices remain; some have been models and mentors for centuries. They are being reclaimed and rediscovered today by many concerned for the renewal of the church and the liberation of the human family.

In *Transforming Grace: Christian Tradition and Women's Experience,* Anne Carr outlines the three tasks of the Christian feminist agenda.[1] The first task is to critique the past from the point of view of feminine experience. The second is to rediscover the history of christian women, for the most part lost through both circumstance and the male bias of historians. The third task is to reconstruct a christian theology and the categories by which theology is done so that they include women's experience and wisdom. All of this is not simply the work and concern of acknowledged feminists. Everyone in the christian community has a stake in assuring that the Church of Christ be illuminated by the widest and deepest possible understanding of christian truth. Nor are these three tasks discrete: the history of christian women, as it is being reconstructed, contains much evidence by which past and present may be judged. It also contains the possibilities for a new, inclusive vision by which the church might understand herself and be led in new paths.

The texts collected in this anthology are a modest contribution to the recovery of women's history. They represent a handful of women who left a written record of their feelings, concerns, spiritual insights and activities. Texts have always been important to the christian tradition; the general neglect of texts by women is symptomatic of the suppression of women's history and it is in hopes of correcting the imbalance that these writings are gathered here.

In choosing texts, I looked for variety: personal narrative, letters, treatises, journals, essays. Together they provide a sense of the richness to be found in women's writings. This means, however, that there is considerable difference in length between the selections. I hope that all are long enough to provide the reader with a real taste for the woman behind the writing; in some instances this seemed to require somewhat longer pieces, especially when the writing was less formal and therefore less cohesive. Another criterion for selection was diversity in the activities and backgrounds of the authors: both single and married women; lay and religious; living public lives or quiet personal ones, in classical, medieval and modern times, whatever their state or age, I wanted women to speak for themselves.

I also wanted to use writings that were generally less well-known. Some of the women represented were public figures in their own day and those singled out for sainthood by the Roman Catholic Church have had a popular following. Perpetua was honored because of her political and personal courage. She braved both the Emperor's and her father's wrath, surrendered her most intimate bonds with her family and displayed her courage as a public witness to Christ in the arena of martyrdom. But even Catholics who prayed to her in one of the centuries-old Eucharistic prayers did not often know, much less read, her personal account of her time in prison. Heloise was celebrated in popular song at the time of her romance with Abelard and that romance continues to engross fiction writers and playwrights. Few know her, however, for her literary and theological skills. The letter included here reflects both her passion and her learning. Teresa of Avila, long respected for her mystical writings and her sanctity, is represented by selected letters. She numbered the socially and politically powerful among her acquaintances and, through her correspondence, brought her good sense and personal influence to bear on the social and political problems of her day, especially on the reform of religious orders. Sarah Grimke published her own feminist pieces at the time they were written, but like other examples of feminine political writing, they fell through the cracks of historical attention and are not yet widely known.

There are also women writers (undoubtedly many more than recorded history leads us to believe) who lived in a smaller, private world, yet whose fidelity to their gifts led them to commit themselves to writing. They too have an important place in this volume. Dhuoda of Septimania was a noble wife and mother relegated by her husband to a medieval walled city and the care of its Archbishop in the ninth century; she overcame many obstacles to become a writer, teacher and counselor for her son. Julian of Norwich, encompassed within her narrow anchorite's cell, became a spiritual director and theologian even while the Inquisition was growing ever more suspicious of teachers who dared to instruct on the basis of their personal religious experience (especially if these teachers were women). For these, writing itself was a courageous, even radical act. Religious teaching had been closed to them by the church's fiat, while a literary education was difficult and rare. By taking pen in hand and writing authoritatively, they challenged the stereotypes and assumptions of their day.

Blandina Segale, S.C., like many another nineteenth century Catholic Sister, wrote almost accidentally and certainly conventionally; in spite of the publication of her journal, she is virtually unknown. It is her daily life that challenges the traditional religious ideology of women. Autonomous, resourceful, and courageous, she acted out a new theology of church almost a hundred years before that theology was discussed and proclaimed. Similarly, it was not the fact that Caryll Houselander wrote that was radical but the sanity and holiness she wrested from a life that almost broke her spirit and her balance. No single piece of her writing totally represents her ultimate balance but all of them reveal her sanity and when she speaks of suffering she speaks with the eloquence of experience.

Her behavior was considered idiosyncratic, even bizarre by her contemporaries, but she integrates her rich mystical and contemplative life into a life of ordinary action and commitment to others. Popular in a certain Catholic milieu of the 1950s, Houselander's work fell into neglect after Vatican II. Possibly she came to seem tame and old-fashioned, especially in the reforming fervor that followed the Council. A re-examination shows, I believe, that she enunciated a theme important to both feminism and continual christian reform: that spirituality is at the heart of all reform and must be rooted in a firm fidelity to one's own unique self.

Ultimately I wanted to introduce to a wider reading public some women whom I found interesting and attractive and who had a particular connection to the experience of women today. Each of the following chapters contains, therefore, an introduction to the author as well as to her social and intellectual context. There is also a general outline of the possibilities for a feminist reading of the text. The interpretation given in the introduction is not meant to persuade readers to a particular position or to close off other possible interpretations; it is merely meant to illuminate the text of the author herself which follows and to provoke questions in the mind of the reader. Then follow some suggestions for discussion and activities which I hope will allow the reader to appropriate the author's work.

Personal taste and bias are operative here, to be sure, as is a particular method of imaginative, as well as historical reconstruction. Texts can only speak to us insofar as we are open to new meanings. They only respond to the questions which we pose. When we ask "What is this woman saying?" we must be prepared to listen to her on her own terms but also with new questions that are our own. We must find out as much as we can about the context in which she lived and wrote so that we can understand her language and her frame of reference. But we must also presume a continuity between the experience of others and our own. We must enter imaginatively into her world, a new world, but we must bring along our own world, our own questions. These women were not feminists, in the contemporary meaning of the word; to name them such would be anachronism. But insofar as today's feminist questions come from an experience which is continuous with that of women in the past, we can ask our questions and expect an answer which is not forced into the text but, rather, waiting there for discovery.

This demands imagination as well as historical and exegetical study. It is through the imagination that other lives and other times come alive, take on concrete reality and become formative as well as informative. Without the texture which imagination can provide, the christian tradition is in danger of becoming abstract and a norm external to our own experience. The imagination contains resources for reform, both institutional and personal. It is through the imagination that we envision possibilities that are new, within the texts and within ourselves. When we "try on" these new possibilities in our collective or individual imaginations, we accustom ourselves to new modes of behavior and become confident that they are realistic and achievable. Wedded to a scholarly attention to the text, its exegesis and historical context, the imagination can enable us to read these women into a new, contemporary existence where they may become models and mentors, collaborators and colleagues, in the project of our own personal liberation and the re-envisioning of the church.

Note

1. San Francisco: Harper and Row, Publishers, 1988, pp. 7-8.

1.

"Not Daughter but Domina": Perpetua's Account of Her Martyrdom

In the month of March, in the year 202 or 203, a small group of newly-baptized Christians were led into the arena at Carthage where they were forced to confront wild beasts before being put to death by the sword. In the group were two young women, Vibia Perpetua, the daughter of a wealthy provincial and her slave, Felicitas. Both of these women were mothers of young children and indeed Felicitas had delivered her infant daughter only three days before her death. This death spectacle was, therefore, especially poignant. Unknown to the spectators, Perpetua had left an account of her experiences while in prison and one of the eyewitnesses there in the arena later took her memoirs, connected them to a similar narrative of Saturus (imprisoned with her) and framed both with an introduction and conclusion to compose the piece which has come down to us under the title of *The Passion of Perpetua and Felicity*.[1]

The editor was long believed to be Tertullian, an early Christian theologian who later became a Montanist.[2] If that tradition

1

is correct, Tertullian was to write, ironically, not only the laudatory introduction to Perpetua's narrative, but some of the representative damning comments about the nature of women and women's role in the church. Thus he serves as a good example of the tension within the church of his time over the place and the valuation of women. On the one hand, there was a continual public recognition of the heroic virtue of individual women, especially the martyrs. On the other, a growing body of literature began to accumulate in which women were increasingly indicted as the source of sin in the world and society and were also held to be inferior to men by nature and, therefore, by God's creative will.

There is evidence to support the idea that there was some transition in the status of women within the text of the New Testament itself. In the earliest days of the church, women seem to have had a somewhat more equal place in the community and its ministry than they would have as restraints were later placed upon their activities, especially as these restraints were reinforced and justified by an increasingly negative theological attitude.[3] Correspondingly, from the second century through the fifth, while the major theological work was being done on the central doctrines of Christian faith, a body of primarily negative teaching on women was also slowly taking shape. The teaching was nuanced, taking account of the courage and virtue of particular women and allowing in different ways for some participation in the official ministry of the church. In the *Constitution of the Holy Apostles,* for example, we are given a prayer for the ordination of a deaconess and a description of her ministry to women in the rite of Baptism and in other needs of women at home.[4] But the teaching was, in sum, rigidly patriarchal: in it, sexuality was considered the key to understanding women's place in the world and their role in the drama of salvation. The teaching generally denigrated women's intellect and depicted them as sexually much more vulnerable than men to the persuasions of the devil. These male theologians usually advised, in consequence, that salvation for women consisted in submission to male authority and, whenever possible, in sexual abstinence.

In an anthology of early theological writings entitled *Women in the Early Church,* Elizabeth A. Clark has identified two principal themes in the theology of women during these formative centuries.[5] The first theme is the natural subjection of woman to man by God's choice at the time of creation. A second and related theme is the sexual weakness of women and their sexual power over men which, together, brought about the Fall and all subsequent suffering for the human family. These two foundational ideas were used to justify all the restrictions placed on women in marriage, society and the church. Woman's place in social institutions, carefully delineated and narrowly circumscribed, was designed, on the one hand, to fulfill and enact God's will in her regard and, on the other, to protect woman from herself and men from her.

Other themes found within the early writings are really corollaries of these first two. Since sexuality is seen as the cause of woman's weakness and subordination, she can only achieve a wider role within the Christian community through celibacy.[6] Virgins and widows are given pride of place: they alone have any liturgical functions to perform and gradually they are replaced by consecrated and cloistered virgins. Widows continue to be honored as the "altars of God" because of their prayer and service, but admonitions of sexual restraint and prohibitions designed to test their sexual self-discipline are many. This citation from the *Didascalia Apostolorum* is representative: "If her husband has been long dead, she may be appointed without delay. But if her husband has died recently, she shall not be trusted; even if she is aged she must be tested by time; for often the passions grow old in those who yield to them."[7] Even celibate women who were given limited roles in the church were rigidly denied the power to teach. It would seem that even total sexual abstinence could not restore the power to woman's intellect that had been weakened through her sexual nature; the telling argument, oft repeated, was that of the author of 1 Timothy who noted that, when woman did have an opportunity to teach, in the Garden of Eden, the results were disasterous.

But extraordinary women did win recognition in the thought and writings of these early centuries. Martyrs, above all, were praised; having achieved the heights of identification with Christ, they were the earliest models of the Christian life. Other women, too, were honored in writing by the men whose lives they had influenced. Augustine described the virtue and persuasive power of Monica, his mother. Gregory of Nyssa wrote a biography of his sister, Macrina the Younger, and acknowledged her competence as a theologian. Olympias was the confidante of John Chrysostom and the recipient of many of his letters. Even Saint Jerome, perhaps the most misogynist of the early male writers, praised several of the holy women he knew in letters and eulogies.[8] Women figure as mentors as well as models in these accounts, thus denying in the restrictions against teaching placed on them in theory. As friend and patron of the early theologians, women played their role primarily behind the scenes (as in all the centuries to come), but they were publicly honored and remembered in the writings of the men they had befriended.

It is easy to see that, in its teaching on women, the Christian community could not resolve a critical inner ambiguity. Nor could it free itself from the pervasive patriarchy of its roots and its social context. In its exegesis of the *Genesis* creation stories, the early church relied heavily on the rabbinic tradition. When the strongly eschatological emphasis of the early days was gradually replaced by a need for order and for the good opinion of contemporary pagans, church leaders probed models of community and authority in the cultures which surrounded them. First they looked to the Jewish religion to which they still felt deeply related and, ultimately, to the Greco-Roman world in which they would flourish. For the first few centuries of Christian history, then, only extraordinary women would be able to escape from the restrictions that kept their religious activity primarily within the private, domestic sphere and prevented their own history from being recorded. Such an extraordinary woman was Perpetua of Carthage.

As noted above, Perpetua left an account of the circumstances of her imprisonment which was later subsumed into a longer piece. It is an extraordinarily rich text. Perpetua not only narrates the external story but also explores the development of her own thought and feelings about the ordeal she was facing. The account became a very important text in the early church; it played a formative role in the early teaching on martyrdom and Perpetua's popularity grew accordingly. By the third or fourth century, a basilica was built to Perpetua's memory in Carthage[9] and several of Augustine's sermons for her feast day (March 7) record his knowledge of the text and his respect for Perpetua. By the third century, her name was invoked, along with that of her slave, Felicitas, in the Eucharistic prayer known as the Roman Canon which would be the solemn prayer of praise and thanksgiving of Christians for centuries to come. Her text is the first known written document by a woman in Christian history.

In this very early text we find the story of a woman's struggle with all the classical tensions in her life. There is the record of Perpetua's struggle between her desire to please her father and her conviction that she must live up to her own conscience. Intertwined with this dilemma is Perpetua's sense of responsibility for her child and the guilt engendered when she realizes that her public witness to Christian truth will deprive her infant son of his mother. Finally, there is evidence of real fear, less of the physical pain to come, than of her weakness in confronting it. It is the manner in which Perpetua deals with these tensions and the candor with which she narrates the stages of her intellectual and affective development that engages the interest of women today and creates a sense of empathy with her.

Perpetua's father is the focal point of the first part of the narrative. Her conflict with him seems to provoke great turmoil and creates a need for self-justification. In a series of visits he proposes a wide range of arguments, expressed with great emotional intensity, designed to recall her to obedience. He pleads his old age and the comfort which he needs from her. He reminds her of his past generosity. He lists her obligations to her family: the grief she will cause those who love her as well as the political retribution she will provoke. The family reputation will suffer if she is condemned—no small loss in Roman society—and they will seemingly lose some of their civil liberties as well as prestige. These are powerful arguments for Perpetua—several times she repeats the sad refrain 'I grieved for him,' 'I mourned'—and she records her relief when her father's visit is over. His arguments are made even more powerful still by his dramatic action: ostensibly putting himself at her mercy he kneels before her and calls her "Domina" ("Lady"). The pattern of arguments and the paternal strategy are all too familiar. What adult woman has not experienced them, even if in circumstances less dramatic?

When his arguments fail, Perpetua's father resorts to action. After Perpetua and her companions are sentenced and returned to prison, her father refuses to return her infant son to her. A two-fold concern for her son has been evident from the beginning of her narrative. She is, at first, concerned for his physical well-being; in prison with her, he is at risk from the darkness, bad air and the difficulty he experiences in nursing. But most of all, she is concerned for his future. Perpetua's son is a potent symbol of the family relationships which have a legitimate claim upon her and which, if they are not outweighed by a genuinely higher claim, must be determinative of her behavior. Intellectually, Perpetua finds a satisfying answer to her dilemma: there is indeed a higher claim upon her and she explicates it in terms of her name. She is called Christian, she affirms, and she must live up to her name. Her father has appealed to Perpetua's *piety,* the loyalty to family which was foundational to Roman ethical living and was represented by the family name. Perpetua's affirmation of her new name represents the higher form of piety to which she obligates herself.

But an intellectual answer neither convinces her father nor heals her inner conflict. Unreconciled to the end, her father remains a source of torment for her. He is "wasted and worn," he tears out his hair and curses his life, and Perpetua, in great emotional conflict "grieved because of his old age" (#19).* Before Perpetua can be free to give herself in martyrdom, the emotional conflict which she reveals with great candor must be resolved. This happens primarily through a sequence of dreams or visions.[10] In these dream-visions the Christian doctrines in which she is to find consolation "take on flesh," as it were, through the power of the imagination. She envisions the way in which her family will be sustained without her; she imagines herself succeeding at the tremendous challenge of the arena. There is even some suggestion that she "sees" a kind of reconciliation with her father. After each of these visions, she "wakes up" refreshed and strengthened for the next stage of the ordeal, having been healed of anxieties which debilitate, even paralyze.[11]

The sequence of dream-visions has an internal structure: the first and fourth visions are concerned with the drama of the arena. In between are two visions which primarily focus on her family obligations; they are visions of her brother, Dinocrates, who had died some years before. But no dream is completely self-contained; fear of her own weakness and self-doubt about her decision tie the dreams together even as they are linked by symbols and imaginative associations.

In the first vision (#9), Perpetua anticipates the challenge which is ahead of her. She pictures that challenge as an enor-

*Numbers in parentheses refer to the primary text, that begins on page 13.

mous ladder, stretching from earth to heaven, at the summit of which is a garden, perhaps the Garden of Paradise transformed as in the *Apocalypse,* for it is full of people dressed in shining white. The serpent, biblical symbol of evil, is not, however, in the garden but at the foot of the ladder where he is the obstacle to her ascent. Even here, at the beginning of her journey to courage, she has some confidence in herself. She senses the serpent is almost afraid of her and she speaks to Saturus, one of her fellow prisoners preceding her on the ladder with the confidence that Christ will preserve her in her ascent. Perpetua reaches the garden where she encounters a male figure who combines aspects of the Good Shepherd (Christ) and of her father as well. She mentions his white hair, recalling her father's appeal to her sympathy. She is nourished by this father/Good Shepherd figure: he gives her cheese from the sheep he is milking and the cheese tastes "indefinable and sweet," words which vaguely suggest the Eucharist.[12] Most of all, the male figure approves of her: "Welcome, my child." It is both an assurance of ultimate victory and the word of approval from her father that she needs to go on.

The two dream-visions of Dinocrates are intimately linked; they occur after Perpetua has experienced a definitive separation from her family—her father has been expelled from the martyrs' hearing and has subsequently refused to send her infant son back to her in prison. She is struggling with the emotional consequences of choosing her fidelity to Christ over her responsibilities to her family. In each, the scene is the same: Dinocrates, her brother who died from a facial cancer some years before, is situated near a pool of water. In the first dream, he is dirty, surrounded by crowds and darkness, still bearing the open wound on his face; he is unable to drink from the pool because the rim is too high (#16). Perpetua realizes that her brother is struggling and is suddenly convinced that her prayers can help. "Perpetua has lost her child, but in her inner life she encounters another child (perhaps an aspect of herself) whom she can help."[13] In the second vision, after a period of daily prayer on her part, Dinocrates is clean and refreshed, the wound has become a scar and the boy is drinking incessantly, not only from the pool but from a golden bowl hung above it (#18).

The imagery here is somewhat classical: the first scene recalls literary descriptions of Hades and there is an echo of the Tantulus story in Dinocrates' inability to drink from the pool. But there are liturgical elements too, especially in the golden bowl and the sense that the water is "living water." What Perpetua receives from the two visions is an imaginative and intuitive assurance that in the spiritual realm to which she is committing herself she can continue to effect the well-being of her family through a kind of transfer of spiritual riches. Her anxiety is slowly being alleviated. She receives another sign by way of confirmation: when her son is suddenly taken away from her, her breasts suffer none of the discomfort associated with weaning (#15). Thus she knows, through physical sign and the assurance of her dreams that she is being freed for her public act of faith and worship in the arena.

The final vision returns to her concern for the coming ordeal. The imagery and feelings of this last experience are a mixture of agony feared and victory anticipated. The way to the arena (as she sees it in her imagination) is "rocky and winding" (#20); in the arena there is "an Egyptian, horrible to look at" (#20) and there is an actual combat (#21). On the other hand, the combat is described in terms of a wrestling match, she has handsome, young supporters and during the combat she floats above the ground in a sudden surge of power. The judge of the contest is the "fencing master" (#20), more a god-figure than an imperial one: he towers above the arena, wears purple, gold and silver and is ready to give Perpetua the emblem of victory—"a green branch on which were golden apples" (#20).

As in the visions of Dinocrates, liturgical elements pervade the final vision. It is the deacon, the ordinary minister of baptism, who leads her to the arena, suggesting that initiation into the community was, inevitably, a commitment to public witness. The anointing with oil, recalling the actual practice of the games, alludes also to the ritual of baptism and her victory is greeted with jubilant singing, suggesting hymns. All of this seems to hint at a conviction that Perpetua's role in the Christian community is essentially a public one. Her baptism is a call to public witness and the physical suffering that such a witness requires is transformed in her imagination into an athletic competition in which she clearly anticipates victory. Today's reader can see in her narrative of this vision the enactment of a public ritual in which Perpetua herself is both the chief sacrifice and the one who offers the sacrifice.[14]

One last element in the final dream-vision requires comment. As Perpetua is preparing for her struggle against the Egyptian she sees herself stripped naked and she becomes a man (#20). One cannot help but wonder what this transformation means to Perpetua; several interpretations have been suggested. It may be a kind of imaginative modesty in which her psyche protects her physical nakedness by transforming her into a man for whom the nakedness of the games was considered appropriate. On the other hand, it may be an acknowledgement that her public role requires that she become a man. Jungian interpretors might suggest that she is becoming androgynous by assuming a male body and a male role, thus attaining a kind of maturity through the complementary side of herself.[16] Is she acting out the patriarchal assumption that her femininity must be overcome before she can be a victor in the games? Or is the masculinity here just a symbol of strength available to her psyche? Whatever the answer—and it is undoubtedly complex—it seems unlikely that Perpetua is rejecting her sexual identity here. The narrative has been an unusually feminine one with its central concerns for her child and for her relationship with her father. There is absolutely no hint of self-hatred discernible in any of the previous dreams or discussions; there is no reason to posit it here.

In her own narrative, Perpetua focuses primarily on her own inner development as she moves to martyrdom. Yet she also records, almost in passing, the response of others to her. She notes that the director of the prison has respect for the power of the Christian prisoners and shows them honor (#19). The editor's account completes the picture and shows us a Perpetua who is bold and inspiring in her leadership, courageous in her death. Indeed, he affirms that he is finishing the story in order to fulfill Perpetua's sacred trust. According to him, she challenges the prison authorities with wit and temper, refusing to wear the dress of pagan ritual as required. She goes joyfully to the arena, a real "darling of God" with lively step and "brightly flashing eyes." She enters the arena, already singing psalms of victory as if to anticipate the end of her final vision and, when the beasts are brought in and the combat begins, Perpetua acquits herself not only with bravery but also with dignity, compassion and something which can only be called "flair." She fixes her hair so that she might not appear to mourn in the moment of victory and Petroff calls her request for a hairpin a gesture that is

> typical of that flair for the dramatic that Perpetua demonstrated in her first confrontation with her father. To a world in which a married woman with loosened hair and torn clothing was the image of grief, where females were the ritual mourners for the dead, Perpetua's gesture denies both grief and death. Her own hand, guiding the sword of the unskilled executioner is consonant with this reading ....[16]

But our last glimpse of Perpetua is tempered by an image more tender, more truly heroic in its gentleness. Perpetua helps Felicitas, her slave in Roman law but her sister in Christ, to her feet and, in almost the final image with which the editor of *The Passion* leaves us, joins in the kiss of peace. The compassion of the martyrs for one another, especially in the face of the violence which surrounds them, transforms the situation. It is the love of the martyrs, after all, and not their courage which makes the barbaric game into an agapic liturgical act. As the eye witness turned editor says: "... they kissed each other so that their martyrdom would be completely perfected by the rite of the kiss of peace" (#37).

The Passion of Perpetua and Felicity is compelling on several levels. In it we see a very concrete and individual woman working out the tensions of her Christian life with candor and feeling. We find someone, not unlike ourselves, who must search within *her own inner resources* to solve dilemmas and balance moral and emotional demands. The rules of social conduct do not help her and she records no clerical intervention by which she is enlightened. It is her own dreams and visions that lead her to wholeness and to her ultimate victory. The narrow ladder in the first dream is telling: since only one person at a time can climb it, it bespeaks the essentially personal decision Perpetua must make. She has only her own religious experience to rely on and she trusts it; she says, "I...knew I could speak with the Lord, whose great favors I had already experienced..." (#8).

At the same time, we see that Perpetua understands her struggle as essentially communal and public. The results of her decision, individual and even lonely as it is, are the leadership she exercises among her companions, the inspiration she offers to all those who witness and the public liturgy of martyrdom she offers, a true second baptism/Eucharist in which she is both priest and offering. Against a background of growing church teaching, in which woman's weakness is emphasized and her subordinate place in society and church justified, Perpetua's words and actions challenge all the stereotypes.

The Martyrdom Of Perpetua[17]

1. If instances of ancient faith which both testified to the grace of God and edified persons were written expressly for God's

honor and humans' encouragement, why shouldn't recent events be similarly recorded for those same purposes? For these events will likewise become part of the past and vital to posterity, in spite of the fact that contemporary esteem for antiquity tends to minimize their value. And those who maintain that there is a single manifestation of the one Holy Spirit throughout the ages ought to consider that since a fullness of grace has been decreed for the last days of the world these recent events should be considered of greater value because of their proximity to those days. For "In the last days," says the Lord, "I shall diffuse my prophesy; the young shall see visions, and the old shall dream dreams."

2. Just as we valued those prophecies so we acknowledge and reverence the new visions which were promised. And we consider the other powers of the Holy Spirit to be instruments of the Church to which that same Spirit was sent to administer all gifts to all people, just as the Lord allotted. For this reason we deem it necessary to disseminate the written account for the glory of God, lest anyone with a weak or despairing faith might think that supernatural faith prevailed solely among the ancients who were honored either by their experience of martyrdom or visions. For God always fulfills what he promises, either as proof to non-believers or as an added grace to believers.

3. And so, brothers and dear ones, we share with you those things which we have heard and touched with our hands, so that those of you who were eye witnesses of these deeds may be reminded of the glory of the Lord, and those of you now learning of it through this narration may associate yourselves with the holy martyrs and, through them, with the Lord Jesus Christ to whom there is glory and honor forever. Amen.

4. Arrested were some young catechumens; Revocatus and Felicitas (both servants), Saturninus, Secundulus, and Vibia Perpetua, a young married woman about twenty years old, of good family and upbringing. She had a father, mother, two brothers

(one was a catechumen like herself), and an infant son at the breast. The following account of her martyrdom is her own, a record in her own words of her perceptions of the event.

5. While I was still with the police authorities (she said) my father out of love for me tried to dissuade me from my resolution. "Father," I said, "do you see here, for example, this vase, or pitcher, or whatever it is?" "I see it," he said. "Can it be named anything else than what it really is?" I asked, and he said, "No." "So I also cannot be called anything else than what I am, a Christian." Enraged by my words my father came at me as though to tear out my eyes. He only annoyed me, but he left, overpowered by his diabolical arguments.

6. For a few days my father stayed away. I thanked the Lord and felt relieved because of my father's absence. At this time we were baptized and the Spirit instructed me not to request anything from the baptismal waters except endurance of physical suffering.

7. A few days later we were imprisoned. I was terrified because never before had I experienced such darkness. What a terrible day! Because of crowded conditions and rough treatment by the solidiers the heat was unbearable. My condition was aggravated by my anxiety for my baby. Then Teritus and Pomponius, those kind deacons who were taking care of our needs, paid for us to be moved for a few hours to a better part of the prison where we might refresh ourselves. Leaving the dungeon, we all went about our own business. I nursed my child who was already weak from hunger. In my anxiety for my infant I spoke to my mother about him, tried to console my brother, and asked that they care for my son. I suffered intensely because I sensed their agony on my account. These were the trials I had to endure for many days. Then I was granted the privilege of having my son remain with me in prison. Being relieved of my anxiety and concern for the infant, I immediately regained my strength.

Suddenly the prison became my palace, and I loved being there rather than any other place.

8. Then my brother said to me, "Dear sister, you already have such a great reputation that you could ask for a vision indicating whether you will be condemned or freed." Since I knew that I could speak with the Lord, whose great favors I had already experienced, I confidently promised to do so. I said I would tell my brother about it the next day. Then I made my request and this is what I saw.

9. There was a bronze ladder of extraordinary height reaching up to heaven, but it was so narrow that only one person could ascend at a time. Every conceivable kind of iron weapon was attached to the sides of the ladder: swords, lances, hooks and daggers. If anyone climbed up carelessly or without looking upward, he or she would be mangled as the flesh adhered to the weapons. Crouching directly beneath the ladder was a monstrous dragon who threatened those climbing up and tried to frighten them from ascent.

10. Saturus went up first. Because of his concern for us he gave himself up voluntarily after we had been arrested. (He had been our source of strength but was not with us at the time of the arrest.) When we reached the top of the ladder he turned to me and said, "Perpetua, I'm waiting for you, but be careful not to be bitten by the dragon." I told him that, in the name of Jesus Christ, the dragon could not harm me. At this, the dragon slowly lowered its head as though afraid of me. Using its head as the first step, I began my ascent.

11. At the summit I saw an immense garden, in the center of which sat a tall, gray-haired man dressed like a shepherd, milking sheep. Standing around him were several thousand white-robed people. As he raised his head he noticed me and said, "Welcome, my child." Then he beckoned me to approach and gave me a small morsel of the cheese he was making. I accepted

it with cupped hands and ate it. When all those surrounding us said "Amen," I awoke, still tasting the sweet cheese. I immediately told my brother about the vision, and we both realized that we were to experience the sufferings of martyrdom. From then on we gave up having any hope in this world.

12. A few days later there was rumor that our case was to be heard. My father, completely exhausted from his anxiety, came from the city to see me, with the intention of weakening my faith. "Daughter," he said, "have pity on my gray head. Have pity on your father if I have the honor to be called father by you, if with these hands I have brought you to the prime of your life, and if I have always favored you above your brothers, do not abandon me to the reproach of men. Consider your brothers; consider your mother and your aunt; consider your son who cannot live without you. Give up your stubbornness before you destroy all of us. None of us will be able to speak freely if anything happens to you."

13. These were the things my father said out of love, kissing my hands and throwing himself at my feet. With tears he called me not daughter, but woman. I was very upset because of my father's condition. He was the only member of my family who would find no reason for joy in my suffering. I tried to comfort him saying, "Whatever God wants at this tribunal will happen, for remember that our power comes not from ourselves but from God." But utterly dejected, my father left me.

14. One day as we were eating we were suddenly rushed off for a hearing. We arrived at the forum and the news spread quickly throughout the area near the forum. A huge crowd gathered. We went up to the prisoners' platform. All the others confessed when they were questioned. When my turn came my father appeared with my son. Dragging me from the step, he begged: "Have pity on your son!"

15. Hilarion, the governor, who assumed power after the death of the proconsul Minucius Timinianus, said, "Have pity on your father's gray head; have pity on your infant son; offer sacrifice for the emperor's welfare." But I answered, "I will not." Hilarion asked, "Are you a Christian?" And I answered, "I am a Christian." And when my father persisted in his attempts to persuade me, Hilarion ordered him thrown out, and he was beaten with a rod. My father's injury hurt me as much as if I had been beaten, and I grieved because of his pathetic old age. Then the sentence was passed; all of us were condemned to the beasts. We were overjoyed as we went back to the prison cell. Since I was still nursing my child who was ordinarily in the cell with me, I quickly sent the deacon Pomponius to my father's house to ask for the baby, but my father refused to give him up. Then God saw to it that my child no longer needed my nursing, nor were my breasts inflamed. After that I was no longer tortured by my anxiety about my child or by pain in my breasts.

16. A few days later while all of us were praying, in the middle of a prayer I suddenly called out the name "Dinocrates." I was astonished since I hadn't thought about him till then. When I recalled what had happened to him I was very disturbed and decided right then that I had not only the right, but the obligation, to pray for him. So I began to pray repeatedly and to make moaning sounds to the Lord in his behalf. During that same night I had this vision: I saw Dinocrates walking away from one of many very dark places. He seemed very hot and thirsty, his face grimy and colorless. The wound on his face was just as it had been when he died. This Dinocrates was my blood brother who at the age of seven died very tragically from a cancerous disease which so disfigured his face that his death was repulsive to everyone. It was for him that I now prayed. But neither of us could reach the other because of the great distance between. In the place where Dinocrates stood was a pool filled with water, and the rim of the pool was so high that it extended far above the boy's height. Dinocrates stood on his toes as if to drink the water

but in spite of the fact that the pool was full, he could not drink because the rim was so high!

17. I realized that my brother was in trouble, but I was confident that I could help him with his problem. I prayed for him every day until we were transferred to the arena prison where we were to fight wild animals on the birthday of Geta Caesar. And I prayed day and night for him, moaning and weeping so that my petition would be granted.

18. On the day that we were kept in chains I had the following vision: I saw the same place as before, but Dinocrates was clean, well-dressed, looking refreshed. In place of the wound there was a scar, and the fountain which I had seen previously now had its rim lowered to the boy's waist. On the rim, over which water was flowing constantly, there was a golden bowl filled with water. Dinocrates walked up to it and began to drink; the bowl never emptied. And when he was no longer thirsty, he gladly went to play as children do. Then I awoke, knowing that he had been relieved of his suffering.

19. A few days passed. Pudens, the official in charge of the prison (the official who had gradually come to admire us for our persistence), admitted many prisoners to our cell so that we might mutually encourage each other. As the day of the games drew near, my father, overwhelmed with grief, came again to see me. He began to pluck out his beard and throw it on the ground. Falling on his face before me, he cursed his old age, repeating such things as would move all creation. And I grieved because of his old age.

20. The day before the battle in the arena, in a vision I saw Pomponius the deacon coming to the prison door and knocking very loudly. I went to open the gate for him. He was dressed in a loosely fitting white robe, wearing richly decorated sandals. He said to me, "Perpetua, come. We're waiting for you!" He took my hand and we began walking over extremely rocky and wind-

ing paths. When we finally arrived short of breath, at the arena, he led me to the center saying, "Don't be frightened! I'll be here to help you." He left me and I stared out over a huge crowd which watched me with apprehension. Because I knew that I had to fight with the beasts, I wondered why they hadn't yet been turned loose in the arena. Coming toward me was some type of Egyptian, horrible to look at, accompanied by fighters who were to help defeat me. Some handsome young men came forward to help and encourage me. I was stripped of my clothing, and suddenly I was a man. My assistants began to rub me with oil as was the custom before a contest, while the Egyptian was on the other side rolling in the sand. Then a certain man appeared, so tall that he towered above the amphitheater. He wore a loose purple robe with two parallel stripes across the chest; his sandals were richly decorated with gold and silver. He carried a rod like that of an athletic trainer, and a green branch on which were golden apples. He motioned for silence and said, "If this Egyptian wins, he will kill her with the sword; but if she wins, she will receive this branch." Then he withdrew.

21. We both stepped forward and began to fight with our fists. My opponent kept trying to grab my feet but I repeatedly kicked his face with my heels. I felt myself being lifted up into the air and began to strike at him as one who was no longer earth-bound. But when I saw that we were wasting time, I put my two hands together, linked my fingers, and put his head between them. As he fell on his face I stepped on his head. Then the people started to shout and my assistants started singing victory songs. I walked up to the trainer and accepted the branch. He kissed me and said, "Peace be with you, my daughter." And I triumphantly headed toward the Sanavivarian Gate. Then I woke up realizing that I would be contending not with wild animals but with the devil himself. I knew, however, that I would win. I have recorded the events which occurred up to the day before the final contest. Let anyone who wishes to record the events of the contest itself, do so.

22. The saintly Saturus also related a vision which he had and it is recorded here in his own hand. Our suffering had ended (he said), and we were being carried toward the east by four angels whose hands never touched us. And we floated upward, not in a supine position, but as though we were climbing a gentle slope. As we left the earth's atmosphere we saw a brilliant light, and I said to Perpetua who was at my side, "This is what the Lord promised us. We have received his promise."

23. And while we were being carried along by those four angels we saw a large, open space like a splendid garden landscaped with rose trees and every variety of flower. The trees were as tall as cypresses whose leaves rustled gently and incessantly. And there in that garden sanctuary were four other angels, more dazzling than the rest. And when they saw us they showed us honor, saying to the other angels in admiration, "Here they are! They have arrived."

24. And those four angels who were carrying us began trembling in awe and set us down. And we walked through a violet-strewn field where we met Jocundus, Saturninus, and Artaxius who were burned alive in that same persecution, and Quintus, also a martyr, who had died in prison. We were asking them where they had been, when the other angels said to us, "First, come this way. Go in and greet the Lord."

25. We went up to a place where the walls seemed constructed of light. At the entrance of the place stood four angels who put white robes on those who entered. We went in and heard a unified voice chanting endlessly, "Holy, holy, holy." We saw a white haired man sitting there who, in spite of his snowy white hair, had the features of a young man. His feet were not visible. On his right and left were four elderly gentlemen and behind them stood many more. As we entered we stood in amazement before the throne. Four angels supported us as we went up to kiss the aged man, and he gently stroked our faces with his hands. The other elderly men said to us, "Stand up." We rose

and gave the kiss of peace. Then they told us to enjoy ourselves. I said to Perpetua, "You have your wish." She answered, "I thank God, for although I was happy on earth, I am much happier here right now."

26. Then we went out, and before the gates we saw Optatus the bishop on the right and Aspasius the priest and teacher on the left, both looking sad as they stood there separated from each other. They knelt before us saying, "Make peace between us, for you've gone away and left us this way." But we said to them, "Aren't you our spiritual father, and our teacher? Why are you kneeling before us?" We were deeply touched and we embraced them. And Perpetua began to speak to them in Greek and we invited them into the garden beneath a rose tree. While we were talking with them, the angels said to them, "Let them refresh themselves, and if you have any dissensions among you, forgive one another." This disturbed both of them and the angels said to Optatus, "Correct your people who flock to you as though returning from the games, fighting about the different teams." It seemed to us that they wanted to close the gates, and there we began to recognize many of our friends, among whom were martyrs. We were all sustained by an indescribable fragrance which completely satisfied us. Then in my joy, I awoke.

27. The remarkable visions narrated above were those of the blessed martyrs Saturus and Perpetua, just as they put them in writing. As for Secundulus, while he was still in prison God gave him the grace of an earlier exit from this world, so that he could escape combat from the wild beasts. But his body, though not his soul, certainly felt the sword.

28. As for Felicitas, she too was touched by God's grace in the following manner. She was pregnant when she was arrested and was now in her eighth month. As the day of the contest approached she became very distressed that her martyrdom might be delayed, since the law forbade the execution of a pregnant woman. Then she would later have to shed her holy and in-

nocent blood among common criminals. Her friends in martyrdom were equally sad at the thought of abandoning such a good
friend to travel alone on the same road to hope.

29. And so, two days before the contest, united in grief they
prayed to the Lord. Immediately after the prayers her labor
pains began. Because of the additional pain natural of an eighth
month delivery, she suffered greatly during the birth, and one of
the prison guards taunted her; "If you're complaining now, what
will you do when you're thrown to the wild beasts? You didn't
think of them when you refused to sacrifice." She answered,
"Now it is I who suffer, but then another shall be in me to bear
the pain for me, since I am now suffering for him." And she gave
birth to a girl whom one of her sisters reared as her own
daughter.

30. Since the Holy Spirit has permitted, and by permitting has
willed, that the events of the contest be recorded, we have no
choice but to carry out the injunction (rather, the sacred trust) of
Perpetua, in spite of the fact that it will be an inferior addition to
the magnificent events already described. We are adding an instance of Perpetua's perseverance and lively spirit. At one time
the prisoners were being treated with unusual severity by the
commanding officer because certain deceitful men had intimated
to him that the prisoners might escape by some magic spells.
Perpetua openly challenged him; "Why don't you at least allow
us to freshen up the most noble of the condemned, since we
belong to Caesar and are about to fight on his birthday? Or isn't
it to your credit that we should appear in good condition on that
day?" The officer grimaced and blushed, then ordered that they
be treated more humanely and that her brothers and others be
allowed to visit and dine with them. By this time the prison war-
den was himself a believer.

31. On the day before the public games, as they were eating
the last meal commonly called the free meal, they tried as much
as possible to make it an *agape*. In the same spirit they were ex-

horting the people, warning them to remember the judgment of God, asking them to be witnesses to the prisoners' joy in suffering, and ridiculing the curiosity of the crowd. Saturus told them, "Won't tomorrow's view be enough for you? Why are you so eager to see something you hate? Friends today, enemies tomorrow! Take a good look so you'll recognize us on that day." Then they all left the prison amazed, and many of them began to believe.

32. The day of their victory dawned, and with joyful countenances they marched from the prison to the arena as though on their way to heaven. If there was any trembling it was from joy, not fear. Perpetua followed with quick step as a true spouse of Christ, the darling of God, her brightly flashing eyes quelling the gaze of the crowd. Felicitas too, joyful because she had safely survived child birth and was now able to participate in the contest with the wild animals, passed from one shedding of blood to another; from midwife to gladiator, about to be purified after child birth by a second baptism. As they were led through the gate they were ordered to put on different clothes; the men, those of the priests of Saturn, the women, those of the priestesses of Ceres. But the noble woman stubbornly resisted even to the end. She said, "We've come this far voluntarily in order to protect our rights, and we've pledged our lives not to recapitulate on any such matter as this. We made this agreement with you." Injustice bowed to justice and the guard conceded that they could enter the arena in their ordinary dress. Perpetua was singing victory psalms as if already crushing the head of the Egyptian. Revocatus, Saturninus and Saturus were warning the spectators, and as they came within sight of Hilarion they informed him by nods and gestures: "You condemn us; God condemns you." This so infuriated the crowds that they demanded the scourging of these men in front of the line of gladiators. But the ones so punished rejoiced in that they had obtained yet another share in the Lord's suffering.

33. Whoever said, "Ask and you shall receive," granted to these petitioners the particular death that each one chose. For whenever the martyrs were discussing among themselves their choice for death, Saturus used to say that he wished to be thrown in with all the animals so that he might wear a more glorious crown. Accordingly, at the outset of the show he was matched against a leopard but then called back; then he was mauled by a bear on the exhibition platform. Now Saturus detested nothing as much as a bear and he had already decided to die by one bite from the leopard. Consequently, when he was tied to a wild boar the gladiator who had tied the two together was pierced instead and died shortly after the games ended, while Saturus was merely dragged about. And when he was tied up on the bridge in front of the bear, the bear refused to come out of his den; and so a second time Saturus was called back unharmed.

34. For the young women the devil had readied a mad cow, an animal not usually used at these games, but selected so that the women's sex would be matched with that of the animal. After being stripped and enmeshed in nets, the women were led into the arena. How horrified the people were when they saw that one was a young girl and the other, her breasts dripping with milk, had just recently given birth to a child. Consequently both were recalled and dressed in loosely fitting gowns.

35. Perpetua was tossed first and fell on her back. She sat up, and being more concerned with her modesty than with her pain, covered her thighs with her gown which had been torn down one side. Then finding her hairclip which had fallen out, she pinned back her loose hair thinking it not proper for a martyr to suffer with dishevelled hair; it might seem that she was mourning in her hour of triumph. Then she stood up. Noticing that Felicitas was badly bruised, she went to her, reached out her hands and helped her to her feet. As they stood there, the cruelty of the crowds seemed to be appeased and they were sent to the Sanavivarian Gate. There Perpetua was taken care of by a cer-

tain catechumen, Rusticus, who stayed near her. She seemed to be waking from a deep sleep (so completely had she been entranced and embued with the Spirit). She began to look around her and to everyone's astonishment asked, "When are we going to be led out to that cow, or whatever it is?" She would not believe that it had already happened until she saw the various markings of the tossing on her body and clothing. Then calling for her brother she said to him and to the catechumen, "Remain strong in your faith and love one another. Do not let your excruciating suffering become a stumbling block for you."

36. Meanwhile, at another gate Saturus was similarly encouraging the soldier, Pudens. "Up to the present," he said, "I've not been harmed by any of the animals, just as I've foretold and predicted. So that you will now believe completely, watch as I go back to die from a single leopard bite." And so at the end of that contest, Saturus was bitten once by the leopard that had been set loose, and bled so profusely from that one wound that as he was coming back the crowd shouted in witness to his second baptism: "Salvation by being cleased; Salvation by being cleansed." And that man was truly saved who was cleansed in this way.

37. Then Saturus said to Pudens the soldier, "Goodbye, and remember my faith. Let these happenings be a source of strength for you, rather than a cause for anxiety." Then asking Pudens for a ring from his finger, he dipped it into the wound and returned it to Pudens as a legacy, a pledge and remembrance of his death. And as he collapsed he was thrown with the rest to that place reserved for the usual throat-slitting. And when the crowd demanded that the prisoners be brought out into the open so that they might feast their eyes on death by the sword, they voluntarily arose and moved where the crowd wanted them. Before doing so they kissed each other so that their martyrdom would be completely perfected by the rite of the kiss of peace.

38. The others, without making any movement or sound, were killed by the sword. Saturus in particular, since he had been the first to climb the ladder and was to be Perpetua's encouragement, was the first to die. But Perpetua, in order to feel some of the pain, groaning as she was struck between the ribs, took the gladiator's trembling hand and guided it to her throat. Perhaps it was that so great a woman, feared as she was by the unclean spirit, could not have been slain had she not herself willed it.

39. O brave and fortunate martyrs, truly called and chosen to give honor to our Lord Jesus Christ! And anyone who is elaborating upon, or who reverences or worships that honor, should read these more recent examples, along with the ancient, as sources of encouragement for the Christian community. In this way there will be new examples of courage witnessing to the fact that even in our day the same Holy Spirit is still efficaciously present, along with the all powerful God the Father and Jesus Christ our Lord, to whom there will always be glory and endless power. Amen.

Questions and Activities

1. We often experience in dreams another part of ourselves which gives us insight into our present stage of growth or which calls us to self-transcendence. Sometimes the dream records a healing or a step forward achieved. Sometimes it illuminates a challenge or a moment of crisis in which the next level of maturity hangs in the balance. Reflect upon one of your own significant dreams in these categories. In what ways was your dream-experience like or unlike that of Perpetua?

2. Imagine yourself in Perpetua's shoes: in prison or otherwise facing death, but with some significant human relationships still unresolved. Imagine some scenes in which you move toward resolving them. With whom and how would these scenes be

played out? Write them up as a kind of Volume II of Perpetua's *Martyrdom*.

3. Read further on what the "Fathers" of the Church had to say about women. Elizabeth A. Clark's anthology would be helpful as would her work on St. Jerome and St. John Chrysostom. Isolate one theme within that material and write a short analysis of it. Alternatively, write a letter to the author or authors in which you explore your own responses to the theme.

4. Research the question of martyrdom within the early church. Where did the ideals of martyrdom come from? How important was Perpetua's narrative to the formation of those ideals? What do we know about the actual experiences of martyrdom (places, dates and impact of the significant persecutions)? In what ways has the early church's experience of martyrdom shaped your thinking about what it means to be Christian?

5. Research the role of women in the ministry of the early church. What roles did women play in the official life of the early church? How were these roles changed as time went on? What influences created these changes? Do the experience and theory of those first centuries offer any help to the discussion about women in ministry today?

Selected Additional Reading

Clark, Elizabeth A. *Jerome, Chrysostom and Friends: Essays and Translations.* Studies in Women and Religion, 2. New York and Toronto: The Edwin Mellen Press, 1979.

Clark, Elizabeth A. *Women in the Early Church.* Wilmington, Delaware: Michael Glazier, Inc., 1983.

Dronke, Peter. *Women Writers of the Middle Ages.* New York: Cambridge University Press, 1984.

Gryson, Roger. *The Ministry of Women in the Early Church.* Trans. by Jean Laporte and Mary Louise Hall. Collegeville, Minnesota: The Liturgical Press, 1980.

Klawiter, Frederick C. "The Role of Martyrdom and Persecution in Developing the Priestly Authority of Women in Early Christianity: A Case Study of Montanism." *Church History* 49 (1980): 251-61.

Laporte, Jean. *The Role of Women in Early Christianity.* New York: Edwin Mellen Press, 1982.

MacHaffie, Barbara. *Her Story: Women in Christian Tradition.* Philadelphia: Fortress Press, 1986.

Petroff, Elizabeth Alvida. *Medieval Women's Visionary Literature.* New York and Oxford: Oxford University Press, 1986.

Tavard, George H. *Women in Christian Tradition.* Notre Dame and London: University of Notre Dame Press, 1973.

Wilson-Kastner, Patricia. et al *A Lost Tradition: Women Writers of the Early Church.* New York: University Press of America, 1981.

Yarborough, Anne. "Christianization in the Fourth Century: The Example of Roman Women." *Church History* 45 (June 1976): 149-65.

Notes

1. A critical edition of the text with English translation can be found in Herbert Musurillo, *The Acts of the Christian Martyrs* (Oxford: Clarendon Press, 1972) 106-131. The translation here is by Rosemary Rader, *A Lost Tradition: Women Writers of the Early Church* ed. by Patricia Wilson-Kastner (New York: University Press of America, 1981) 19-30. Used by permission of UPA.

2. Montanism was an early heresy that sought perfection in mandatory celibacy and various theories of illumination.

3. See Elisabeth Schussler Fiorenza, *In Memory of Her* (New York: Crossroads, 1983) for a feminist reconstruction of the earliest history of the church.

4. Ed. by James Donaldson in *Ante-Nicene Fathers,* v.7 (Grand Rapids, MI: Wm.B. Eerdmans Publishing Co., 1979) 431. The *Constitutions* is a collection of material covering an extended period of time, but probably not later than the fourth century.

5. Wilmington, Delaware: Michael Glazier, Inc. The naming and description of the themes are mine but they are based on the divisions of textual material in Clark's anthology.

6. See Jo Ann McNamara, "Sexual Equality and the Cult of Virginity in Early Christian Thought." *Feminist Studies* 3, 4 (Sp-Su, 1976) 145-58.

7. Quoted in Jean LaPorte, *The Role of Women in Early Christianity* (New York: Edwin Mellen Press, 1982) 60.

8. He praised them most of all, of course, for their asceticism but also for their intelligence and learning. See Anne Yarborough, "Christianization in the Fourth Century: The Example of Roman Women." *Church History* 45 (June, 1976) 149-65.

9. Clark, *Women* 97.

10. Dream and vision are alternative word-choices of the various translators. Whichever translation is used, the point is that the healing comes through an experiential and imaginative mode.

11. Few today would discredit all visions as hysterical or as signs of neurosis. According to Elizabeth Alvilda Petroff, *Medieval Women's Visionary Literature* (New York: Oxford University Press, 1986): "visions constitute a vehicle for the transformation of the self.... Visions are also responses to real-life situations: they may be compensatory or offer creative solutions to difficulties or provide images for identity but they always come in response to something, and they always set in motion a new relationship to the original event that called them forth" 22-3.

12. I take issue with Peter Dronke here. In *Women Writers of the Middle Ages* (New York: Cambridge University Press, 1984) 9, he sees the cheese image (from Aristotle) as indicative of new birth, a celestial birth, and rules out a Eucharistic implication. Since the early church considered the Eucharist the food of immortal, celestial life, I see no conflict. Perpetua's images often blend classical and

Christian in a manner typical of dreams as acknowledged by Dronke in other instances.

13. Petroff, *Visionary Literature* 62.

14. There is suggestive evidence that martyrdom conferred the power of the keys and that, at least in Rome, a confessor (someone who was imprisoned for the faith but released before he could be killed) was elevated to the rank of presbyter after his release. A different understanding of this connection seems to have been one of the differences between the Montanists and Orthodox Catholicism. See Frederick Klawiter, "The Role of Martyrdom and Persecution in Developing the Priestly Authority of Women in Early Christianity: A Case Study of Montanism." *Church History* 49 (1980) 251-61.

15. Wilson-Kastner, *Lost Traditions* 10-11.

16. *Traditions* 63.

17. Reprinted from *A Lost Tradition: Women Writers of the Early Church,* trans. by Rosemary Rader. Copyrighted in 1981 by University Press of America Inc. Used by permission.

2.

"A Troublesome Puppy": Dhuoda of Septimania

Somewhere around the year 842 a noblewoman residing in Provence, finding herself separated from her two sons, decided to write a book which she titled the *Liber Manualis*.[1] The title means "handbook;" such manuals of instruction were a popular genre during the eighth and ninth centuries in Latinized areas of Europe. Dhuoda of Septimania, wife of one of the magnates of Louis the Pious, used the popular form as a vehicle to transmit the spiritual, moral and courtly teaching which she was unable to provide to her sons face-to-face. She thus transformed her maternal vocation into a literary one and left a legacy that outlived her sons.

We know little of the family or background of Dhuoda,[2] only what she reveals in the text. She married Bernard of Septimania in 824 in the imperial chapel at Aachen. Her first son, the William to whom her book is addressed, was born a year and a half later and his brother, Bernard, in 841. Bernard was a newly-born infant when he was separated from him mother. In the interim, her husband had been caught up in the dynastic fighting endemic to the period of Louis the Pious and which intensified after his death. Bernard wavered in his allegiance

31

throughout those years. He variously supported Charles the Bald and Pepin of Aquitaine and was finally beheaded for treason by Charles in 844, not long after Dhuoda finished her handbook.

In 841, in one of his periods of support for Charles the Bald, Bernard sent his older son to the prince as a kind of hostage of his own good intentions. He took his second son and namesake with him at the same time, presumably for safe-keeping. Bereft of her sons and living in the city of Uzes under the protection of its bishop, Dhuoda turned to writing as a way to alleviate her grief at the enforced separation.[3]

Her decision to write for her sons seems a significant departure from the conventions of her day. Aristocratic women were often expected to administer vast estates when their husbands were absent for the purposes of war and there were some women, like Charlemagne's daughters, who were literate. But it is still generally held that a literary education was a rare privilege available only to clerics and certain male members of the aristocracy.[4]

Yet education may have been more available for aristocratic women than the common wisdom acknowledges. The true picture of women's history does not yet completely exist, partly because the evidence has not been preserved, partly because it has often been passed over or read in such a way as to reinforce existing presuppositions. Dhuoda's *Handbook for a Noble Son,* of which there are three extant manuscripts, teases us with the possibility that she is not an extraordinary phenomenon of the early Middle Ages but an example of a larger tradition that was subsequently lost. Even if this were true, however, the decision to express a maternal vocation through a literary one argues for a confident self-understanding.

Dhuoda is not only acquainted with some of the major Christian writers of the time (Augustine, Gregory the Great, Isidore of

Seville);[5] she also has a strong sense that the wisdom to be found in books is absolutely necessary to Christian formation. She tries to embue William with this same sense; over and over again she recommends that he read widely and that he strive to possess many books.

Her self-confidence is substantiated by a careful reading of the text. It is, to be sure, filled with self-deprecating assertions of humility and inadequacy. Anyone familiar with medieval literature will recognize in some of these assertions the rhetorical commonplace. But Dhuoda's use of this device seems to reflect her sense of history, a sense which is at the same time metaphysical and concrete. Sometimes she considers her own unworthiness a result of her humanity. She considers it arrogance for any human being to dare to talk about God and so she speaks specifically about her own unworthiness. She is unworthy because she is "frail," as are all human beings, because she is "in exile," both from her husband and from her heavenly home, and because she is "turning to dust." The entire book is redolent with a sense of denouement: everyone is turning to dust; all are becoming like shadows. Dhuoda herself is approaching her death, her transition to dust and ashes. Hers is a sense of the mutability of all human things in the face of the immutability of God, about whom she dares to write. But this mutability of all human things is, for Dhuoda, neither general nor vague. Rather, her awareness that the world is passing away is historical and social. In the Carolingian world that is itself in decline, she is literally both weak and insignificant because her family has been on the downside of historical forces and no longer has either power or authority. She explicitly attributes her lack of merit—which she describes repeatedly in a manner that strikes the modern writer as obsequious or debasing—to the historical shifts of fortune to which she and her family have been subject. It is in no way a condition of her gender. She was a woman who believed herself capable of fulfilling the public roles of writer, counselor and, especially, teacher, at least in William's life. To take on these tasks she has consciously to confront the prevailing ideology; and, though she justifies her temerity, making it clear that she knows she is taking an unusual, perhaps even a radical step, she never apologizes for it.

Dhuoda describes a writer as a person of unusual gifts and one who has public responsibility. Both of these characteristics she clearly ascribes to herself. In the selections which follow she says that writing takes "sharpness of mind" and she calls it a "perilous public contest" (#8). By use of such language, she likens writing to the tournaments, acts of war or public debates that were part of her experience. She also describes the sudden increase of human genius required to turn ordinary people into writers (#10). She speaks of herself as a writer who has struggled to write well. She talks about the elements of good writing that she considers important: metrics that make for poetry and the fluidity of prose phrases. The *Liber Manualis* is a consciously crafted book.

It is also a book crafted for a wider audience than that of her son. The handbook is far more than the personal letter that some have called it. In several places, Dhuoda addresses the wider audience directly, asking prayers and mercy for her sons and herself. Elsewhere she recommends that William give the book to others who, like himself, are struggling to be true Christian knights in a difficult moral climate. Finally, in the very passage toward the end of the book in which she frames her epitaph, she notes that readers other than her family can profit from meditating on her words (#33). Even in this, one of her more intimate passages, she is aware of the public character of her work.

The second role that Dhuoda takes to herself is that of counselor, in the sense of political advisor. William has been sent as a hostage to the court of Charles—a court riddled with treachery and dissension—and his mother tells him that his only salvation at that court may depend on good counselors. One of his first tasks at court, then, will be to find such advisors for himself. Additionally, he will be called upon to act as a counselor; as a first son of one of the noblest families, his role is not just to fight for his liege lord but to give him good counsel. She speaks of the scarcity of good counselors, but affirms that they can still be found in the descendents of very noble families. She exhorts William to look for persons of good virtue, consulting both old and young. Finally, she defines a good counselor as one who leads others to virtue and gives counsel that is both pertinent to the matter at hand and conducive to leading people to heaven. Having explained the role of counselor, she then says:

> There are some who consider themselves counselors and they are not. They judge themselves to be wise and they are not. If I say less, I am more ...[6]

Here Dhuoda applies to herself Paul's defense of his own apostolic qualifications (2 Cor 11:23). The parallel is telling: like Paul, she is forced to justify herself but, also like him, she is full of confidence in her ability to play an important public role.

The role of counselor is not unrelated to the third and most important role that Dhuoda assumes for herself in the course of the text—the role of teacher. This is a role she takes even greater pains to document and which would have been closed to her not only by custom but more particularly by ecclesiastical law. The church's prohibition of teaching for women began early and perdured. In Paul's first letter to Timothy (2:11-14), two reasons are given for forbidding women to teach. The author says that since woman was created after man, she was inferior to him. Then he points out that when woman did exercise the teaching role in the Garden as described in *Genesis,* she taught humankind to sin. This initial misreading of the creation story had been reinforced by a large body of early Christian material, very formative of ninth-century thought.[7] A few samples of that early thought easily demonstrate that of all the roles to which women might have aspired the one that was forbidden most explicitly was that of teacher.

Tertullian, for instance, who includes widows among the official ranks of the clergy (*ordines*), repeats in numerous places the prohibition against teaching.[8] In fact, he prohibits any exercise of ministerial power, especially any exercise of sacramental significance. Though Tertullian considered exorcism a power of the whole community not intrinsically restricted to priests, it was to be exercised by men only. After he joined the Montanists, Tertullian made exception for the function of prophecy but even then he surrounded the right of women to prophecy with all sorts of precautions. As Gryson says, "From one end to the other of his religious evolution, Tertullian remained adamant in his refusal to acknowledge the right of women to teach in church or to perform a sacramental act." Similarly Origen, who accepted a ministry for widows with certain public functions (primarily hospitality and good works), forbade women to teach. He noted that older women may sometimes have to teach young girls, who were essentially housebound, but he makes it quite clear that such teaching is primarily the inculcation of appropriate behavior. He is adamant that women can never teach men. One such clear prohibition reads:

> ... for it is improper for a woman to speak in an assembly, no matter what she says; even if she says admirable things or even saintly things, that is of little consequence, since they come from the mouth of a woman.[9]

Augustine is probably the patristic author who most influenced the early Middle Ages; he is also Dhuoda's favorite. Augustine's thought on the human person as the "image of God" was to become the heart of medieval anthropology and in his work on the *Literal Meaning of Genesis* he affirms that insofar as woman possessed a rational mind, she was made to the image of God. But her body, with its inferior sexual characteristics, made her subordinate to man by nature.[10] Later in the same work he seems to hedge on the clarity of that assertion by raising the possibility that woman before the Fall was not yet fully the image of God—hence, her ease in succumbing to the Serpent—but was in the process of gradually acquiring the knowledge of God (by which she would become truly "image") through the tutelage of her husband.[11] A quote long ascribed to Augustine though probably from Ambrosiaster,[12] demonstrates the conclusions that could be drawn from Augustine's more nuanced, indeed almost tortured thinking.

> How can one say about the woman that she is in the image of God when she is subject to the domination of her husband and is not allowed to have any *authority*. She cannot teach, testify, act as a surety or serve as a judge. Hence, she surely cannot rule.[13]

Ambrosiaster's point here is whether women can rule. He brings in their inability to teach as evidence to the contrary. The operative word for him is "authority," something that comes from within the human person and cannot, therefore, be conferred by law or custom, though the latter, properly, reinforced nature in this matter. For Ambrosiaster, authority comes from the image of God within us, because God alone is the source of all authority. The male has authority because he is in the image of God while the female is *not* in the image of God, has not the inner source of authority and therefore she cannot teach. He understands this not as a matter of law or custom but of metaphysics. By nature, woman lacks a certain intrinsic perfection that is the source of the teaching ministry.

It is precisely against that background of decisive teaching that Dhuoda sets herself up as a teacher. She clearly sees her teaching role as an extension of maternal obligations; indeed, that is her justification for assuming it. That such an action demands justification she acknowledges in the prologue, the only place, incidentally, where she refers to herself as a member of the weaker sex (#1).[14] But she goes on to offer William the manual of instruction with the simple explanation that, after all, she is his mother. She offers it diffidently at first, comparing it to the game of chess to which he might have daily recourse in order to escape the tedium of everyday tasks (#1). She has thus minimized her actions to that of a mother offering entertainment to her child. Later, however, she becomes bolder, asserting that it is her role to lead him into a deeper understanding of God, in spite of her unworthiness. Indeed, she soon dares to affirm that she will be his best teacher, best in the sense that the power of her teaching will have special ability to touch his life because of "her burning heart ..." (#24), which imparts to her words a unique character.

Finally she elevates her experience to a general principle, saying that if she can teach as a mother, all mothers can teach. She seeks precedent for that statement both in antiquity and in tradition. In chapter 47, Dhuoda discusses the two births and the two deaths that every human being experiences—physical birth and death and spiritual birth and death. She puts forth the simple principle that the one who is the most active in the first birth ought to be similarly concerned and active in the second birth. She cites several mothers of antiquity who were honored in the church for having brought about the baptism and second birth of their children and she concludes with the sweeping statement that Christian women have been teachers and spiritual guides to their children in all generations.

> Then, now and always many women unceasingly give daily birth to their sons in holy church through the gospel, as it is said, by the preaching of sacred doctrines and by the example of frequent good works.[15]

Her use of the phrase "the preaching of sacred doctrines" is telling, since that is an official and public task within the church.

Not only is the role of teacher appropriate for mothers, not only does affection give special power to their words, but a mother, says Dhuoda, has a special skill for teaching that comes from her practical knowledge of the child's development. Traditionally, religious education has been compared with the act of giving nourishment. The soul is fed with wisdom, as the body with meat and grain, and who better than a mother knows how to suit the appropriate food to the child's stage of development? Paul spoke in maternal imagery when applying this metaphor to his own teaching. He told the Corinthians that he gave them milk rather than solid food because they were too immature for the solid food of difficult doctrine. Dhuoda applies the metaphor to herself; she has broken down the sublime teaching concerning the gifts of the Holy Spirit and the beatitudes into modest teaching so that William can grasp it a little at a time, as if he were beginning with milk and maturing until he was ready for heavenly food. The words sound most appropriate on her lips.

It seems quite evident that Dhuoda is aware that she is taking on the role of teacher and thereby exposing herself to censure. She takes pain to connect this function with the role to which both society and church assigned her and would therefore accept, the mother's role. In the course of writing her manual she seems to grow in confidence, moving from a desire to show that her teaching is not harmful, to a conviction that, as a mother, her teaching will have a special power and will lead William to God. Finally she arrives at a confidence that enables her to teach on her own authority and in the name of good pedagogy. Like many others, Dhuoda has become a teacher by teaching.

Dhuoda knows that religious and spiritual truth is the particular province of the teaching authority of the church or, by special grace, of the mystics. By her own admission, Dhuoda is no mystic. The wisdom about divine things that she is attempting to communicate to William is human wisdom, acquired through arduous study, tenuously held and, therefore, taught with some trepidation and a great deal of humility.

Both of us must search for God, my son; in his will we take our place, we live and move and have our being. Unworthy and insubstantial as a shadow, I seek him in order to be strong. Unceasingly, I ask his help in order to know and understand. This is absolutely necessary for me (#10).

Dhuoda reveals herself in this passage and elsewhere as a woman of great intellectual curiosity. There is tension in her self-understanding as thinker and teacher. On the one hand she knows her serious limitations: they are both personal and a consequence of her human condition. On the other hand she has studied and worked hard and knows that she has achieved some insight and understanding. This tension is apparent in a piece of original exegesis she gives on Mark 7:24-29 (#10), the story of the Syro-Phoenican woman who approached Jesus, asking him for healing for her daughter. In the original story, Jesus calls the woman a dog who is unworthy to receive the food destined for the children.

Dhuoda sees the woman as an image of herself. She comes in search, not of healing, but of spiritual teaching and wisdom. Building upon the strong biblical association between bread and divine truth, she describes herself as a troublesome little puppy who excels at catching the crumbs of wisdom that fall. Further, she says that all those who search for God's wisdom are so many dogs scrapping for the crumbs; the priests are nearer to the table [the altar], Dhuoda says, but they too are puppies like herself. Her final appeal is to the mercy of God. As he gave speech to dumb animals (she recalls Nm 22, 28), so he can give wisdom to her. Like the Syro-Phoenician woman, she turns her inferior social position and her personal limitations into strength, a claim on the God of biblical narrative whose preference is consistently for the "under-dog." The God of Christian revelation fills Dhuoda's entire treatise. On page after page, the image of God is recalled as the omnipotence before which all human claims to power are mere pretense (e.g., #17), the eternal truth before which all human accomplishments are dust and ashes (e.g., #8 and #13). Here, in a very positive note, that same God is the benevolent, all-encompassing providence in which Dhuoda stands and from which she dares to speak for herself with confidence.

Dhuoda's *Handbook for a Noble Son* deserves wide recognition in the history of woman's struggle to assume her rightful place in the world. Whether we regard her as an anomaly in her time or as a tantalizing hint of feminine accomplishments lost through neglect or misunderstanding, she reveals the energy and talent available to society in its women. These gifts were sometimes utilized but more often neglected; it took troublesome puppies like Dhuoda to transcend the limitations which law and custom imposed.

Dhuoda of Septimania's *Liber Manualis*

Selections from Prologue, Preface and Chapter One

1. Many things that are clear to many people are concealed from me; others like me, with darkened intellect, lack understanding—if I speak of this less, yet I am more so. Always present with me is the one who opens the mouth of the mute and makes fluent the tongues of children. Though I am weak of intellect and unworthy even among worthy women, I, Dhuoda, am nevertheless your mother, William, my son. To you I now direct my conversation in this handbook. Just as chess remains for the moment the most suitable and appropriate of recreations for young people or as some women are accustomed to look in the mirror to remove blemishes, refresh their beauty and thus pay their worldly debt by satisfying their husbands, in just such an habitual manner do I want you, burdened as you are by a profusion of profane and worldly activities, to read this little

book which I have addressed to you so that you will remember me. That is, I want you to read it as frequently as young people play chess or women use their mirrors.

2. Though your collection of books may increase by many volumes, may it please you frequently to read the small book I send you and with the help of the all-powerful God, may you become powerful in understanding it for your own benefit. You will find in it whatever you choose to know in abbreviated form; you will also find a mirror in which to scrutinize the salvation of your soul so that you can discover not only how to please the world in all things but also the One who has formed you out of clay. It is absolutely necessary, William, my son, that you show yourself equally distinguished in matters which lead in both directions; you must be equally useful to the world and always be capable of pleasing God in all things.

3. I have taken great care to direct a word of salvation to you, William, my son; the chief concern of my soul, vigilant and ardent as it is, has been the desire to compose a written account of your birth by God's grace in this bound book. Therefore it behooves me to continue as I have previously planned.

4. In the eleventh year of the happy reign of our lord Louis, by Christ's graciousness, the year of five concurrent days on the third calends of July, in the palace at Aix-en-chapelle, I was joined as wife in lawful marriage to my lord and your father, Bernard. And in turn, in the thirteenth year, the third calends of December, God helping me as I believe, you came forth from me into this world, my most yearned for, first-born son.

5. The calamities of this miserable time continued to roll on and reach their crest and in the midst of many disagreements and fluctuations of fortune in the kingdom, the above-mentioned emperor followed the path common to all. For during the twenty-eighth year of his reign, without reaching the fullness of his life, he completed his life as a debt to the world. And after his

death, in the following year, your brother was born in the eleventh calends of April, the second after you to come forth from my womb (God being merciful), this time in the city of Uzes. While he was still an infant, before he had received the grace of baptism, Bernard, the lord and father of you both, had you brought to him in Aquitaine accompanied by Elefantus, bishop of Uzes, and other of his faithful followers.

6. When I had remained in that city a long time, separated from you by command of my lord who was already rejoicing at his public combat, I decided to assuage the grief of separation by the writing of this small book—comparable to the measure of my understanding—which I now send to you.

Selections from Chapter One: On Loving God

7. God ought to be both loved and praised not only by the choirs of heaven but also by every human creature who walks on earth even as they move toward heaven. You, my son, are one of those whom I challenge to search eagerly with whatever strength you have to scale the fixed summit along with those who are worthy and capable of loving God. Like them, may you be strong in attaining the kingdom which will remain forever.

8. I speak now as if I were in your presence and in the presence of those to whom you will offer this book for reading: I humbly beg to suggest that from the height of your nobility and your youthfulness, you may not condemn me nor reproach me for undertaking too casually such a perilous public contest, that is, for beginning a work demanding sharpness of mind, namely that I dare to address written words about God to you. Certainly I know better than anyone else the condition of my human frailty; I reproach myself unceasingly for I am but poor dust and ashes. I know that if patriarchs, prophets and all the other saints from the creation until now could not fully understand the pattern of holy things, how much less can I do so, insignificant and of low

birth as I am. And if, as the scriptures say, the heaven and the heaven of heavens cannot contain God because of his greatness, what could I, unskilled as I am, possibly be capable of saying about him?

9. We read in Genesis that when blessed Moses, fresh from his intimate companionship in speech with God, wanted to see him face to face, he spoke this way. "If I have found favor in your sight, show yourself to me that I might see you." And the response to him was: "You cannot see my face, because no one can see me and continue to live." And if it is like this on the heights what can you expect from those like me upon the earth? Denied a vision like this, my soul grows very feeble; in my mind, feeling burns.

10. Both of us must search for God, my son; in his will we take our place, we live and move and have our being. Unworthy and insubstantial as a shadow, I seek him in order to be strong; unceasingly I ask his help in order to know and understand. This is absolutely necessary for me. It is not unusual that a troublesome puppy, under the master's table with the others, often succeeds at catching and eating the crumbs that fall. So powerful, indeed, is the one who made the mouth of dumb animals to speak, and given understanding. He who prepares a table in the desert for his faithful followers, giving them a satisfying measure of wheat in time of need, can also satisfy from his own goodwill my inclination as his handmaid. At least I may be under his table, that is to say, inside holy church, able to watch even if from afar the small dogs there (that is, the ministers of his holy altars). And under that table I can collect crumbs of spiritual understanding—beautiful, lucid and valuable words, appropriate for both me and you. I know this because God does not abandon his impoverished ones.

11. He is the same now as he was in the past, and remains so into the future, always here and everywhere. Every good and profitable possibility has its origin in him. And in him all things

find their completion, as he himself says: "I am the alpha and omega," And again, "I am who am." The scripture adds: "He who is sent me," and many more examples.

12. God is great and above all, my son William, because he looks favorably on the lowly and knows the high and mighty, that is to say, the proud, only from afar. The frail person is raised up and God withdraws himself from the mighty. Compassionate, he lowers himself and descends to the one who needs him. Therefore, frequently submit yourself that you may always be raised up by him. For he knows the disorderliness of our make-up, both yours and mine. As scripture says, "His eyes look down upon the children of men, seeing if there is one who is wise and seeks him."

Indeed, he observes our actions from first sight until the evening, that is, from the rising of the sun until its setting, which certainly means also from the moment of our departure from the womb until the last moment of our death. But this "from first light until the evening" also means that he watches over all of us from the moment of Adam, the first formed, until the person who will be born and die at the end of the world. He knows whatever human frailty thinks, says and does, recognizing his own among the multitudes, gathering them from the lowest places to the highest, allotting to them the kingdom and rewarding those who fight for worthy goods according to their individual merits.

13. As the apostle Paul says, my son, no mortal being has ever yet been able to comprehend fully the sublimity and greatness of God. "Oh the height of the riches of the wisdom and knowledge of God. How incomprehensible are his judgments and unsearchable his ways." And again: "For who has known the mind of the Lord, or who may be his counselor?" Who in the skies is equal to him or who can be like him? The answer is understood: no one. Why? Because he alone knows the hearts of his human children and he is the most high over all the earth.

14. Fragile as a shadow though I may be, my son, it is for me here to lead you into whatever deeper understanding you may achieve. I cannot offer you a lecture perfectly worked out—I am not capable of that even if it were appropriate for me to do it. Rather I will now try to imitate such a work by putting together the most helpful ideas.

15. I admonish you continually to mull over the words of the holy gospels and the writing of the fathers concerning these powers, elements and bodily senses. By thinking, speaking and acting rightly, you may believe the triune nature of the everlasting God, who remains one in trinity and triune in unity. He is the one whom no one can measure; it is he, as scripture attests, whom the morning stars praise together and to whom all the sons of God give joyful praise. He is the one who laid the foundations of the earth and took its measure, who enclosed the sea within bounds and dressed it in cloud. And if he is in himself such a being and rules over all things in such a manner, he can bring you to the pinnacle of perfection, nourishing and increasing your being to an always greater degree.

16. When once you have begun to consider who or what God is, how great and of what quality, when once you are unable to understand him fully nor find another equal to him, you will know, through this very inability to knowk, that He is God. He is the one, as a certain poet said, who commanded and they were created; he spoke and all was fashioned—heaven and earth, the underwater depths, the orb of sun and moon.

17. Our way of speaking in the world is such that we think about all things in relation to our power and purposes—which is against the true reality of things. Thus someone in the world may struggle and assert with confidence "the kingdom is mine" and again "in my whole kingdom." He does not stop to reflect that the kingdom and all the transitory realities therein belong to the Lord. Nabachodonosor, once unbelieving and the worst of scoundrels when prostrate and conquered, regained true under-

standing saying, "He himself is the King governing and ruling, with the power to raise up whomsoever he will and to bring down those who walk in pride. The kingdom is his and he can give it to whomever he will." Another man affirms, "the earth is mine" and does not consider carefully the words of the psalmist: "The earth is the Lord's. To the Lord also belong the bird and the fish; he gives the former pastures in the forest and the latter walk the pathways of the sea. For in his hand are all the ends of the earth; he rules and directs all who dwell within it." Contrarily on earth we say and they say "this is mine; all of it is." They speak truly, of course, because it is and yet it isn't. These things pass away and they remain; they belong to someone for a little while but not forever; they pass away at the right moment but not in every moment.

18. I think at length about those whose stories I have heard read and others I have known myself among my ancestors and yours, my son, who behaved as if they were all-powerful in the world and they were not. Perhaps they are with God because of their merits but they no longer hold bodily converse with the world. For them and for others I say the prayer for the dead upon my knees. Indeed for myself, although I may be thought the least of my family, in their fall and mortal ruin, I see the things to come.

19. Therefore, he who is the powerful king, always undiminished, is the one to be feared, loved and believed in as most certainly immortal. It is he who rules and does whatsoever he wishes. Indeed, in his will and his power all things are established. There is no one who can resist his will saying, "Why have you done this?" He is the god of the universe: to him belong power and kingdom and empire. Of that power and kingdom, the most holy David spoke with assurance: "His power is eternal power which may not be taken from him; his kingdom will not dissolve." There are many similar affirmations.

20. And what will I add to all of this, fragile earthen vessel that I am? I am already turned in the direction that many have taken before me, as if already one of their companions. If the heavens and earth were like a giant leaf of parchment unrolled into the air and if curved bridges had been sharpened and dipped into different inks, and if all the people born into all the cultures of the world were to be made writers by a sudden increase of human genius—all of which is clearly impossible and against nature—they would still be unable to capture [in writing] the greatness and the width and the height and the depths of the sublime, all-powerful One. Nor could they tell the story of the richness, knowledge, piety and mercy of him who is called God. Since he is like this and so great that no one can grasp his essence, I urge you to fear and love him with your whole soul, your whole intellect and in all your ways and actions. Bless him and say over and over again, "For you are good and your mercy is forever!"

21. Believe that he is above you, below you, within and outside of you for he is the reality above, the foundation, the interior reality and the reality outside. He is the reality above because he presides over and rules us all. He is on high and as the psalmist says, his glory is above all the heavens. He is the foundation because he bears us all: in him we live, we move, we have our being, and in him we make our stand. He is the interior reality because we are filled with his good things, yes filled to satisfaction as the scripture says: "With the fruit of your works the earth is filled and you fill every creature with blessing." He is the reality around us because his impregnable wall surrounds us all; he makes us secure, protects and defends us all. As it is written: "he circles us with a wall and like a shield he spreads his encircling care." Such is the faith I, your mother, have in God—blessed may he be forever—a faith which far exceeds the limits and poverty of my understanding.

22. I also admonish you, my beautiful and lovable son William: among the every-day cares of this world, do not be reluc-

tant to acquire for yourself many books by the most holy doctors, your teachers, in which you may discern and understand more and better ideas about God the creator than what is written above. Beg for this learning, choose it and love it. If you do this, it will be for you a guardian, a leader, your companion and homeland, the way, the truth and the life. It will bring to you munificent prosperity in the world and all your enemies will be converted to peace.

23. Additionally, as it is written in Job, gird your loins like a man; be humble in heart and chaste in body; be upright in your grandeur and adorn yourself with splendor.

24. And what more? Dhuoda, your orator is always here, my son, and if I fail you by departing—a future certainty—you will have this little moral book as a memorial. By reading it and by praying to God, you will be able to behold me, body and mind, as in a mirror. The duties you owe me you will find here in detail. You will have many teachers, my son, who will offer you instructions that are lengthier and of greater usefulness, but none like mine in character nor given with such a burning heart as I, your mother, give you, my firstborn son.

25. Read these words which I send you—read, understand and put them into practice. And when your little brother, whose name I do not know, has received the grace of Christ in baptism, do not be reluctant to instruct, support and love him, challenging him always from the good to the better. When he is of an age to speak well and to read, show him this bound copy of the manual which I have put together and in which I have written your name. Urge him to read it for he is your own flesh and your brother. I, your mother, urge you both as if you were both [already able to respond] that you raise up your hearts, at least from time to time, among the burdens and cares of this life. Keep your eyes on the one who reigns in heaven, who is called God. May the all-powerful one himself, whom I speak of often if unworthily, make you happy and joyous at this present moment

along with your father, my master and lord, Bernard. May everything you do prosper. And after the journey of this life is finished may you enter rejoicing into the heaven of the holy ones. Amen.

Selections from Chapter Ten

26. Because of the sweetness of my great love and my desire [to see] your beauty, I have put myself aside as if forgotten. But now, with "the doors closed," I desire again to enter within myself. Even if I am not worthy to be counted among those numbered above, nevertheless I ask that you include me in that number, numbered among them through affection; I ask you to pray unceasingly for the healing of my soul.

27. It has not escaped you how, because of my continual infirmities and certain other causes—according to the word of the one who said, "in danger from my own nation, in danger from gentiles,"—I have had to bear all these and similar things, weak in body and hindered by [lack of] merits. With God's help and through the power of your father Bernard, I have confidently escaped all these [dangers], but I remember [the times] I was taken by force. As time went on, I have been negligent in divine praise, and what I ought to have done during the seven [canonical] hours, I have done lazily seven times seventy times. Because of this, I beg with suppliant feeling and all my strength, that you take pleasure in praying God's mercy on all my offenses and negligence so that he will deign to raise me, broken and weighed down as I am, to the heights.

28. While you know that I am still alive, strive zealously and with vigilant heart, not only in vigils and prayers but also in alms for the poor that I may be freed bodily from the chain of my sins and may deserve to be received unreservedly and in a kindly manner by the merciful judge.

29. Your frequent prayer and that of others are necessary for me now; they will be more so, much more so, afterward in what I believe is speedily about to come. With great fear and sadness about what might happen to me in the future, my spirit is shaken from every side and I am uncertain about how I may be freed at the end. Why? Because I have sinned in thought and word. Useless speech itself leads to sinful action. Though all this may be true, I will never despair of God's mercy: I don't despair now and I will never despair. And I know that I will eventually regain [his mercy] at some time, because I leave a survivor like you; there is no one who will struggle on my behalf as you will, noble son, and as will your many descendants.

30. I find myself heavily weighed down with debt in the interest of my lord and master Bernard. I took on these debts so that I might not fail in my feudal obligation to him in the March and many other places, and also so that he would not separate himself from me and from you as is the custom among others. In genuine needs, I have frequently borrowed much from the hands of both Jews and Christians. I have paid back as much as I could and I will continue to do so. But if after my death, something remains to be acquitted, I beg you diligently to seek out my creditors. When you have found them, pay back absolutely everything not only from my estate—if anything remains—but also from what you have or may acquire justly with God's help.

31. What more? What you ought to do on behalf of your little brother I have admonished you above and I do so again. I ask that if he grows to maturity, he also may deign to pray for me. It is as if I already admonish both of you together to have offered for me the frequent pouring out of sacrifices and offering of hosts.

When the Redeemer orders me summoned from this world, may he deign to prepare refreshment for me and may he who is called God have me pass over with the saints to the eternal kingdom. May this come to be through your prayers and the worthy prayers of others.

The Manual is finished here. Amen. Thanks be to God.

32. *The Names of the Dead*

Note here the names of certain deceased persons omitted from among those named above. They are: William, Cunegunda, Gerberg, Withburg, Thierry, Guacelm, Warner, Rothlind.

There are some from your genealogy who are still alive with God's help; their called remains in all things the business of him who created them as he wished. For them, my son, we can only say with the psalmist: "We who are living, we bless the Lord, now and forever."

When someone of your stock passes, it happens only with the power of God when he orders it, as is the case with your uncle, Lord Heribert. If you survive him, order his name written into the list transcribed above, that he might be prayed for.

33. *The Epitaph for My Tomb*

When I myself finish my days, please order my name written on that list of the dead above. What I wish—and I ask it with all my strength as if I were present to you—is that in the place where I am buried, on the stone covering the tomb which encloses my body, you order these verses written so deeply that those who see this epitaph will pour out worthy prayers to God for me who am unworthy.

And if someone reads this Manual which you now read, let him meditate on the words which follow and commend me to God, that I might be released. I already feel as if I were enclosed within a tomb.

34. *Read Here, Reader, the Verses of My Epitaph*

Formed of earth, here in this little earthly mound,
Is the earthy body of Dhuoda thrown.
Infinite King, receive her.
For the earth has received her fragile clay
Into its depths
Gracious King, pardon her.

She is bathed from her wounds; only the tomb,
With its absolute darkness remains.
O King, absolve her sins.

You who come and go by here, of every age and sex,
I ask you to pray thus:
O Great and Holy One, dissolve her chains.

Pierced by a deep, dire wound, she ended life
Entombed in bitterness.
O King, forgive her sins.

That the dark serpent himself not seize her soul,
Praying will you please say this:
Merciful God, come to her aid.

Let no one pass by until he reads this.
I conjure all of you to pray, saying:
Kind God, give her rest.

O indulgent God, order perpetual light
To be lavished on her with the saints at the end.
May she receive the "Amen" after the funeral rites.

Questions and Activities

1. Write a letter to one of the fathers of the church described in this chapter. Answer his objections to having women as teachers, especially teachers of religious truth, by appealing to

your own experience (the teachers you have known, your own experience of teaching).

2. The roles of teaching and writing are no longer closed to women but many roles still are. Write a defense in the style of Dhuoda for promoting women to one or other of the positions still effectively closed. Note that she bases her justifications not on self-interest or self-aggrandizement but on the common good and the welfare of others.

3. Do some reading on the social position of women during the early middle ages. How does the life of Dhuoda contradict some of the patterns which historians assume about women during that time? What elements in her own life and in her own personality served to liberate her from these patterns? Are any of these elements still available to women seeking liberation?

4. Dhuoda uses her understanding of motherhood as the springboard for understanding woman's place in the larger social sphere. Write a reflective essay in which you explore the social implications of the biological role of motherhood. In what ways is it a limiting role? In what ways does it expand woman's responsibilities and influence? Does the role of motherhood have anything to say to women who are not mothers?

Selected Additional Reading

Bowers, Myra Ellen, ed. *The Liber Manualis of Dhuoda: The Advice of a Ninth-Century Mother for Her Sons.* Ann Arbor, Michigan: University Microfilms International, 1977.

Dronke, Peter. "Dhuoda." *Women Writers of the Middle Ages.* Cambridge: Cambridge University Press, 1984. 36-54.

Lucas, Angela M. *Women in the Middle Ages: Religion, Marriage and Letters.* New York: St. Martin's Press, 1983.

Marchand, James. "The Frankish Mother: Dhuoda." *Medieval Women Writers*. Katherine M. Wilson, ed. Athens, Georgia: University of Georgia Press, 1984. 1-29.

Riche, Pierre. *Daily Life in the World of Charlemagne* Trans. by Jo Ann McNamara. Philadelphia: University of Pennsylvania Press, 1978.

_____. *Education and Culture in the Barbarian West (sixth through eighth centuries)*. Trans. by John J. Contreni. Columbia: University of South Carolina Press, 1976.

_____, ed. *Liber Manualis*. Sources Chrétiennes, 225. Paris: Editions du Cerf, 1975.

Suzanne Wemple. *Women in Frankish Society*. Philadelphia: University of Pennsylvania Press, 1984.

_____. "The Contemplative Life: The Search for Feminine Autonomy in the Frankish Kingdom." *Anima* 6. (Spring, 1980) 131-136.

Notes

1. A critical edition by Pierre Riche, together with French translation, is available in *Sources Chrétiennes* 225 (Paris: Editions du Cerf, 1975). An alternative edition with English translation has been done by Myra Ellen Bowers, *The Liber Manualis of Dhuoda: Advice of a Ninth-Century Mother for Her Sons* (Ann Arbor, MI: University Microfilms International, 1977). Citations in the text are to my own translation based on the Bowers edition.

2. We know a good deal more about her husband's family. As a prominent military leader and Count, he figured in the chronicles of the time. English translations of these are found in *Carolingian Chronicles,* translated by Berhard Walter Scholz (Ann Arbor: University of Michigan Press, 1970) and *Charlemagne's Cousins,* translated by Allen Cabaniss (Syracuse: Syracuse University Press, 1967); Cf. also J. Calmette, *De Bernardo, Sancti Wilelmi filio* (Toulouse, 1902).

3. #6 in the primary text to follow. Subsequent paragraph references will be given in parentheses in the text.

4. See Pierre Riche, *Education and Culture in the Barbarian West,* trans. by John J. Contreni (Columbia: University of South Carolina Press, 1976).

5. See the introduction in the *Source Chretiennes* edition for a more complete analysis of her sources.

6. Chapter 17 of the Bowers edition, 92.

7. See Suzanne Wemple, *Women in Frankish Society,* (Philadelphia: University of Pennsylvania Press, 1983) 9-25; also Angela M. Lucas, *Women in the Middle Ages* (New York: St. Martin's Press, 1983) 3-18.

8. See Roger Gryson, *The Ministry of Women in the Early Church,* trans. by Jean LaPorte and Mary Louise Hall (Collegeville, MN: The Liturgical Press, 1980) 17-22.

9. A fragment on 1 Cor 14, 34 preserved in a catena and quoted by Gryson, 29.

10. Trans. by John Hammond Taylor, *Ancient Christian Writers,* 41 (New York: Newman Press, 1982) 99.

11. *Ibid.* 175.

12. The name given to the author of some early commentaries on Paul as well as of *The Questions on the Old and New Testament* wrongly ascribed to Augustine.

13. *Questions on the Old and New Testament,* 45.3, quoted in Suzanne Wemple 23, emphasis mine.

14. Dronke, commenting on this passage, says "Dhuoda...is passionately serious about the three-fold conviction she expresses here: her understanding is imperfect; yet God can remedy her imperfection by grace; and she must write, whatever her intellectual and personal defects, because her relationship to William is unique...." 41.

15. Chapter 47 of Bowers, 260.

3.

"A Love . . . Publicly Exposed": Heloise

The twelfth century came to western Europe like a rich and vibrant spring. Kenneth Clarke in his series on civilization calls it "The Great Thaw" and like the spring, it was the culmination of slow and often unrecorded growth during those preceding centuries still persistently called "the dark ages." The changes which had already begun in almost every area of life began to flower in profusion in the twelfth century and nowhere else were they more luxuriant than in education, religion and literature.

In the schools, the entire course of studies was changing; the traditional divisions of subject matter called the seven "liberal arts" were being revised and a new emphasis given to the development of skills in dialectic, a method of reasoning and argumentation. Furthermore, the context of education was changing as well. Learning, grounded in "the arts" and leading to theology, had flourished primarily in the monasteries where the culminating text was the Sacred Scriptures, the primary purpose was the illumination of Christian living, and the method of preference was the consultation of traditional authorities. The twelfth century saw the transition to the urban cathedral schools (in the process of becoming universities) where, though the ultimate text was still the Scriptures, the purpose was gradually becoming more academic, the love of learning in itself, and the method more reliant on human reason and the use of dialectic.

This is not to imply that the twelfth century was in any sense becoming secular. It was a period of intense religious activity. Monastic reform was popular and widespread and in many instances it was prompted by a scholarly return to the textual sources. The Cistercian reform was rooted in a desire for the thorough implementation of the Rule of Benedict. There was a renewed enthusiasm for the "apostolic life," that is, the simple, devout Christian life associated with the period of the Apostles as recorded in the New Testament.[1] The eremitical life received new attention and flourished again, particularly in the north of France.[2]

With all its energy and movement, the twelfth century seems to have opened up new possibilities for women. Eleanor of Aquitaine would have been extraordinary in any age; queen, consort of two kings and mother of two others, she had a unique range of possibilities open to her. But as a celebrated, literate patron of the arts, learning and the good life, she exemplified much that we identify as twelfth century achievement. She maintained a court that was a seed-bed for the development of "courtliness" and promoted the new arts of ritualized love-making as well as the troubadour poetry that celebrated it. Some of the poets in this new style were themselves women[3] and the convents were graced no less than the courts with women of vision and poetic gifts. Hildegarde of Bingen wrote poetry and essays explaining her cosmic visions; they were scientific and spiritual textbooks for her day. People traveled great distances to consult her. Hroswitha of Gandersheim wrote plays in the style of Terence and though she tried to tame him somewhat for her cloistered audience, she wrote both forcefully and felicitously.[4] Among these celebrated twelfth century women, Heloise takes her place.

We know little about Heloise's early life beyond the fact that she was born not long before 1100 and educated at the convent of Argenteuil. Fulbert, the Canon of Notre Dame in Paris, claimed her as his niece and, through his patronage, she met Peter Abelard whose pupil she became. By the time she was introduced to Abelard, her skills in writing were already well-known. The nuns at Argenteuil had done their work supremely well; and though Abelard's star was in the ascendency and his own scholarly reputation already well established, he did not hesitate to accept the position of her tutor. In spite of her connections in the city of Paris and her literary reputation,[5] Heloise's opportunity to do "higher studies" (philosophy) was extraordinary in the annals of the twelfth century and thrust her into the public eye. She was to remain a public, even notorious, figure for some years as her personal story unfolded.

Today she is probably better known for her personal life than for her learning. She has been celebrated as the reckless and romantic heroine who abandoned herself to a flamboyant love affair with Abelard. His castration at the hands of her kinsmen forms the dramatic climax to that love story, after which Heloise retired to monastic life and ultimately became the Abbess of the monastery of the Paraclete. Her personal life has been a perennial inspiration to novelists and playwrights.[6] On the other hand, we have the testimony of her contemporaries that she continued to be honored for her learning and, ultimately, for her virtues. No less a personage than Peter, the highly-respected Abbot of Cluny, praised her posthumously for her piety, learning and common sense. She possessed all of these talents and more.

Her complexity is revealed in a brief exchange of letters with Abelard shortly after she and the nuns were settled at the Paraclete. The letters expose the many sides of Heloise: the passionate woman wounded by the treatment she received, not primarily at the hands of her family, but from Abelard himself; the skillful logician and classical scholar who can marshal the precedents from both the pagan and Christian traditions into a persuasive and many-sided argument; the religious woman committed to maintaining the religious fervor of the Paraclete community through schooling and humane discipline.

The authenticity of these letters has been questioned. The reasons put forth against her authorship are varied, but a popular one is that the author of the passionate self-disclosures in the first letter could not be the same person who discourses so rationally on theological and monastic topics in the later two. Peter Dronke's assessment is the one that prevails here: after a painstaking study of the style of all of Heloise's letters, both certain and doubtful, Dronke believes that she indeed wrote the letters to Abelard.[7]

The first letter, which dates from about 1113, is, as Heloise tells us, a response to the publication of Abelard's *History of My Misfortunes*.[8] It is remarkable for its degree of self-revelation, its poignancy and its persuasive arguments. It exemplifies the "new learning" of the twelfth century which, while it continued the medieval tradition of biblical allegory, showed a new appreciation of classical letters and ideals as well. With a blend of vigor, optimism and diplomacy, Heloise writes to Abelard to convince him that he should continue to show his love for her through letters, if not through visits. She does this through a felicitous marriage of Christian and classical wisdom and style. In her range of arguments, she reveals her passion but, even more, her thoughtful reflection on her own experience, demonstrating her understanding of the motivation and moral character of human action.

Like Dhuoda before her and Julian after, Heloise thinks in biblical categories and uses the allegorical interpretation of scriptural stories and sayings to understand and express her own life experience. This tradition is particularly rich in the twelfth century; it attains a high-water mark in the Cistercian monastic literature with Bernard's great homilies on the *Song of Songs*, as the allegory of the mystical life. All theology was understood as commentary on Sacred Scripture; biblical history, taken as a whole, showed the continuity of God's salvation. The events of creation, exodus, the earthly life of Jesus and his paschal mystery were seen as paradigms repeated in the individual lives of all Christians. Thus, the scriptures were continually read in the light of contemporary experience and personal experience was interpreted by reference to the scriptures.

Throughout the first letter, Heloise expresses herself in the phrases and images of the Scriptures. She tells Abelard, for instance, that his letter was "full of gall and wormwood" (#2).[9] She gathers a collection of allusions (#9) by which she interprets Abelard's foundation of the Paraclete as the building of a new Solomonic temple. When trying to understand why Abelard supervised her entrance into the monastic life before he himself took monastic vows, Heloise wonders aloud whether he thought her likely to look back, as Lot's wife had done, to the pleasures of the flesh. Nourished as all Christians were on Bible and liturgy, Heloise does not in any way move beyond the tradition when she communicates her experiences and feelings in biblical language and imagery.

But the first letter of Heloise is also an excellent example of the growing medieval appreciation of the classical world. The great classics of the Roman empire had long provided the textbooks by which medieval students had learned the rudiments and niceties of the Latin language. Classical allusions and rhetorical figures were, therefore, commonplace to anyone who learned to write in Latin. But as Heloise builds her arguments against Abelard's behavior, she speaks of the virtues of the pagan authors as well as of their style and she cites their moral values which she parallels to traditional teaching. She cites Seneca to remind Abelard that even pagans recognize the power of a letter to render present an absent friend (#6). In this regard, Abelard's virtue is not yet up to pagan standards. She notes (#12) that the early Fathers of the church took great pains to write for the spiritual edification of women and expresses astonishment that Abelard should not have followed their example, especially as he was responsible for the foundation of the Paraclete. Thus as Heloise builds her arguments, she cites pagan and Christian authorities alternately; for her, as for the twelfth century generally, the common cultural wisdom rested equally on the two pillars of Christian revelation and classical Roman philosophy.

At the height of her persuasion, she even gives a kind of priority to pagan wisdom. On the relationship of men and women in marriage, Heloise quotes Aspasia, a Roman courtesan whom she calls a "philosopher" and whose opinion she names "wisdom." For Heloise, marriage is perfect not because of the sacredness of the sacramental bond but because of the human excellence of the individuals who contract the marriage (#16). True fidelity is intellectual rather than physical; it requires that one evaluate one's spouse as superior to all others. Otherwise, as Heloise comments on Aspasia, there is a kind of continual spiritual infidelity as one or other partner keeps open the possibility that someone better will come along. Thus does Heloise explain that in spite of physical distance and Abelard's impotence, theirs is a perfect marriage. Its perfection is based on Abelard's excellence and Heloise's unwavering appreciation of his gifts (she mentions specifically his poetic talent and the eminence of his reputation). As Heloise describes what their marriage has been and ought to continue to be, she appeals to the Ciceronian ideal of friendship.[10]

But her letter does not theorize directly about friendship or debate the validity of its tenets as derived from Roman ideals. Rather she applies this ideal to her relationship with Abelard (in a way that argues a prior consensus between them) to reinforce her arguments that he should come to visit her or, at the very least, write often. She writes with increasing intensity that friends must share a common destiny. At first she uses this idea to encourage him to share his sufferings with the nuns at the Paraclete, arguing that he will thus be able to bear his sufferings the more easily (#5). Later she says that it is souls, not only destinies, that are shared between friends. "For my soul was not my own but yours and even more now, if it is not with you, it does not exist" (#23). Friendship, for Heloise, is not just one of the greatest human goods; it is the very condition of human happiness.

Like the ancients, Heloise believes that true friendship requires self-denial, even self-forgetfulness. It also mandates absolute generosity and ought not to be sullied by any thought of gain, whether of money, pleasure or privilege. She speaks of "a certain great obligation, which became even more binding when it was reinforced by the lasting bonds of the sacrament of marriage" (#12). She speaks of "obligation" in the singular, but indeed, she is speaking of the entire relationship which bound them even before marriage, an exceedingly complex relationship as she reveals in her opening greeting. He is her master, having been, at first, her teacher and has become her father through his founding of the Paraclete; he was her husband, even before their official, secret marriage and now is her brother in Christ as they strive to succeed in fulfilling the obligations of religious life. But most of all, he has been her friend; this is the relationship that subsumes all others. She says quite clearly that marriage has only reinforced what was already contracted in friendship (#12). Therefore, it too requires self-forgetfulness and Heloise has responded to love's demands with a totality that seems even to surprise her as she writes of it: "And what is even more wondrous, my love turned against itself, becoming such madness that it put aside, without hope of recovery, what alone it hungered for ..." (#13). In contrast to her total giving, Peter lacks the most rudimentary generosity. Though words were cheap to one of his facile eloquence, he is stingy even with words; so she can expect no generosity in deeds.

The gift of self in friendship and marriage precludes any thought of gain. Heloise reminds Abelard that she had no desire for his possessions, in complete contrast to the marriage contracts of the day (#14). She implies that her friendship for him was not lustful, though it was, originally, erotic; but now that sexual love is not possible, her friendship remains even more intense and, therefore, more authentic than Abelard's whose present behavior casts serious doubt on the selfless character of his earlier attraction (#21). She does not pretend that her earlier love for him was completely selfless; she did hope to share in his reputation and prestige. Ironically, that hope has now added to her suffering; once "famous everywhere" because of his love songs, she is now publicly an object of pity.

In the treatise on *Spiritual Friendship,* Aelred of Rievaulx argues that Christian friendship is a virtue of such excellence that it can almost be equated with charity, that charity which is, according to St. John, the very name of God. For him, there are a few distinctions to be made between friendship and charity but he holds that friendship is the very apex of charity, that height of holiness where natural goodness and grace are one and inseparable. Similarly, Bernard of Clairvaux in his *Treatise on the Love of God* develops the proposition that human love (or friendship) and divine love were not two separate, much less mutually exclusive, realities but that human love was a stage on the road to perfect charity, a genuinely virtuous activity that was subsumed into and not negated by perfect love for God. Heloise also sees a clear relationship between her love for God and her love for Abelard, drawing a parallel between them that shocks many readers. In her attempt to show Abelard how perfect has been her love for him, she tells him that her conversion to monastic life and her progress along its stages has been entirely for love of him and therefore she expects no reward from God. She describes her obedience, the heart of Benedictine spirituality: as the nun vowed obedience to God in all things, so Heloise has given unconditional obedience to Abelard: "... I have done everything because of you and remain absolutely obedient to you even now" (#22). And as genuine monastic obedience involves total renunciation, so Heloise's obedience to Abelard has involved a total renunciation of the goods of sexuality and possessions.

> I have forbidden myself *all* pleasure so that I might serve you. I have kept back nothing for myself except the privilege of being your special possession (#24).

Indeed, she implies that as she had given herself to Abelard, she has been turned over to God through no action of her own but through a kind of contract made by Abelard and God between them; as she says "... you gave God title to me by monastic investiture ..." (#22).

It is precisely thoughts such as these which have made many question the authenticity of this letter; they are certainly extravagant assertions. But, as indicated above, the question of the intimate relationship between divine and human love was one under discussion in the most deeply religious circles of the day and if Heloise gives that discussion an unusual twist, we cannot rule out her intention to shock Abelard into taking her seriously again. Indeed, her request that Abelard fulfill his spiritual obligations, not only to her, but to all the nuns at the Paraclete, is a theme of the entire letter. She reminds him in biblical language and imagery that he has an apostolic role to play to the Paraclete; she cites Paul's relationship to the Corinthians as his model (#10) and calls him to be a good vineyard-keeper to the vines he has planted (#11). When she uses their past relationship as a basis for his present obligations to her, the language is consistently erotic, but she knows that the relationship is transformed and her ultimate goal is spiritual growth, both for herself and for the nuns of the Paraclete.

She begs for some such advice as the early fathers used to give to holy women, for she is "already wavering" (#12). The lack of supernatural motivation that she describes in herself is what she has experienced "up to now" (#22); there is something of a hint here that she is in the process of growing more truly spiritual. She tells Abelard that he is wrong to have so much confidence in her; or perhaps, rather, that she was wrong to create such confidence in him since it has meant greater neglect on his part (#24). She had somehow given him cause to take her monastic virtue for granted. Finally, she tells him that she needs only a comforting message and she will "quickly be at leisure for God again" (#25). The concept is monastic: contemplation is to be at leisure for God and is the result of proper discipline. Heloise truly desires to be at the service of God; but she cannot arrive at that state—or doesn't want to!—without the support of Abelard. If she uses every weapon in her arsenal to win that support, it is not too surprising nor, upon reflection, shocking. Bernard had used erotic language to describe the mystical life with God; Heloise also uses it to convince Abelard to use his power over her to her ultimate well-being. "Is it not so much more appropriate for you to arouse me now to the service of God as you did then to the service of lust?" (#25)

We see in the thought of Heloise in the first letter, not a radical departure from the values and style of her day, but a certain twist given to those values and style so that they are fitted into the framework of her own experiences. There is an attempt to mine the riches of both classical and Christian traditions for categories by which to understand and evaluate her motives and her behavior. Heloise is moving in the direction of ethical analysis. Abelard, of course, wrote one of the most significant ethical pieces of the century, his *Ethica,* the first work of the time to consider seriously the importance of intention in determining the ethical character of an act. Abelard wrote the *Ethica* in 1137, after his affair with Heloise, but ethical theory seems to have been a part of their discussions prior to separation. In this letter, Heloise appeals to an ethic of intentionality in a way that indicates she believes that they both agree on its validity. Her words are clear: "Though I am considered most guilty, I am most innocent, as you know. For it is not the thing done but the intention of the doer which makes the crime" (#20). In this letter of persuasion, she makes no attempt to persuade him that intentionality is the critical issue, so we may assume that she knows his mind in this matter. Indeed, since the theory seems to have come from their common investigation of issues, we may wonder to what extent she has helped to *form* his mind on this point.[11] Whichever way the influence worked, she makes a firm distinction between how she is viewed by others ("I am considered most guilty") and how he must judge her, according to their mutually held theory. She seems to welcome him as her judge; because of the friendship between them, she affirms that he alone knows and, in fact, has tested her heart (intentions) and therefore he alone is the appropriate judge.

The sticking-point in an ethics based on intention is that intention is normally beyond external verification. Therefore, only the person making the choice would be in a position of judging its ethical character; subjectivism is the problem. Heloise suggests that her intentions may be judged by their enduring results in what ethicists call the public forum, i.e., in the world of visible action. By this criterion, Heloise says, her love is perfect. She puts her case: at the beginning of their affair, it was not clear whether true love or only lust motivated the lovers. Now when no sexual satisfaction is possible, her total self-denial at Abelard's command and for his sake proves that her love has been pure from the beginning (#24). This is a very person-centered ethics; no laws are mentioned, even to be rationalized away. Heloise does not analyze the social consequences of her actions. There is no echo here of the penance manuals of the time, no hint of the notion of shame associated with the violation of the norms of the community or one's class.[12] Since the letter was not intended as a complete treatise on ethics, we may not assume that other elements of ethical thinking would not have come into play were Heloise framing a theoretical work. Yet the letter demonstrates the great extent to which she emphasized her own experience as the core of ethical reflection.

In many ways, Heloise is representative of her age but she is certainly not typical of the women in it. Not for many centuries (at least as far as we know), would someone again be as educated as she. Though there were some women in the twelfth century, like Eleanor of Aquitaine, who played decisive roles, no one else was so thoroughly absorbed the intellectual and moral changes of the day. She used the intellectual resources available to her to illuminate her own particular, feminine experience. Heloise is a forerunner of later changes in women's lives. She questioned the moral norms of her day, not merely because they constrained her, but because they contradicted the understanding which had come to her from a rational analysis of her own experience. She did not hesitate to be completely personal, nor completely reasonable. In a later letter, she will apply the same norms of experience and reason to an analysis of the rules of monastic life for women. In the first letter, she explored those norms as they applied to her feelings and her relationship with Abelard. She took the theoretical discussions out of the academic environment in which they flourished and played them out in her life. Her experience of the consequences would often be replicated; her courage, rarely.

Heloise's First Letter to Abelard

1. To Abelard, her lord, or rather her father, her husband or rather her brother, from Heloise, his servant or rather his daughter, his wife or rather his sister.

2. My beloved, someone recently brought me, quite by chance, the letter which you sent to comfort a friend. I knew it was yours as soon as I saw the invocation and I began to read it with the ardor with which I would equally embrace the writer himself.

I intended to recreate, at least through his words, the image of the one whose reality I had been deprived of. Almost everything mentioned in the letter was full of gall and wormwood, referring as it did to the wretched story of our conversion as well as to the unremitting crosses which you alone carry. In truth, you carried out in the letter the promise you had made to your friend in the beginning, namely [to make him see] that in comparison with your own troubles, his are small and negligible.

3. You first explained something of the persecutions you experienced at the hands of your teachers followed by the most treacherous injury done to your very body; then you discussed the cursed envy and no less dangerous pen of your fellow students, Alberic of Rheims and Lotulf of Lombardy. You did not omit what was done to your glorious theological work through their instigation or how you yourself were given something almost like a prison sentence. Then you proceeded to narrate the machinations of your abbot and false brothers, the most serious attacks on your reputation that were stirred up against you by those two false apostles, the rivals previously mentioned, and the scandal which occurred, for the most part because you violated custom in the naming of your oratory for the Paraclete. After that, you brought the miserable story to an end by exposing the intolerable persecutions waged against you, and continuing even until now, by one who is surely the most cruel overseer and by those worst monks imaginable whom you call "brothers."

4. In my judgment, no one could read or hear those tales with dry eyes. They re-awakened my own sorrows in proportion to the many details they narrated; they greatly increased that sorrow insofar as they recounted how your dangers increase even until now. As a consequence, all of us here have been driven to despair of your life: daily we expect the last words about your death and await the rumors, our hearts pounding with fear within our bosoms.

5. Therefore, through Christ who still protects you in some way, we who are his handmaids and yours beseech you to write frequently about those situations which still buffet you on all sides, like a boat about to sink. Let us, who alone remain on your side, share in your sorrows or your joys. For sorrows which are shared usually bring some consolation and whenever a burden is carried by many it may be borne more lightly or even put aside. Even if this storm has quieted a little, the more quickly the letters come, the more joyfully they will be received. Whatever you may write about, it will be no small means of healing because at least you will show that you still remember us. Indeed, Seneca himself teaches us by example how welcome are the letters of absent friends; he writes to his friend Lucilius these words:

> 6. I thank you for your frequent letters. They are the one way in which you can be present to me, because whenever I receive your letter it is as if we are immediately one. If pictures of absent friends are welcome even though they revive our memories of and longing for those who are gone and give a false and empty comfort, so much more welcome are the letters which absent friends send us in their own handwriting.

7. Thank God that there is at least this way of restoring your presence to us, a way which no malice can prevent, nor no difficulty hinder; therefore let no negligence slow you down.

8. You have written your friend a prolific letter of consolation, seemingly about his adversities but also about your own. Though you intended your painstaking remembering to provide consolation for him, you added much to our desolation; what you wanted to be a medicine for his wounds became instead a means of inflicting new wounds of sorrow on us and renewed our old wounds as well. I beg you to heal what you have hurt even while you have your hands full trying to cure someone else. You have done what is fitting both as friend and companion; you have paid

the debt of friendship as well as that of fellowship. But you have assumed a greater debt to us who are most fittingly called, not friends but most precious friends, not companions but daughters —or whatever word can be thought up that is sweeter and holier.

9. If doubt remains about how how great this debt is by which you have obligated yourself, there is no lack of argumentation or witnesses; and even if all of these remain silent, the reality of the thing itself cries out. After God, you alone are the founder of this place, you alone are the builder of this oratory, you alone the architect of this congregation. You have built nothing on another's foundation. Everything here is your creation. This wasteland which lies so open to wild beasts and robbers knew no human habitation nor did it have any dwelling on it. In the very lairs of wild beasts, in the hiding places where robbers lurked, you have erected a divine tabernacle and dedicated a temple to the Holy Spirit. You brought to this building-project no riches from kings or princes—though you had influence with the greatest and the wealthiest—and so whatever was built should be credited to you alone. This in spite of the fact that those who gathered here for your teaching, whether clerics or scholars, were certainly used to ministering to all your needs. And even those who were living off of ecclesiastical benefices, who did not know how to offer but only to receive, who extended their hand for taking but not for giving, even these became insistent and generous in their offers of help.

10. Yours, truly yours, is this young planting which is dedicated exclusively to a holy way of life; up till now you have put in a large number of young shoots and frequent watering is necessary if they are to thrive. This planting would be weak, even if it were not new, because it is composed completely of the frail feminine sex. Therefore, frequent and diligent cultivation is needed just as the Apostle himself said: "I planted, Apollos watered, and God, however, gave the increase." The Apostle planted the Corinthians, to whom he was writing, and founded

them in faith by his preaching of doctrine. Afterward, Apollos, the disciple of that apostle, watered them by sacred exhortations and thus divine grace was showered on them, bringing an increase in virtue.

11. But you cultivate the vines of another's vineyard which you have not planted and these vines have turned against you in bitterness. Thus your admonitions are fruitless and your sacred words without effect. You teach and admonish rebellious men who do not profit from it. In vain you scatter the pearls of divine eloquence before pigs. You who spend yourself so thoroughly on the stubborn, consider what you owe to the obedient. Think about what you owe to your daughters, you who squander so much on your enemies. And even though I omit the rest, think of how obligated you are to me, so that the debt which you have contracted to these women communally, you may most devoutly satisfy to one who is yours alone.

12. In your greater excellence, you know better than our humble selves how many impressive treatises the fathers wrote for the teaching and exhortation of women—or even for their comfort—and with what care they composed them. This makes your initial forgetfulness, when our conversion was as yet in its fragile beginnings, even more astonishing. I was amazed that neither reverence for God, nor our love, nor, finally, the example of the holy fathers, caused you to offer me some words of comfort face to face, nor even a letter when you were absent. And yet, I was already wavering, almost done in by prolonged grief. I am the one to whom you were bound, as you know, by a certain great obligation, which became even more binding when it was reinforced by the lasting bonds of the sacrament of marriage; you know, too, that you have been made subject to me by the great love with which I have always surrounded you, a love which has been publicly exposed as excessive.

13. You know, my beloved, as everyone knows, how much I have lost in losing you. You know how that wretched event, the

greatest act of treachery known anywhere, robbed me of myself as well as of you. Indeed, the suffering is greater because of the manner of the loss than because of the sentence [of separation] itself. Truly, the greater the cause of sorrow, the greater the remedies that must be used for the consolation of it. These consolations must come from no one but you: since you alone are the cause of the sorrow, you alone have the grace of consolation. Inasmuch as you are the only one who has saddened me, you are the only one who can make me happy or console me. It is also you alone who owe me the most, especially now that I have carried out everything you ordered so completely that I even found strength in your command to throw myself away since I was unable to oppose you in anything. And what is even more wondrous, my love turned against itself, becoming such madness that it put aside, without hope of recovery, what alone it hungered for; at your command, I instantly changed my dress along with my mind so that I could prove that you alone possessed both my body and my soul.

14. God knows that I asked nothing whatever of you except yourself; my desire for you was pure, undefiled by any desire for your possessions. I expected neither marriage bonds nor marriage portion; at the end, I strove, not to satisfy my own pleasure and wishes, but yours, as you yourself know. And if the name of wife seems holier and more valid [to others], the word mistress will always remain sweeter to me or even, if you do not get angry at it, the name of concubine or prostitute. I hoped by these names to humble myself more fully before you and, in consequence, to win fuller gratitude from you as well as to do less damage to the glory of your reputation. Even you yourself did not forget this, if the letter which you sent to console your friend is any example; in that letter, of which I reminded you above, you did not refuse to explain *some* of the reasons by which I tried to prevent you from binding us in an unfortunate marriage. You did not, however, speak of the *many* reasons I gave for my preference for love over marriage, for liberty over chains. I call

God as my witness that if Augustus, ruler of the entire world, thought me worthy of the honor of marriage and conferred on me his entire territory as my possession forever, I would consider it more precious and more honorable to be called your whore than his empress.

15. For someone is not made better by riches or power; the latter depend on luck, but goodness is a matter of virtue. A woman should be considered no more than a slave put up for sale if she marries a rich man more willingly than a poor one or desires a man's possessions in marriage more than the man himself. Truly a woman led to marriage by such desires ought to be given wages rather than gratitude. It is surely clear that such a woman pursues a man's things rather than the man himself and would, if she could, willingly prostitute herself to a richer man. This is what Aspasia the philosopher clearly has in mind in the logical argument she put forth to Xenophon and his wife (according to Aschines Socraticus). When she proposed a way of reconciling them to one another, she ended her argument in this fashion:

16. Unless you decide that the one you have is the best one for your needs and that you each have the best woman and the best man, you will always indeed go over again and again in your mind whether there may be a better man or woman on earth who may be chosen.

17. Her thought is holy indeed and more than philosophical; it ought rather to be called wisdom than philosophy. When perfect love thinks this way, it is a holy error and a blessed fallacy in those who are married. Then the marriage bonds are kept through modesty of spirit rather than through bodily continence. Error has brought some people to that point; clear truth brought me there. What others believed about their husbands, I believed about you; but the whole world also believed it, or rather, knew it to be true of you. Therefore my love was all the more true to the degree that it was free of error.

18. Who could equal your fame, either among kings or philosophers? What region or city or village was not hot to see you? Who, I ask you, did not hasten to lay eyes on you when you went out into the public or did not crane his neck and strain his eyes to follow your departure? What wife or virgin did not covet you in your absence or glow with excitement in your presence? What queen or very powerful woman did not envy me my joys or my bed?

19. I admit that you had two special gifts with which you could immediately entice the minds of however many women you liked, namely the gifts of speaking and of singing, talents which have rarely been given to philosophers as we know. Though only as a kind of game refreshing you, so to speak, from the work of philosophic exercises, you left many love songs and poems composed in meter and rhythm. Because of the great sweetness of the lyrics as well as of the tunes, your name was always on everyone's lips and even illiterate people could not forget the sweetness of your melodies. Because of this most of all, women sighed for love of you. And since the largest number of these songs sang of our love, I became famous everywhere in a short time and many women burned with envy against me. For what gift of body or mind did not adorn your young manhood?

20. Does not my present misfortune compel those women who envied me then to suffer along with me now the loss of such delights? Does not the compassion that is my due now soften every previous enemy, man or woman? Though I am considered most guilty, I am most innocent, as you know. For it is not the thing done but the intention of the doer which makes the crime. Therefore justice ought to weigh not what was done but what was in the heart. But what I have had in my heart toward you, you alone can judge for you have put it to the test. I commit everything to your examination; I yield in all things to your testimony. Give me one reason, if you can, why after our conversion to a life in religion—which you alone insisted upon—I have been

so neglected and forgotten that you have not spoken to me so as to revive my strength nor sent me a letter to console me. Tell me, I say, if you can, or rather I will tell you what I feel and what everyone suspects.

21. Desire joined you to me more powerfully than friendship, the fires of lust more powerfully than love. Therefore, when what you desired ceased to be possible, your display of affection vanished with it. Beloved, this is not my conjecture alone but is what everyone believes; it is not one opinion among many but the universal view, not only in private but publicly acknowledged. If only this were my personal opinion and others found excuses for your love, that would lessen my sorrow. If only I could fabricate excuses for you and thereby cover up your cheap behavior toward me! Pay attention to what I am about to ask, I beg you, and you will see how small and easy a thing it is. Since I am cheated of your presence, at least send me, as you promised, a sweet image of yourself in words—you have enough of those! Yet, I wait in vain for generous deeds if I must put up with your stinginess even in words.

22. Up to this point, I have believed that you would do much for me, since I have done everything because of you and remain absolutely obedient to you even now. It was not religious devotion but your command which dragged me to the austerities of the monastic way of life while I was still a young girl. Judge my situation for yourself: if you do nothing for me, are not my efforts in vain? I cannot expect any reward from God for what I have done because love for Him has been no part of my motivation up till now. Rather I followed you when you were hastening after God, indeed I beat you to the taking of the religious habit. As if moved by the memory of Lot's wife who turned back, you gave God title to me by monastic investiture and profession before you yourself made that commitment. I confess that I suffered violently and was ashamed that you had so little confidence in me in this one situation. God knows that, at your command, I

would not have hesitated either to precede you or follow you as you hastened to the region where Vulcan presides.

23. For my soul was not my own but yours and even more now, if it is not with you, it does not exist. In truth, without you there is no purpose for its existence. I beg you to treat my soul well so that it may remain with you and it will flourish in your possession if it finds you kind, if you repay gracious act for gracious act, a small grace in return for my great ones, mere words in return for deeds.

24. I suppose, my love, that if your love was less sure of me, you would take greater care of me. But now that I have restored your confidence even more fully, I shall have to put up with greater neglect! I beg you to remember what I have done and consider how much you owe me. When I enjoyed carnal pleasure with you, many were uncertain whether I acted through love or lust, but now the end of the affair indicates what kind of beginning it had. I have forbidden myself *all* pleasure so that I might serve you. I have kept back nothing for myself except the privilege of being your special possession. Weigh carefully your own injustice, truly, if when I merit more, you repay less, indeed practically nothing, since what I ask is so small a thing and so easy for you to do.

25. I beg you in the name of God Himself to whom you have offered yourself to restore your presence to me in the only way you can: write me some comforting message, at least agree to do so, and then my obedience will be revived and I will quickly be at leisure for God again. When you came after me for sinful pleasures in the past, you deluged me with letters, you kept putting "your Heloise" on everyone's lips in poems that you continually published. Every street and every single house echoed my name. Is it not so much more appropriate for you to arouse me now to the service of God as you did then to the service of lust? Weigh carefully, I beg you, what you owe, pay attention to

what I am asking, and I will finish a long letter with a short ending; Farewell, my only one.

Questions and Activities

1. Although it is generally accepted that human experience is one of the important sources of ethical thinking, it is only very recently that women ethicists have begun to question the male bias of ethical theory up to now as well as to analyze the particularities of feminine experience as a source of insight into moral norms. There are some works in the Suggested Reading list which reflect this new understanding. Read one or more of them and write a personal essay of response.

2. Read the rest of the correspondence between Heloise and Abelard, including the *History of My Misfortunes*. Take one of the themes of the introductory essay, or one of your own, and trace it through two or more of the other letters.

3. Do an analysis of your own ethical position. What norms and values seem to operate in your own thinking? Do you know where you acquired them? To what extent has education played a part in your moral development? Are any of your norms and values identifiable as particularly "feminine" or derived from feminine experience? If possible, involve a trusted male of your acquaintance in a dialogue on these questions. Does such a dialogue give you any insight into your own moral development?

4. Imagine yourself interviewing Heloise for a segment on CBS' "Sixty Minutes." What would you like to ask her? How do you think she would answer? What would she think of the position of women today? Write up the interview.

Selected Additional Reading

Abelard and Heloise. *The Letters of Abelard and Heloise.* Trans. by B. Radice. Harmondsworth: Penguin Press, 1974.

Aelred of Rievaulx. *Spiritual Friendship.* Cistercian Fathers Series, VI. Kalamazoo, Michigan: Cistercian Press, 1978.

Andolsen, Barbara Hilkert, Christine E. Gudorf and Mary D. Pellauer, eds. *Women's Consciousness, Women's Conscience.* Minneapolis: Winston Press, 1985.

Baker, Derek, ed. *Medieval Women.* Oxford: Basil Blackwell, 1978.

Bogin, Meg. *The Women Troubadours.* New York and London: W.W. Norton, 1980.

Dronke, Peter. *Women Writers of the Middle Ages.* New York: Cambridge University Press, 1984.

Farley, Margaret A. *Personal Commitments: Beginning, Keeping, Changing.* San Francisco: Harper and Row, 1986.

Gies, Frances and Joseph Gies. *Women in the Middle Ages.* San Francisco: Harper and Row, 1978.

Gilligan, Carol. *In a Different Voice.* Cambridge, Massachusetts: Harvard University Press, 1982.

Gilson, Etienne. *Heloise and Abelard.* London: Holt Publishing Co., 1951.

Lucas, Angela M. *Women in the Middle Ages.* New York: St. Martin's Press, 1983.

MacHaffie, Barbara. *Her Story: Women in Christian Tradition.* Philadelphia: Fortress Press, 1986.

Muckle, J.T. *The Story of Abelard's Adversities.* Toronto, Canada: The Pontifical Institute of Medieval Studies, 1964.

Stuard, M.A., ed. *Women and Medieval Society.* Philadelphia: University of Pennsylvania Press, 1976.

Waddell, Helen. *Peter Abelard, A Novel.* New York: Literary Guild, 1933.

Notes

1. Cf. Marie Dominique Chenu, "Monks, Canons, and Laymen in Search of the Apostolic Life," *Nature, Man and Society in the Twelfth Century* (Chicago and London: University of Chicago Press, 1968) 202-238.

2. Jacqueline Smith, "Robert of Arbissel: *Procurator Mulierum,*" in *Medieval Women,* ed. by Derek Baker (Oxford: Basil Blackwell, 1978) 175-184.

3. See Meg Bogin's anthology entitled *The Women Troubadours* (New York and London: W. W. Norton and Co., 1980). Bogin's introduction gives a brief but helpful introduction to the background of the women troubadours.

4. See *The Plays of Roswitha,* trans. by Christopher St. John (New York: Cooper Square Publishers, Inc., 1966).

5. "She read and wrote Latin with precision, knew her Greek and Roman classics, had her ideas from Ovid, her stoicism from Seneca, and probably her science from Aristotle," says Mary Lukas in "Farewell to Heloise," *Catholic World* 213 (July 71) 174-177.

6. See, for example, Helen Waddell's *Peter Abelard, a Novel* (New York: Literary Guild, 1933) and George Moore, *Heloise and Abelard* (New York: Liveright Publishing Co., 1932). "Heloise" by James Forsythe was presented at the Gate Theatre in New York on September 24, 1958, and Ronald Millar's dramatization of the Waddell novel, entitled "Abelard and Heloise," opened on Broadway in 1971.

7. *Women Writers of the Middle Ages* (London and New York: Cambridge University Press, 1984) 107-109.

8. See J.T. Muckle, *The Story of Abelard's Adversities,* a translation with notes of the *Historia Calamitatum* (Toronto, Canada: The Pontifical Institute of Medieval Studies, 1964).

9. The recent edition of the Latin text of the letters as well as of the *Historia Calamitatum* is by J. T. Muckle in *Medieval Studies* 12 (1950) 163-213. His English translation of the letters, "The Personal Letters between Abelard and Heloise," is also in *Medieval Studies* 15 (1953) 47-94. It is my own translation of the first letter which follows and to which references are made by paragraph number.

10. Others in the twelfth century were similarly attracted to this ideal and friendship became a theme of some of the most representative writing of the century. The first book on friendship to come out of the Christian tradition, Aelred of Rievaulx's *Spiritual Friendship*, trans. by Mary Eugenia Laker (Washington, D.C.: Cistercian Publications, Consortium Press, 1974), appears at this time from within the Cistercian school; it is a conscious updating of the Ciceronian work and even, like Heloise, considers marriage a species of friendship.

11. Heloise's actual influence upon the *Ethica* may be impossible to determine, but it should not be ruled out. See the remarks of Kenneth Rexroth in "Abelard and Heloise," *Saturday Review* 51 (Feb., 1968): 14-15. "Our only record of her intelligence is her letters where she is patently the superior of Abelard."

12. See John F. Benton, "Consciousness of Self and Perceptions of Individuality," in *The Twelfth Century Renaissance,* Robert L. Benson and Giles Constable, eds. (Harper and Row: New York, 1980) 263-298, for an exposition of the question of the growing importance of the personal in twelfth-century morality. His examples, however, give no indication of the kind of personalism found in this letter.

4.

"So Far as My Intelligence and Understanding Will Serve:" Julian of Norwich

[1]The late fourteenth century was not particularly propitious for the advancement of women. The twelfth century with its promise of change and enlightenment had ended by leaving women's lot pretty much as it had been. The flourishing of religious reform within and without the monastic tradition had inspired large numbers of women to experiment with new forms of religious life, but at the century's close, religious options for women remained few and substantially unchanged. In 1100, for instance, Robert of Arbrissel established a renowned double monastery at Fontevrault to provide a more controlled and cloistered environment for the women who had originally gathered around him in a spontaneous and unstructured manner. Once founded, Fontevrault quickly became one aristocratic monastery like many others for women: "From the simple, crude constructions which had sufficed in the early years, and which

became unattractive because of their insecurity, instability and non-conformity, grew an abbey of great complexity, marked by its respectability, traditionalism and aristocratic character."[2] In a similar pattern of innovation and repression, Cistercian nunneries arose almost from the beginning of Stephen Harding's reform, yet they were first ignored, then impeded by Cistercian legislation and, though fairly large in number, continued to exist only on the fringe of Cistercian life until the end of the Middle Ages.[3] The women who were attracted to the spontaneous and unstructured Franciscan movement received immediate encouragement from Francis himself, but his attitude changed quickly and even his beloved Clare found it almost impossible to win the right to practice absolute poverty, something finally granted only to her own house as a special privilege.[4]

Outside of convents, women's innovations in religious living fared even worse. The Beguines, for example, were a substantive movement of twelfth-century laywomen who wished to remain "in the world" while engaging in good works and the practice of the evangelical virtues. Though the majority of these women remained completely orthodox, their experiment became synonymous with heresy and their name itself may well be a derivation of the word "Albigensian."[5] As the enthusiasm and energy that the twelfth century winds of reform had kindled in women were increasingly restricted, not to say repressed, the mystical life became the only avenue open to those who desired lives of intense devotion. The fourteenth century became remarkable for the numbers and importance of its women mystics; names such as Catherine of Siena, Gertrude the Great, Machtilde of Magdeburg and Mechtilde of Hackeborn are well known. At the same time, there were other women, like Margery Kempe, who seemed to live in the shadowland of mysticism; outside of the monastery with its education in Bible and liturgy, these women had few resources by which to discern or discipline their own experience. Led by an unrestained imagination, Margery fell victim to scruples and gave herself over to excessive practices.[6]   Still other women moved completely outside the church's official pale and joined groups such as the Cathari where their mystical longings were not only given scope and direction but were interpreted as signs of a ministerial vocation.[7] Since the Cathari regarded sexuality as a Satanic creation, sexual identity could have no meaning in their rites; Cathari women seemed willing to surrender their sexual reality for the privilege of developing their intellectual and spiritual leadership. In this, of course, they were not unlike their more orthodox sisters in the cloister.

The fourteenth century reeked of morbidity.   External events encouraged an obsession with death and a frenetic attempt to escape it.   It was the time of the Black Plague, the Hundred Years' War, the Inquisition and the danse macabre.   Julian of Norwich lived in a world that produced scrupulosity as well as extreme forms of passion piety, often involving self-mutilation.   Yet she proposed a practical soteriology that is both optimistic about material creation and serene in the face of sin and death.[8]   History has recorded little of Julian.   She seems to have been a recluse at the church of St. Julian in Conyngsford, Norwich.[9] She shows some elements of a Benedictine background and perhaps left the local Benedictine monastery to follow her eremitical vocation.   She claims to be unlettered but her style is not that of an untutored woman but rather that of someone with a more than passing acquaintance with the art of rhetoric.   She dates the visions which she describes in the *Showings* at May 13, 1373 at which time, she says, she was thirty and one-half years old. She would therefore have been born in 1341-2.[10] Civil records in the city of Norwich testify that she was the beneficiary of four bequests, the last in 1416, indicating she was still alive at that time.[11] But the central event of her life, that which shaped all of her thought thereafter, occurred when she was just turned thirty and already established in her anchor-hold. Julian fell victim to a near fatal illness; as she neared death, a crucifix was offered to her and she suddenly experienced that the reality around her receded into darkness, the cross alone illuminated. Then followed sixteen visions, the narration of which is at the heart of her text.

There are, in fact, two versions of her revelations. We do not know how soon after the event she recorded them in her first version, but the second, longer version was completed considerably later, the final editing taking place probably in 1393.[12] Between the visions and the final interpretation lie some twenty years of Christian living during which Julian not only devoted herself to contemplation but also ministered to many who came for spiritual counsel.[13] *Showings,* then, is the fruit of reflection nourished by prayer and ministry, a genuinely theological project undertaken by one who, as she says of herself, "... wanted to live to love God better and longer, so that [she] might through the grace of that living have more knowledge and love of God ...."[14]

The final version of *Showings* is unified by Julian's understanding of creation as God's primary and paradigmatic work. For Julian, creation reveals God's essential nature which she repeatedly describes as power, wisdom and love (or goodness). The revelation of God in creation is definitive: nothing, not even human sin, can impede God's benevolent purpose. All of history is the unfolding of Divine Providence and an understanding of creation is the basis of our profound trust in God's providential care in spite of our own experience of sin. A lengthy quotation is justified by its cogency in bringing together these key themes of the *Showings:*

> The thirteenth revelation is that our Lord God wishes us to have great regard for all the deeds which he has performed in the most noble work of creating all things and it treats of the excellence of man's creation, which is superior to all God's works; and it is about the precious amends which he has made for man's sins, turning all our blame into everlasting honor. Here he says: Behold and see, for by the same power, wisdom and goodness that I

> have done all this, by the same power, wisdom and good-
> ness I shall make all things well which are not well, and
> you will see it. And in this it is his wish that we should
> preserve ourselves in the faith and truth of Holy Church,
> not wishing to know his mysteries except as that is fitting
> for us in this life.[15]

Julian here highlights the importance of a respect for the created
order, in which the human person itself is the preeminent
achievement. It is God himself who requires of us this "great
regard" for the creation of the human person and the God who so
requires is one who has revealed himself in a special way to
Julian as a lord ever "homely" and "courteous" (this is the
vocabulary of the original Middle English).[16] This "homely"
creator is also the one who has made "precious amends" for our
sins. As Genesis describes God calling the created, orderly
universe out of impersonal, primeval chaos, so Julian's God
promises an even more amazing order which will be brought out
of the personal chaos which we continue to unleash in our own
lives and upon our world: "I will make all things well which are
not well and you shall see it."

Julian develops the notion of redemption as a new creation at
some length. She draws an explicit parallel between initial creation and the redemption won by Christ's death and resurrection.

> ...we know that when man fell so deeply and so wretched-
> ly through sin, there was no other help for restoring him,
> except through him who created him. And he who created
> man for love, by the same love wanted to restore man to
> the same blessedness and to even more. And just as we
> were made like the Trinity in our first making, our
> Creator wished us to be like Jesus Christ our savior in
> heaven forever, through the power of our making again.[17]

Jesus is both the instrument of our first creation and our savior
through the second creation. He is therefore our mother in the

first (because he gives us being and life) as well as in the second (because he gives us newer, eternal life which he nourishes from his own body in the Eucharist).[18] Julian does not originate the theme of Jesus as our Mother. It was used by Anselm of Canterbury to whose work Julian's forms an interesting contrast. Anselm analyzed both Incarnation and redemption in terms of justice, retribution, and condign merit; Julian derives from the same mysteries a theology of mercy, forgiveness, and the internal renewal of the fallen creature.[19]

If the primary and most significant work of God is the act of creation, then the creator/creature relationship is, for Julian, the most important one in the spiritual life of Christians. Creaturehood is often misunderstood as depreciating the nobility of the human person. Certainly, if we reflect upon the story of the primal sin in Genesis, Adam and Eve seem to find their status as creature somehow a condition to be avoided or overcome. But we find no such sense in the *Showings*. Here, the creator/creature relationship is always a source of delight for God[20] and a well of grace for the Christian.

Julian considers this the key for understanding the grace given to Mary, the mother of God. In chapter four, Julian describes a vision she has of the preeminence of Mary.[21] In this vision she sees Mary at the Annunciation caught up in prayer and contemplation. According to Julian, God gives her a spiritual insight into the content of Mary's contemplation and she is led to understand that at the moment of Incarnation Mary is engaged in contemplating the creative act of God in her own regard. Julian believes that Mary's grace-filled assent to the divine invitation flows from her acceptance of creaturehood. In this act of assent she reverses the dynamic of the primal sin. The Incarnation which her acceptance brings about is thus the fulfillment of creation rather than the breaking-in to human history of a new order of divine activity. Mary is praised above all creatures precisely by reference to her preeminence in the created order rather than her role in the plan of salvation. Or instead, the latter is seen as in perfect continuity with the former. Further on in the text, Julian adds that it is Mary's profound sense of creaturehood (which includes a sense of the greatness of God and her own smallness) that is the foundation of all her grace and of her fulness of virtue.[22] There is no mariolatry here. Mary's meaning is not to be found in her exceptions but in her fidelity to the human condition.

Julian's appreciation of God's act of creation leads her to an optimistic understanding of human nature, not only in the abstract but in the concrete, existential situation of human sinfulness and ambiguity. Like all spiritual writers from Augustine on, Julian's anthropology begins with the human person as the *imago Dei*. Like Augustine, she insists that from the first moment of creation all human beings have a natural orientation toward the creator which grace only intensifies and develops. Love of, and desire for, God are part of the natural human endowment from the beginning.

> ... and therefore we may with reverence ask from our lover all that we will, for our natural will is to have God, and God's good will is to have us, and we can never stop willing or loving until we possess him in the fullness of joy. And there we can will no more, for it is his will that we be occupied in knowing and loving until the time comes that we shall be filled full in heaven.[23]

But she does not ignore the dark side of the human condition. She often reflects that human persons are changeable; blinded, weak, and ignorant, they are incapable of fidelity and constancy.[24] They continually experience the effects of the Fall and are victimized by conflicting feelings. Indeed, "during our lifetime here we have in us a marvelous mixture of both well-being and woe."[25] Yet to her the mixture is always "marvellous" indeed and she grows ever more confident that in Christ's power "we never assent" to our sinfulness but rather cling tenaciously to God's will "in our intention."[26] She is unceasingly puzzled by God's insistance that love prevents our sinfulness from being definitive. Equally mysterious to her is our persistence in sin, after we have been given to understand God's immense love. Though she is admonished by the Lord himself to consign this paradox to his mercy and to refrain from attempting to penetrate his mysterious will, she continues to return to the theme throughout the book.

Much that is representative of Julian's thought, comes together in the parable of the Lord and the servant.[27] According to Julian, God shows her the vision of the Lord and the servant in response to a very specific question. She is burdened by a perceived contradiction between what she has understood from her visions about God's mercy and the ordinary teaching of the church about sin. From the church and from her own feelings, she has learned that the guilt of sin is a universal burden, but from her visions and the twenty years of subsequent contemplation upon them she has become intimate with a Lord who continually offers mercy rather than blame. So she asks the Lord: "And if it be true that we are sinners and blameworthy, good Lord, how can it be that I cannot see this truth in you, who are my God, my maker in whom I desire to see all truth?" (#1)

God's response is a bodily vision of a stately Lord reclining at ease and attended by a respectful servant. "The Lord looks on his servant very lovingly and sweetly and mildly" and then gives him a task to perform. The servant runs off to complete the task and in his very eagerness "he falls into a dell and is greatly injured." And yet the servant, though "feeble and foolish," remains meek and as attentive to the lord in his intention as he was before; therefore the lord does not consider him blameworthy "for the only cause of his falling was his good will and his great desire" (#2). The lord decides he must reward the servant for goodness of intention and for the suffering endured, lest the lord himself appear discourteous. What an extraordinary description;

Adam falls through carelessness because he is too eager to obey![28] Julian makes it very clear that though the servant is wounded in every aspect of nature, still "his will was preserved in God's sight" (#8). From this she can only conclude that it is we who punish ourselves for our sin, or rather experience the punishment in the pain, while God longs only to console and strengthen the servant whom he never ceases to love. Even the kindly Julian is amazed and is admonished by the lord to study "all the attributes, divine and human, which were revealed in the example, though this may seem to you mysterious and ambiguous" (#8). With a docility akin to that of the servant in the parable, Julian does this for twenty years.[29]

The parable of Chapter 51 is remarkable not only for its content but, perhaps even more, for the methodological care which Julian exercises in telling it. She is careful to distinguish what she is given to see in a bodily vision and what she is given to understand in her spirit (#1). She further distinguishes the inchoate understanding with which she is left at the end of the seeing (#6) from the fullness of understanding which was to come only later. She notes that she was given the keys to later understanding ("three attributes") and states that she allowed those keys to guide her subsequent reflections. The road to understanding, for Julian, led her to bring together the vision itself (the first "attribute"), the "inward instruction" she was to continue to receive (*i.e.*, the on-going process of interior reflection) and "the whole revelation from the beginning to the end" (#7). In very simple language, Julian has outlined her understanding of the traditional process of theology. It begins with "the given," that is, revelation; gradually illuminated through prayer and reflection, it is then tested by Christian living. In the final analysis, the single truth must be fitted into the entire body of Christian teaching, the whole divine story.

The meanings which she extricated from the parable by her contemplation cannot be systematically analyzed. They are uncovered, bit by bit, as she lays back the layers of meaning. They flow from her in rich association rather than logical progression. She narrates her understanding by replaying the vision for us several times. In the first telling, the lord and the servant are described in general terms (the lord "sits in state," the servant "stands respectfully"). This is the story of God and the first human person in whom all are incorporated. It is the description of the sinful human condition, but the way out is already indicated here. It is the ancient way of loving knowledge already put in classical form by Augustine: to know God and to know oneself. But for Julian, to know God is to see oneself as loved, forgiven, and accepted by God. "And this is a great sorrow and a cruel suffering to [the servant] for he neither sees clearly his loving lord, who is so meek and mild to him, nor does he truly see what he himself is in the sight of his loving lord" (#8).

At this stage of the reflection, she concentrates on the loving look with which the lord encompassed the fallen servant and she begins to realize that the loving relationship she has witnessed between God and Adam is the same relationship enjoyed by all people, even in their sin. Julian notes that there are two aspects to God's looking; the first, which she identifies as "earthly" is reserved for the creature Adam and another, which she calls the "heavenly," is for the son Jesus who also falls. From this point on in the parable Adam and Jesus are identified and the falling of Adam is an explicit parallel to the "falling" of the Son "into the valley of the womb of the maiden who was the fairest daughter of Adam..." (#16).

As if the contemplation of the idea of Incarnation reminds Julian of the importance of the earth in the plan of God, her next series of reflections have the earth (in the sense of the ground or soil) as their thematic connection. The earth is alluded to in a variety of forms (the created globe, a garden plot, a tomb), but it is also a metaphor for the human family, "which is mixed with earth" (#11). She notes that in the vision the lord (Father) is sitting on the ground (#10). Having made humanity to be his own proper dwelling-place, the lord can only sit patiently and wait for the return of the human family as it comes forth again out of the earth. Then, as if in a dream, the whole parable is played out again. This time the servant stands before the lord in rags and tatters, the shabby garments of one who is both field-hand and pilgrim (#13). Again the servant is sent and this time the task is described. The passage deserves detailed comment and so requires complete citation.

> There was a treasure in the earth which the lord loved. I was astonished, and considered what it could be; and I was answered in my understanding; it is a food which is delicious and pleasing to the lord. For I saw the lord sitting like a man, and I saw neither food nor drink with which to serve him. This was one astonishment; another astonishment was that this stately lord had only one servant, and him he sent out. I watched, wondering what kind of labor it could be that the servant was to do. And then I understood that he was to do the greatest labor and the hardest work there is. He was to be a gardener, digging and ditching and sweating and turning the soil over and over, and to dig deep down, and to water the plants at the proper time. And he was to persevere in his work, and make sweet streams to run, and fine and plenteous fruit to grow, which he was to bring before the lord and serve him with to his liking. (#14)

We hear echoes of the parable of Jesus about the treasure hidden in the field. The earth contains some treasure (humankind itself?) that the lord (the Father) desires, some fine fruit that the lord desires to eat. The servant is sent to acquire it, but this requires gardening, "the greatest labor and the hardest work" (#14).[30]

If the servant here is Adam, then the reference to the gardener is clear: Adam, though he be evicted from the garden, has still a gardener's work to do and it is described here less as a punishment than as a means of acquiring the treasure much beloved by the lord. Irrespective of sin, the proper environment for the human family is the earth, which is a garden made fertile and productive by human labor and God's grace. If the servant is Christ, the son, then perhaps the treasure is those he will save by being buried in the earth, those who will become one body (one earth) with him and therefore become also the fruit of that earth, the banquet of the Father. In either case the earth and its fruitfulness are clearly the proper environment and task for humankind, the primary gift of God which is fulfilled, not negated, by the gift of redemption.

Julian concludes her chapter with a careful allegorizing of all the concrete details of the parable. Her allegories demonstrate her understanding of the whole of Christian truth as a single story which begins with creation and will not end until each one of us sits with Christ "in his city in rest and peace" (#24). The lives of all creatures interpenetrate with one another and are the life of Adam and of Christ re-enacted in new times and new places. A hermit, Julian understands how the smallness of our lives constrains us, like "Adam's old tunic" (#22), and would have us understand the eternal significance of our limited, grimy lives, filled with "passing woe and sorrow" (#19). Together, all of our lives make up the heroic epic which is the drama of salvation. This is a genuine theological vision: human experience in all its concrete reality is understood as the sacrament of God's eternal love for the world. It is theology at its best: grace and experience are fused, reason and imagination work together to apprehend, and the whole theological enterprise is tested by Christian life. In a church beset by dichotomies and unable to hold together the various tensions of its existence, Julian offers a theological alternative unifed by her experience and warmed by her personal vision of God.

The Fifty-First Chapter

1. And then our courteous Lord answered very mysteriously, by revealing a wonderful example of a lord who has a servant, and gave me sight for the understanding of them both. The vision was shown doubly with respect to the lord, and the vision was shown doubly with respect to the servant. One part was shown spiritually, in a bodily likeness. The other part was shown more spiritually, without bodily likeness. So, for the first, I saw two persons in bodily likeness, that is to say a lord and a servant; and with that God gave me spiritual understanding. The Lord sits in state, in rest and in peace. The servant stands before his lord, respectfully, ready to do his lord's will. The lord looks on his servant very lovingly and sweetly and mildly. He sends him to a certain place to do his will. Not only does the servant go, but he dashes off and runs at great speed, loving to do his lord's will. And soon he falls into a dell and is greatly injured; and then he groans and moans and tosses about and writhes, but he cannot rise or help himself in any way. And of all this, the greatest hurt which I saw him in was lack of consolation, for he could not turn his face to look on his loving lord, who was very close to him, in whom is all consolation; but like a man who was for the first time extremely feeble and foolish, he paid heed to his feelings and his continuing distress, in which distress he suffered seven great pains. The first was the severe bruising which he took in his fall, which gave him great pain. The second was the clumsiness of his body. The third was the weakness which followed these two. The fourth was that he was blinded in his reason and perplexed in his mind, so much so that he had almost forgotten his own love. The fifth was that he could not rise. The sixth was the pain most astonishing to me, and that was that he lay alone. I looked all around and searched, and far and near, high and low, I saw no help for him. The seventh was that the place in which he lay was narrow and comfortless and distressful.

2. I was amazed that this servant could so meekly suffer all this woe; and I looked carefully to know if I could detect any fault in him, or if the lord would impute to him any kind of blame; and truly none was seen, for the only cause of his falling was his good will and his great desire. And in spirit he was as prompt and as good as he was when he stood before his lord, ready to do his will.

3. And all this time his loving lord looks on him most tenderly, and now with a double aspect, one outward, very meekly and mildly, with great compassion and pity, and this belonged to the first part; the other was inward, more spiritual, and this was shown with a direction of my understanding toward the lord, and I was brought again to see how greatly he rejoiced over the honourable rest and nobility which by his plentiful grace he wishes for his servant and will bring him to. And this belonged to the second vision. And now my understanding was led back to the first, keeping both in mind.

4. Then this courteous lord said this: See my beloved servant, what harm and injuries he has had and accepted in my service for my love, yes, and for his good will. Is it not reasonable that I should reward him for his fright and his fear, his hurt and his injuries and all his woe? And furthermore, is it not proper for me to give him a gift, better for him more honourable than his own health could have been? Otherwise, it seems to me that I should be ungracious.

5. And in this an inward spiritual revelation of the lord's meaning descended into my soul, in which I saw that this must necessarily be the case, that his great goodness and his own honour require that his beloved servant, whom he loved so much, should be highly and blessedly rewarded forever, above what he would have been if he had not fallen, yes, and so much that his falling and all the woe that he received from it will be turned into high, surpassing honour and endless bliss.

6. And at this point the example which had been shown vanished, and our good lord led my understanding on to the end of what was to be seen and shown in the revelation. But despite this leading on, the wonder of the example never left me, for it seemed to me that it had been given as an answer to my petition. And yet at that time I could not understand it fully or be comforted. For in the servant, who was shown for Adam, as I shall say, I saw many different characteristics which could in no way be attributed to Adam, that one man; and so at that time I relied greatly on three insights, for the complete understanding of that wonderful example was not at that time given to me. The secrets of the revelation were deeply hidden in this mysterious example; and despite this I saw and understood that every showing is full of secrets. And therefore I must now tell of three attributes through which I have been somewhat consoled.

7. The first is the beginning of the teaching which I understood from it at the time. The second is the inward instruction which I have understood from it since. The third is all the whole revelation from the beginning to the end, which our Lord God of his goodness freely and often brings before the eyes of my understanding. And these three are so unified, as I understand it, that I cannot and may not separate them. And by these three as one I have instruction by which I ought to believe and trust that our Lord God, that out of the same goodness and for the same purpose as he revealed it, by the same goodness and for the same purpose will make it clear to us when it is his will.

8. For twenty years after the time of the revelation except for three months, I received an inward instruction, and it was this: You ought to take heed to all the attributes, divine and human, which were revealed in the example, though this may seem to you mysterious and ambiguous. I willingly agreed with a great desire, seeing inwardly with great care all the details and the characteristics which were at that time revealed, so far as my intelligence and understanding will serve, beginning with when I

looked at the lord and the servant, at how the lord was sitting and the place where he sat, and the colour of his clothing and how it was made, and his outward appearance and his inward nobility and goodness; and the demeanour of the servant as he stood, and the place where and how, and his fashion of clothing, the colour and the shape, his outward behaviour and his inward goodness and willingness. I understood that the lord who sat in state in rest and peace is God. I understood that the servant who stood before him was shown for Adam, that is to say, one man was shown at that time and his fall, so as to make it understood how God regards all men and their falling. For in the sight of God all men are one man, and one man is all men. This man was injured in his powers and made most feeble, and in his understanding he was amazed, because he was diverted from looking on his lord, but his will was preserved in God's sight. I saw the lord commend and approve him for his will, but he himself was blinded and hindered from knowing this will. And this is a great sorrow and a cruel suffering to him, for he neither sees clearly his loving lord, who is so meek and mild to him, nor does he truly see what he himself is in the sight of his loving lord. And I know well that when these two things are wisely and truly seen, we shall gain rest and peace, here in part and the fullness in the bliss of heaven, by God's plentiful grace.

9. And this was a beginning of the teaching which I saw at the same time, whereby I might come to know in what manner he looks on us in our sin. And then I saw that only pain blames and punishes, and our courteous Lord comforts and succours, and always he is kindly disposed to the soul, loving and longing to bring us to his bliss.

10. The place which the lord sat on was unadorned, on the ground, barren and waste, alone in the wilderness. His clothing was wide and ample and very handsome, as befits a lord. The colour of the clothing was azure blue, most dignified and beautiful. His demeanor was merciful, his face was a lovely, pale

brown with a very seemly countenance, his eyes were black, most beautiful and seemly, revealing all his loving pity, and within him there was a secure place of refuge, long and broad, all full of endless heavenliness. And the loving regard which he kept constantly on his servant, and especially when he fell, it seemed to me that it could melt our hearts for love and break them in two for joy. This lovely regard had in it a beautiful mingling which was wonderful to see. Part was compassion and pity, part was joy and bliss. The joy and bliss surpass the compassion and pity, as far as heaven is above earth. The pity was earthly and the bliss was heavenly.

11. The compassion and the pity of the Father were for Adam, who is his most beloved creature. The joy and the bliss were for the falling of his dearly beloved Son, who is equal with the Father. The merciful regard of his lovely countenance filled all the earth, and went down with Adam into hell, and by his continuing pity Adam was kept from endless death. And this mercy and pity abides with mankind until the time that we come up to heaven. But man is blinded in this life, and therefore we cannot see our Father, God, as he is. And when he of his goodness wishes to show himself to man, he shows himself familiar, like a man, even though I saw truly that we ought to know and believe that our Father is not a man. But his sitting on the ground, barren and waste, signifies this: He made man's soul to be his own city and his dwelling place, which is the most pleasing to him of all his works. And when man had fallen into sorrow and pain, he was not wholly proper to serve in that noble office, and therefore our kind Father did not wish to prepare any other place, but sat upon the ground, awaiting human nature, which is mixed with earth, until the time when by his grace his beloved Son had brought back his city into its noble place of beauty by his hard labour.

12. The blueness of the clothing signifies his steadfastness; the brownness of his fair face with the lovely blackness of the

eyes was most suitable to indicate his holy solemnity; the amplitude, billowing splendidly all about him, signifies that he has enclosed within himself all heavens and all endless joy and bliss; and this was shown in a brief moment, when I perceived that my understanding was directed to the lord. In this I saw him greatly rejoice over the honourable restoration to which he wants to bring and will bring his servant by his great and plentiful grace. And still I was amazed, contemplating the lord and the servant as I have said.

13. I saw the lord sitting in state, and the servant standing respectfully before his lord, and in this servant there is a double significance, one outward, the other inward. Outwardly he was simply dressed like a labourer prepared to work, and he stood very close to the lord, not immediately in front of him but a little to one side, and that on the left; his clothing was a white tunic, scanty, old and all worn, dyed with the sweat of his body, tight fitting and short, as it were a hand's breadth below his knee, looking threadbare as if it would soon be worn out, ready to go to rags and to tear. And in this I was much amazed, thinking: This is not fitting clothing for a servant so greatly loved to stand in before so honourable a lord. And, inwardly, there was shown in him a foundation of love, the love which he had for the lord, which was equal to the love which the lord had for him. The wisdom of the servant saw inwardly that there was one thing to do which would pay honour to the lord; and the servant, for love, having no regard for himself or for anything which might happen to him, went off in great haste and ran when his lord sent him, to do the thing which was his will and to his honour; for it seemed by his outer garment as if he had been a constant labourer and a hard traveller for a long time. And by the inward perception which I had of both the lord and the servant, it seemed that he was newly appointed, that is to say just beginning to labour, and that this servant had never been sent out before.

14. There was a treasure in the earth which the lord loved. I was astonished, and considered what it could be; and I was answered in my understanding: It is a food which is delicious and pleasing to the lord. For I saw the lord sitting like a man, and I saw neither food nor drink with which to serve him. This was one astonishment; another astonishment was that this stately lord has only one servant, and him he sent out. I watched, wondering what kind of labour it could be that the servant was to do. And then I understood that he was to do the greatest labour and the hardest work there is: He was to be a gardener, digging and ditching and sweating and turning the soil over and over, and to dig deep down, and to water the plants at the proper time. And he was to persevere in his work, and make sweet streams to run, and fine and plenteous fruit to grow, which he was to bring before the lord and serve him with to his liking. And he was never to come back again until he had made all this food ready as he knew was pleasing to the lord; and then he was to take this food, and drink, and carry it most reverently before the lord. And all this time the lord was to sit in exactly the same place, waiting for the servant whom he had sent out.

15. And still I wondered where the servant came from, for I saw in the lord that he has in himself endless life and every kind of goodness, except for the treasure which was in the earth, and that was founded in the lord in a marvellous depth of endless love. But it was not wholly to his honour until his servant had prepared it so finely and carried it before him into the lord's own presence. And except for the lord, there was nothing at all but wilderness; and I did not understand everything which this example meant. And therefore I wondered where the servant came from.

16. In the servant is comprehended the second person of the Trinity, and in the servant is comprehended Adam, that is to say all men. And therefore when I say 'the Son', that means the divinity which is equal to the Father, and when I say 'the ser-

ant', that means Christ's humanity, which is the true Adam. By the closeness of the servant is understood the Son, and by his standing to the left is understood Adam. The lord is God the Father, the servant is the Son, Jesus Christ, the Holy Spirit is the equal love which is in them both. When Adam fell, God's Son fell; because of the true union which was made in heaven, God's Son could not be separated from Adam, for by Adam I understand all mankind. Adam fell from life to death, into the valley of this wretched world, and after that into hell. God's Son fell with Adam, into the valley of the womb of the maiden who was the fairest daughter of Adam, and that was to excuse Adam from blame in heaven and on earth; and powerfully he brought him out of hell. By the wisdom and the goodness which were in the servant is understood God's Son, by the poor labourer's clothing and the standing close by on the left is understood Adam's humanity with all the harm and weakness which follow. For in all this our good Lord showed his own Son and Adam as only one man. The strength and the goodness that we have is from Jesus Christ, the weakness and blindness that we have is from Adam, which two were shown in the servant.

17. And so has our good Lord Jesus taken upon him all our blame; and therefore our Father may not, does not wish to assign more blame to us than to his own beloved Son, Jesus Christ. So he was the servant before he came on earth, standing ready in purpose before the Father until the time when he would send him to do the glorious deed by which mankind was brought back to heaven. That is to say, even though he is God, equal with the Father as regards his divinity, but with his prescient purpose that he would become man to save mankind in fulfillment of the will of his Father, so he stood before his Father as a servant, willingly taking upon him all our charge. And then he rushed off very readily at the Father's bidding, and soon he fell very low into the maiden's womb, having no regard for himself or for his cruel pains.

18. The white tunic is his flesh, the scantiness signifies that there was nothing at all separating the divinity from the humanity. The tight fit is poverty, the age is Adam's wearing, the wornness is the sweat of Adam's labour, the shortness shows the servant-labourer.

19. And so I saw the Son stand, saying in intention: See, my dear Father, I stand before you in Adam's tunic, all ready to hasten and run. I wish to be on earth to your glory, when it is your will to send me. How long shall I desire it? Very truly the Son knew when was the Father's will, and how long he would desire it, that is to say as regards his divinity, for he is the wisdom of the Father. Therefore this meaning was shown for understanding of Christ's humanity. For all mankind which will be saved by the sweet Incarnation and the Passion of Christ, all is Christ's humanity, for he is the head, and we are his members, to which members the day and the time are unknown when every passing woe and sorrow will have an end, and everlasting joy and bliss will be fulfilled, which day and time all the company of heaven longs and desires to see. And all who are under heaven and will come there, their way is by longing and desiring, which desiring and longing was shown in the servant standing before the lord, or, otherwise, in the Son standing before the Father in Adam's tunic. For the longing and desire of all mankind which will be saved appeared in Jesus, for Jesus is in all who will be saved, and all who will be saved are in Jesus, and all is of the love of God, with obedience, meekness and patience, and the virtues which befit us.

20. Also in this marvellous example I have teaching within me, as it were the beginning of an ABC, whereby I may have some understanding of our Lord's meaning, for the mysteries of the revelation are hidden in it, even though all the showings are full of mysteries.

21. The sitting of the Father symbolizes the divinity, that is to say to reveal rest and peace, for in the divinity there can be no

labour; and that he shows himself as a lord symbolizes our humanity. The standing of the servant symbolizes labour, and that he stands to the left symbolizes that he was not fully worthy to stand immediately in front of the lord. His rushing away was the divinity, and his running was the humanity; for the divinity rushed from the Father into the maiden's womb, falling to accept our nature, and in this falling he took great hurt. The hurt that he took was our flesh, in which at once he experienced mortal pains. That he stood fearfully before the lord and not immediately in front, symbolizes that his clothing was not seemly for him to stand in immediately in front of the lord, nor could nor should that be his office whilst he was a labourer; nor, further, might he sit with the lord in rest and peace until he had duly won his peace with his hard labour; and that he stood to the left symbolizes that the Father by his will permitted his own Son in human nature to suffer all man's pain without sparing him. By his tunic being ready to go to rags and to tear is understood the rods and the scourges, the thorns and the nails, the pulling and the dragging and the tearing of his tender flesh, of which I had seen a part. The flesh was torn from the skull, falling in pieces until when the bleeding stopped; and then it began to dry again, adhering to the bone. And by the tossing about and writhing, the groaning and moaning, is understood that he could never with almighty power rise from the time that he fell into the maiden's womb until his body was slain and dead, and he had yielded his soul into the Father's hand, with all mankind for whom he had been sent.

22. And at this moment he first began to show his power, for then he went down into hell; and when he was there, he raised up the great root out of the deep depth, which rightly was joined to him in heaven. The body lay in the grave until Easter morning; and from that time it never lay again. For then the tossing about and writhing, the groaning and the moaning ended, rightly; and our foul mortal flesh, which God's Son took upon him, which was Adam's old tunic, tight-fitting, threadbare, and short,

was then made lovely by our savior, new, white and bright and forever clean, wide and ample, fairer and richer than the clothing which I saw on the Father. For that clothing was blue, and Christ's clothing was now of a fair and seemly mixture, which is so marvellous that I cannot describe it, for it is all of true glory.

23. Now the lord does not sit on the ground in the wilderness, but in his rich and noblest seat, which he made in heaven most to his liking. Now the Son does not stand before the Father as a servant before the lord, pitifully clothed, partly naked, but he stands immediately before the Father, richly clothed in joyful amplitude, with a rich and precious crown upon his head. For it was revealed that we are his crown, which crown is the Father's joy, the Son's honour, the Holy Spirit's delight, and endless marvellous bliss to all who are in heaven.

24. Now the Son does not stand before the Father on the left like a labourer, but he sits at the Father's right hand in endless rest and peace. But this does not mean that the Son sits on the right-hand side as one man sits beside another in this life, for there is no such sitting, as I see it, in the Trinity; but he sits at his Father's right hand, that is to say right in the highest nobility of his Father's joy. Now the spouse, God's son, is at peace with his beloved wife, who is the fair maiden of endless joy. Now the Son, true God and true man, sits in his city in rest and in peace, which his Father has prepared for him by his endless purpose, and the Father in the Son, and the Holy Spirit in the Father and in the Son.

Questions and Activities

1. After a careful reading of the Julian text, write your own commentary on the parable of the Lord and the servant or on a parable from the Gospel. Let the starting point of your commen-

tary be a response to the question "What personal experience that I have had is illuminated by this parable?"

2. Read the entire long version of Julian's *Showings* as well as *The Book of Margery Kempe*. Write an essay in which you point out some of the similarities and/or differences between these two writers from the same time and place, who, according to Margery, had met at least once.

3. Julian is often spoken about in connection with the anonymous author of *The Cloud of Unknowing* which is also a fourteenth century English mystical work. Read both Julian's book and *The Cloud*. What is the single most important difference between these two works? How does each respond to the difficulty of dealing with sin and guilt? What is the image of God presented in each?

4. Imagine that, like many of her contemporaries, you pay a visit to Julian of Norwich, seeking advice for living. What questions do you have for her? What do you think her reponses might be? Write up your visit as a scene with dialogue.

Selected Additional Reading

Barker, Paula S. Datsko. "The Motherhood of God in Julian of Norwich's Theology." *Downside Review* 100 (October, 1982) 290-304.

Cunningham, Lawrence S. "Julian of Norwich: 'Revelations of Divine Love.'" *The Christian Century* 94 (March, 1977) 215.

Dreyer, Elizabeth. "Julian of Norwich: Her Merry Counsel." *America* 139 (August, 1978) 55-57.

Julian of Norwich. *Showings*. Trans. and ed. by Edmund Colledge, O.S.A. and James Walsh, S.J. New York: Paulist Press, 1978.

Kempe, Margery. *The Book of Margery Kempe*. Trans. by Barry Windeatt. New York: Penguin Press, 1986.

Mayr-Harting, H. "Functions of a Twelfth-Century Recluse." *History* 60 (October, 1975) 337-352.

Reynolds, Anna Maria. "Love is His Meaning." *Clergy Review* 5 (1973) 363-369.

Llewelyn, Robert. *Love Bade Me Welcome*. New York: Paulist Press, 1985.

Llewelyn, Robert, ed. *Woman of Our Day*. Mystic, Connecticut: Twenty-Third Publications, 1987.

Mayeski, Marie Anne. "Creation Motifs in the Spirituality of Julian of Norwich." *The Journey of Western Spirituality*, A. W. Sadler, ed. Chico, California: Scholars Press, 1980, 107-118.

Notes

1. This article is a substantial revision of my article entitled "Creation Motifs in the Spirituality of Julian of Norwich." in *The Journey of Western Spirituality*, ed. by A.W. Sadler (Chico, CA: The Scholars Press, 1981) 107-118. Used with permission of the College Theology Society.

2. See Jacqueline Smith, "Robert Baker: *Procurator Mulierum*," *Medieval Women*, ed. by Derek Baker (Oxford: Basil Blackwell, 1978) 182.

3. See Williston Walker *et al, A History of the Christian Church,* 4th ed. (New York: Charles Scribner's Sons, 1985) 294.

4. See Walker 316 and Regis Armstrong and Ignatius Brady (eds), *Francis and Clare: The Complete Works* (New York: Paulist Press, 1982) 171-172.

5. See Walker 318-19; also Jean Leclercq *et al, The Spirituality of the Middle Ages* (New York: The Seabury Press, 1968) 354-56.

6. See the *Book of Margery Kempe*, trans. by Barry Windeatt (New York: Penguin Press, 1986). Cf also Louise Collins, *The Apprentice Saint* (London: Michael Joseph, 1964).

7. Walker 300-305.

8. See Elizabeth Dryer, "Julian of Norwich: Her Merry Counsel," *America* 139 (Aug. 5, 1978) 55.

9. See H. Mayr-Harting, "Functions of a Twelfth-Century Recluse," *History* 60 (Oct., 1975) 337-352 for a discussion of the social and economic place of anchorites in medieval England.

10. Julian of Norwich, *Showings,* trans. and ed. by Edmund Colledge, O.S.A. and James Walsh, S.J. (Paulist Press, New York, 1978) 177.

11. *Showings* 19.

12. See *Showings* 23.

13. See H. Mayr-Harting, 337-352.

14. *Showings* 179.

15. *Showings* 176.

16. See Paula S. Datsko Barker, "The Motherhood of God in Julian of Norwich's Theology," *Downside Review* 100 (Oct., 1982) 295-6, for a brief background to the meaning of these two words.

17. *Showings* 194-5.

18. *Showings* 298.

19. I am indebted for this specific contrast with Anselm to a paper by Lillian Bozak-Deleo delivered at the national meeting of the College Theology Society, Loyola College, Baltimore, Maryland on May 31, 1987.

20. *Showings* 256.

21. *Showings* 182.

22. *Showings* 187.

23. *Showings* 186.

24. See *Showings* 205 and 260.

25. *Showings* 279.

26. *Showings* 179-80.

27. It is Chapter 51 of the Longer Version. Reprinted with permission of Daughters of St. Paul. References in the text are to paragraph numbers as added for this Anthology.

28. Julian was aware that her understanding of Adam's fall was original. This may have been what prompted her to omit the parable and commentary from the Earlier Version (see below, n. 29). In numerous places in the text she asserts that she does not want to contradict the official teaching of the church; but she also affirms uncompromisingly what she has been *led* to understand. She could not have been unmindful of the presence of the Inquisition.

29. See the Introduction to *Showings* by Edmund Colledge and James Walsh for an interpretation on the significant omission of the parable from the earlier, shorter version: "Two judgments are possible: Either the allegory is Julian's own later invention to justify the doctrines (in which case, in representing the allegory as she does as a part of the revelation, Julian would be guilty of falsification), or she suppressed the allegory when she wrote the short text for reasons no longer obtaining when the long text was composed. There is plain evidence that the second judgment is the right one," 23.

30. Julian may well have known this by experience. Anchorites often maintained their own gardens to provide their simple meals.

5.

"A Restless Gadabout": Teresa of Avila

Perhaps more than most people, Teresa of Avila cannot be understood apart from her place and her times. Born in 1515 into a family of eleven children, she grew up in an atmosphere of love and books and the desire for glory. The external environment of Avila, and indeed of Spain itself, was marked by expansionism and a strong movement of Catholic reform. In 1492, the Moors were overcome at Granada and in the same year Columbus set sail under Spanish protection. Teresa would grow up familiar with the sight of Torquemada, the Grand Inquisitor, who was often in Avila, supervising the burning of heretics. The New World and the accomplishments of the *conquistadores* formed the horizon of her world and by the age of five she had conceived a passionate love for war and glory.[1]

Her life was also shaped in a significant way by the books she read. In early adolescence, she devoured the chivalric romances that flooded Spain; *Amadis de Gaul* nourished her romanticism as the spiritual classics would later nourish her devotion. The Catholic reform in Spain was, at least in part, driven by humanistic ideals (the Bible had been translated into Spanish as early as 1252) and her family read regularly and widely. The first thing that she notes about her father is that "he was fond of reading good books and had some in Spanish so that his children could read them too."[2] In her later life, when deeply involved in the reform of Carmel, she would insist on having confessors and directors who were as learned as possible for, as she asserts, "I have always been attracted by learning, though confessors with only a little of it have done my soul much harm, and I have not always found men who had as much of it as I would have liked." She wrote prolifically herself. Her best known works are the *Life*, the *Way of Perfection*, the *Interior Castle* and the *Book of the Foundations*. She says that she wrote her own works only at the bidding of confessors and superiors; this may well be what one author calls "a rhetoric of protection" rather than a sign that she was an unwilling author.[5] Literature was important to her; it was appropriate that she was given the rare (for women) title "Doctor of the Church."

Significant though books were to be for Teresa, she was ever a woman of action. The energy of the *conquistadores* coursed through Spain at least as much as the vigor of the Reformers. At six, she turned to the lives of the saints and particularly enjoyed the stories of the martyrs who, as she thought, got heaven "very cheaply." She conceived a plan to accomplish her own martyrdom and set off for "the country of the Moors" having convinced her older brother Rodrigo to accompany her.[6] They were brought back home by an uncle who happened to be passing by and she deeply regretted the loss of the basilica which she had hoped would be built in their honor. This incident clearly reveals her character traits and the themes of her life: the leadership she would exercise even in a strongly patriarchal society, her desire for glory, more or less spiritualized at various times in her life, and her '*determinacion*,' an almost doggedly relentless pursuit of her own goals.

But it would be some time before the direction of her life was clear, even to herself. She was, for a long time, a woman who was pulled in two antithetical directions. Like Augustine before her, she acknowledged that she wanted to love and be loved but, in the concrete, she was more sure of what she did not want than what she did. (Actually she says that what she really wanted was to be a man so that she could be a conquistador!) In adolescence she was surrounded by the adulation of her teenaged cousins and she flirted and entertained various possibilities for romance, but she did not want to marry. She considered it an intolerable servitude and said that she feared it. Later on she would describe the condition of a married woman as a reminder to her nuns that they ought not to complain about what she considered the trifling difficulties of the cloister. In her mind, they had all escaped the "great trials of the world" which was the lot of a woman in an unhappy marriage. Neither did she, however, wish to become a nun; that decision, according to Teresa, was only the result of a cold and determined act of the will.

Entry into religion, however, did not heal her divided heart. She would continue to be pulled with equal force toward the human love and admiration that she had experienced from childhood and toward the love and spiritual consolations which Christ, the Lord whom she called "His Majesty," began to pour out upon her with a liberality, indeed a prodigality, that only embarrassed her. For the first twenty years of her convent life she moved from parlor to chapel in a regular rhythm. In the former, she basked in adulation and gossip; in the latter, she found herself ardently wooed by an eternal love. Periods of intense illness marked the failure of her psyche to deal with the tension.

Only in her forties did Teresa face the crisis of limits which her temperament, her energy and her passion forced upon her. Characteristically, she describes this point of decision in terms of "really living" and the lack of freedom which is the result of the inability to choose decisively. As Teresa says: "I wanted to live for I knew quite well that I was not living at all but battling with a shadow of death; but there was no one to give me life and I was unable to take it for myself."[8] There are echoes here of many women's stories. Like so many other women, Teresa here discovers that her liberation depends upon herself and is essentially a question of autonomy, of making her own choices. But most of all, this reflection of Teresa's reveals the paradigm central to all Christian autobiography: the discovery of the divided heart, the hunger for life and freedom and the recognition that these latter are gifts of grace to be had only through complete surrender.

But surrender to God is never, and was not for Teresa, the beginning of a passive life. Having first committed herself to a life of intense prayer, Teresa soon discovered the proper outlet for her passion and her energy, now channeled through single-hearted devotion to God's will. In that age of reform and counter-reform, Teresa became a reformer. With the foundation of St. Joseph's in Avila, Teresa began a series of reformed Carmelite convents that included houses in Seville, Toledo and Segovia; her last foundation was at Burgos. In 1567, with the help of St. John of the Cross and St. Peter of Alcantara, she began to shape the reform of the men's monasteries as well.

Though the Catholic reform had begun early in Spain, it received renewed energies in reaction to the Protestant Reformation and from the activity of the Council of Trent. By 1562, the year of the last session of the Council, a number of individuals had been inspired to revive the Primitive Rule of Carmel which centuries of accommodations had mitigated. To this ideal, Teresa now dedicated herself. The reform of Carmel was, in a sense, the fruit of Spanish humanism; it was an attempt to restructure life according to ancient documents and ideals. Like the Protestant Reform, it was an attempt to recover the experiential base of Christian life but Teresa's notion of reform was more typically Catholic. She believed that religious experience was more easily achieved by the traditional discipline of religious life. There is ample evidence that Teresa was motivated in her reform by the Protestant movements taking place in the north. She cites two intentions in her reform of Carmel: first, to minimize the ravages of Protestantism; and second, to curb the desire for freedom which was clamoring throughout the land. Her second intention reflects her own memory of the struggle for inner freedom: in her understanding, the divided heart inhibits true freedom which consists in a disciplined and wholehearted search for God.[9] In the preamble to the *Way of Perfection,* she recommends to the prayers of her daughters in Carmel those who have to defend the faith, especially the theologians and the preachers. Thus, her work in reforming the Carmelite monasteries was a conscious and energetic response to her world and times.

She soon learned, however, that the enemies of reform were within her own sheepfold. The first foundation of St. Joseph's at Avila stirred up a hornet's nest. Teresa noted: "All this made such a commotion in the city that people talked about nothing else. Everybody was condemning me and going to see the Provincial and visiting my convent."[10] She was amazed at, as she put it, "all the trouble the devil was taking to hurt a few poor women."[11] But she did not doubt that all the trouble she encountered, especially from otherwise "good" people within the church, was an evil to be combatted; never for long did she seriously doubt herself and the rightness of her life's work. Teresa waged her reform with energy and responded to the persecution from her superiors with fire, cunning and humility. In an age when obedience to all paternal authority was part of the very definition of a woman's life and virtue, Teresa had the autonomy to forge ahead on her own path and to resist the powerful suasions of those in authority. It is in her letters that we see most clearly this evidence of her liberation.[12]

The letters selected for inclusion here almost all come from the year 1578 and the first half of 1579. They record some of Teresa's energetic activity as well as her thoughts and feelings during a moment of extreme crisis in the reform of Carmel. The Reform had been unpopular with the friars and nuns of the Observance (Mitigated) from the beginning. They had accused Teresa of "innovations"—always a condemning adjective in religious life but more so in the atmosphere created by the Protestant Reformation. They saw that the austerities and idealism of the Reformers were an implicit condemnation of their own interpretations of the Rule, significantly modified through centuries of small accommodations. In spite of this opposition, Teresa had managed to keep the reform moving until 1576 through the support of the Carmelite General, Father Rubeo, Father P. Jeronimo Gratian, the Apostolic Visitor,[13] and of many devoted followers among the rich and powerful, especially aristocratic women. In 1577, however, one of Teresa's strongest protectors, the Papal Nuncio Odmaneto, died and was replaced by the unsympathetic Cardinal Sega; the full strength of the Mitigated Carmelites was revealed in the fury which broke out against her. By this time, the issue was the desire of the Reformed, both men and women, to become an independent province; the opposition wanted to undermine the entire reform by retaining one province, controlled by the Mitigated Friars. They also hoped to destroy the reputation of Teresa and her nuns. Sega was particularly antagonistic: he was told that Teresa was "a restless gadabout," (#252).* He declared her disobedient, contumacious, and accused her of inventing evil doctrines, of going out of her cloister in spite of the prohibition of the Council of Trent, and of teaching, although St. Paul had forbidden women to do so. Though she acted always through obedience and observed all the legalities imposed, she was an assertive religious superior. She had taken one of the few paths to authority open to women in the church, but in the exercise of that authority, she was accused of unfeminine behavior.

Matters came to a head when an election was held at the Convent of the Incarnation, the very house that had been Teresa's original religious home. The Provincial of the Calced Friars was sent to preside at the election and against his wishes, the nuns of

---

*Numbers in parentheses refer to correspondence from The Letters of Saint Teresa of Jesus, Vol. II. Letters are identified by their numbers in that collection.

the Incarnation elected Teresa the prioress. When persuasion failed, the Provincial excommunicated the nuns, who still refused to bend to his will, and an impasse ensued. About the same time, John of the Cross was imprisoned by his Carmelite brothers; in order to coerce him into betraying both the reform and the reputation of Teresa, they gave him only bread and water and flogged him daily. Eventually he escaped by tying strips of his blanket together and letting himself down through a small window; he then made his way to Avila where Teresa was staying. From her cloister at Avila, Teresa could only conduct her battle for the reform through her correspondence. But her supporters grew fewer and weaker, and her letters to the King during this time remained unanswered as Philip attempted to keep his distance from the controversy.

The darkest year that Teresa and the Reformers faced was 1578. It was the year in which the scandal of the Ahumbradas of Llerena came to light, a vivid example of how the ideals of extreme asceticism could often give way to immorality. Teresa's enemies tried to tar her with the brush dipped in the notoriety which the Ahumbradas generated. All of Teresa's writings, the letters as well as the spiritual treatises, were filled with injuctions to common sense, the need to sleep and eat properly, the need for meat especially when excessive spiritual experiences seemed to be present. It was a lesson reinforced, if not learned, as she witnessed the unraveling of other contemporary reforms, such as that of the Ahumbradas, more impressive in their asceticism, perhaps, but less stable and permanent.

Also in 1578, a brief from the Papal Nuncio removed Gracian from his role as Apostolic Visitor of the reformed Carmelites and, almost simultaneously, Father Rubeo, the General of the Carmelite Order who had originally approved the reform, died and with him the last hope of conciliation between the Reformed and the Mitigated. Sega, the new Nuncio, excommunicated Gracian who went into hiding. Bereft of almost all human help, Teresa repeatedly appealed to the Pope for an independent province. But the Holy Father, continuing to filter all his decisions through his Nuncio, failed to respond to the Reformers' requests. On the 24th of December, Teresa was given a decree which placed all the Discalced Carmelites under the direction of the Provincial and Superiors of the Mitigated Friars in Castile and Andulasia. As the year ended, the hopes of the Reformers seemed to end as well.

The year 1579 began badly. The persecutions and violence against the Discalced Nuns continued: there were recriminations and excommunications. In an attempt to discredit Teresa, confessors and superiors of the Calced Carmelite men tried, and in some instances succeeded, to force the nuns in various reformed convents to swear false testimony against the foundress. With such a conflict of authorities waging around their heads, the nuns in the various convents were divided, individuals and factions turning against one another in their loyalty to Teresa or in their desire to appease the legitimate authority of the Nuncio and Carmelite superiors. These strategies and events tore Teresa apart. She saw her nuns victimized, her precious reputation destroyed, her friends imprisoned or forced into hiding because of their affection for her. Some of the letters of this time reveal her agony. Some read like excerpts from spy fiction; she is forced to use code (the Calced are repeatedly referred to as "the cats") and to send her letters by secret messenger. Yet throughout these dark and terrible months, her firm, almost dogged, devotion to the reform is sustained—as is her wit and humor. A seemingly inexhaustible reservoir of peace is somehow at her disposal.

Seven letters are included here,[15] all but the last sent from Avila where Teresa stayed all during the terrible struggles over the separation of the Reform Carmelites from those of the Observance. Three of the letters are to Father Jeronimo Gracian, who championed their cause, even when he was officially rejected by the Nuncio, and who finally helped in the legal work of setting up the Consitutions of the Reform. Both the first and the last letters are to Gracian and act as a kind of framework for the collection here. The first records the beginnings of the attempt to form a separate province for the reform; the last, after the battle for separation is won, is concerned with the phrasing and organization of the Consitutions. Three others are those sent to the superiors and nuns of the Reformed convent in Seville, a house that experienced much of the inner dissension and outward persecution that marked the years 1578 and 1579. There is one letter to Pablo Hernandez, a Jesuit of Toledo who had assisted with the foundation of the convent in that city and whose help and influence Teresa sought during the time of turmoil.

In all of the letters, we see Teresa in the many roles she played: administrator, political strategist, tender friend, religious superior, and convinced reformer. We also see a woman frustrated by the restrictions placed upon her, having to act behind the scenes, as it were, through the men who were friendly to her cause but who did not always act in the ways she found appropriate or sufficiently effective. Thus, in the first letter (#224), she tries to outline the proper strategy for Gracian and freely admits that she is "suffering agonies at not being free to do what [she is] telling other people to do." Later (#253), she takes issue with him for not following her advice, for acting contrary to her own political acumen and swimming "against the current." All this makes her "dreadfully upset."

Even when the major battle has been won and the separation achieved, she still had to work through Gracian to have the Consitutions read as she would have them read. They were being written by the members of the General Chapter of the Discalced Men and did not reflect a sensitivity to the consciences of the nuns who were often given to scruples. In her negotiations over the text of the Constitutions, she shows a respect for the delicate consciences of her nuns that was unusual for the times. Her letter (#351) to Gracian transmits her concern that the nuns be free to choose the best possible preachers, from whatever order, so that their spiritual needs may be met. It also gives further indications of Teresa's attitude toward food; she was never austere for austerity's sake (note her concern for good gardens and a modicum of comfort in Letter #224) and wanted the widest possible latitude given to superiors so that any tendency to scrupulosity might be avoided. Teresa's common sense has long charmed her biographers and commentators. In these selections we see her concern about the design of the kitchen stove (#233). One of her own superiors in another convent has come up with an improved design and Teresa wants her brother to get permission to visit and copy the stove. Again, she is bothered by the excessive "spiritual favors" apparently experienced by one of the nuns and prescribes a healthy portion of meat to counteract what might well be a psychosomatic, rather than a religious, experience. In Teresa's mind, no higher praise could be spoken of a religious woman than that she be both "virtuous and sensible" (#233).

It is, perhaps, in her role of political strategist that Teresa most obviously exceeded the expectations of her sex; it was, no doubt, her political activities that earned her the epithets of "gadabout," innovator, and insubordinate woman. In the interests of the Reform, she used every strategy at her disposal and showed her acumen in understanding the use of power. Prayer was central to Teresa's strategy; but she also used the enormous charm that was hers, her "friends in high places," and her understanding of human motivation to achieve her foundations and her reform. Her writings are permeated with her stories of, and gratitude to, those rich and powerful (especially women) whose money and influence made numerous foundations possible.

In these letters, written in the years of crisis, she shows herself adept at persuading others while allowing them to save face, to preserve that "honor" that was so important to the Spanish temperament. Letter #224 is particularly instructive here. In it we see Teresa directing Gracian's activities toward the setting up of a separate Discalced province. She is not afraid to have the King approached directly, provided it is done right and through appropriate intermediaries. She is concerned lest Gracian lose "prestige," an important element in the delicate negotiations taking place. She wants all the proper procedures and legalities followed; she wants everyone involved to believe themselves honorably dealt with, even as the conflict is unfolding. In the letter (#233) to M. Maria de San Jose (the designer of the stove), she delicately alludes to gifts needed for rewarding those whose help for the reform needs to be encouraged. When she writes to the Jesuit Pablo Hernandez (#252), she engages in those elaborate, often oblique, compliments which were so much a part of the social intercourse of her day. She remarks on Gracian's Jesuit education, says that she has been "formed and trained" by the Company herself and expresses her esteem for the members of the Company in spite of occasional difficulties between them and her own reform. Teresa's respect for the Society of Jesus was genuine; here we see her turning her esteem into the kind of compliments designed to achieve her worthwhile ends.

In all these endeavors, Teresa remains totally a spiritual woman and religious superior even while she develops as an astute and convinced reformer. In all the letters she writes, there are continual expressions of affection toward her nuns. In that to Mother Maria (#233) we see that her concern for good discipline was sometimes distorted by the limited understanding of her times, as when she counsels fear and blood-letting as the way to control the nervous maladies of one of the members of the community. At the same time, she could motivate and encourage exceptionally well. She exhorts the nuns at Seville to rely on God in their trials (#264); she praises them as the true *conquistadores* of their time, she upbraids them for complaining when they have not yet been called to shed their blood. Her language is that of the Spanish code of honor. She exhorts humility in the face of calumny, but with a confidence that the truth will be known and their reputations preserved. She is like a military leader, marshaling her troops and urging them ever forward. But the martial imagery cannot obscure the truly mystical vision that guides her as a reformer and that is revealed most clearly in Letter #274 about the two nuns at Seville.

In that letter she must deal with the aftermath of the dissension caused in some of the convents by the conflict in authorities that had divided the Carmelites during the battle over the separate Province. Here as elsewhere, we see the way in which Teresa's activities in behalf of the Reform were thoroughly permeated with the rich experiences of her mystical life. The letters counsel continued joy and peace; they reflect an urgency about prayer. But most of all, they record Teresa's refusal to accept an easy division of the world into enemies and friends. Enemies there were and she was not loathe to identify them. She wonders aloud to Hernandez whether the Nuncio might not, through honest investigation, find out who indeed was in need of reform and end by punishing the Calced (#252). She reminds the nuns at Seville that God will swallow up their enemies as he did King Pharoah (#264). But when faced with the enemy within the house, two nuns who had created internal dissension and whom she might legitimately punish, Teresa counsels only forgiveness and kind treatment. Let honest work and companionship with other, loving nuns bring the recalcitrant Beatriz and her companion back to the fold (#264).

Known primarily as a mystic, Teresa is, at heart, an active reformer in the tradition of Catherine of Siena and Mahatma Ghandi.[16] She saw the life of prayer and the requirements of reform as contiguous realities in her life, each nourishing the other. Despite a variety of diverse duties and responsibilities, her life was not disunified but whole and integrated. She learned detachment and inner peace in prayer; these produced courage and persistence in her external activities. The mystical life wedded her to Christ; his will required her to act "manful-ly"—one of her favorite adjectives—and to bear the burden of her actions. The church has long honored women for their ac-complishments in spirituality. It has not often appreciated the course of controversial action and confrontation to which their spirituality has led them. Having for too long accepted the dualism of body and soul, of private and public religion, the church has not sufficiently acclaimed the public accomplishment of private and spiritual women. Teresa of Avila stands as a model of liberation in both the interior life and the world of ac-tion.

Letter 224. To P. Jeronimo Gracian; from Avila, April 15, 1578.

Jesus be with your Paternity, my Father. Since the Father Prior of Mancera went, I have spoken about this matter of the province to Master Daza and Doctor Rueda, for I should be sorry if your Paternity were to do something which anybody could say was wrong. Even if the outcome of it were successful, I should be more distressed about that than about all the set-backs our plan is meeting with, through no fault of our own.

They both say it seems to them a bold thing to do unless there is some special clause in your Paternity's commission which al-lows it. Doctor Rueda made a special point of this, and he is a man whose opinion I greatly value, as I find him very judicious in everything. And, of course, he is a man of great learning. He says the question is one of jurisdiction and so it is very difficult for an election to be held about it. Unless this is done by authority of the General or the Pope, it cannot be done at all: the voting would be invalid. The (Calced) friars would only have to go to the Pope and cry out that we were running counter to obedience by choosing superiors for ourselves when we had no right to do so. The thing sounds bad; Doctor Rueda thinks it would be harder to obtain confirmation for such a proceeding than to get leave from the Pope for the formation of a separate province. That, he says, the Pope would be quite willing to give if the King were to write a line about it to his Ambassador (to the Holy See.) It should be easy to get him to do so by telling him how the Discalced are being treated by these friars (of the Observance). If the King were approached, he might be glad to do this for us. At any rate, such a step would be a great help to the reform, for the friars (of the Observance) would have more respect for (the Discalced), and would give up the idea that they can be suppressed.

I fancy it might be a good idea if your Paternity were to communicate with Father-Master Chaves about this, taking him that letter of mine which I sent by the Father Prior. He is a very prudent person, and, as the King has such regard for him, he might perhaps get what we want. Then, armed with his Majesty's letters, these friars of ours could go to Rome, as has been arranged. I should not like them on any account to fail to go, for, as Doctor Rueda says, the most direct way (to our goal) is to approach the Pope or the General.

I assure you, if Father Padilla and the rest of us had set to work to get this settled with the King, it would have been done long ago. Your Paternity, indeed, might take the matter up yourself, and also approach the Archbishop, for if, after our Provincial has been elected, he will still need to have the King's confirmation and approval, it would be better to obtain that approval now, and then, if it cannot be obtained, our failure will not be remarked upon so much as if it were refused after he had been elected, which would put us under a cloud. Your Paternity, too, would lose a great deal of prestige for having attempted to do what was not possible and not having realized this beforehand.

The Doctor says the election would be looked upon more favorably if it were conducted by the Dominican Visitor or someone like that than if the Discalced hold it themselves. He also says that, as I have remarked, a great deal of weight is attached to these questions of jurisdiction and it is important that the person at the head of things should have authority for holding his position. It frightens me to think that your Paternity will be blamed, and with some reason. (When you are unjustly blamed on the other hand, I am not frightened at all—in fact, it gives me new courage.) So I have lost no time in writing this so that you may give the matter careful consideration.

Do you know what I have been wondering? If by chance any of the things I have written to our Father General can have been used against us. They might have been shown to some of the Cardinals. They were perfectly proper, but I feel inclined to send him no further communication until these negotiations are over. Also it would be a good idea, if an opportunity presented itself, to make the Nuncio a present. I have observed, my Father, that when you are in Madrid you get about a great deal in a single day. You could talk to people here and there, and there are those you know at court, and then Father Fray Antonio could speak to the Duchess; all that might go a long way towards persuading the King to do this, as he wants the Reform to continue. Father Mariano, too, has his ear, and he could put the case to him, and implore his help, and remind how that little saint, Fray John, is still a prisoner. He should tell him they are so furious about the visitation that they go about doing these stupid things, which they could not if (the Discalced) had (someone at their) head. After all, the King will listen to anyone, and I don't know why Father Mariano, in particular, should neglect the opportunity of talking to him and asking for his aid.

But what palaver I am making, and what nonsense I am writing your Paternity—and yet you bear with everything from me! I can tell you I am suffering agonies at not being free to do what I am telling other people to do. And now, as the King is going so far away, I am wishing something had been done earlier. May God bring this about for us, as He has the power to do.

We are very eagerly looking forward to those ladies' arrival, and the sisters here are most anxious that your Paternity's sister should not be allowed to leave without our giving her the habit. Your Paternity would never believe how much they would do for you. I feel extremely grateful to them, as they are very numerous, and also very needy, and yet they are so anxious to have someone belonging to your Paternity that they never think of that. Oh, and that little Teresa—what things she says and does! I should be glad (to have your sister here) too, for if she goes to Valladolid I shall not be able to enjoy her company—she may even be so far out of reach that I shall never see her at all. However, I can do nothing about it and I am discouraging the nuns (from being hopeful), for she has been accepted at Valladolid already, and will get on very well there, and they would be most disappointed (if she did not go), particularly Casilda. We shall keep a place here for Juliana—though I am not saying anything to them about this matter of Juliana—for I think it would be very hard for Senora Dona Juana if she were to go to Seville, and Juliana herself might perhaps be sorry when she was older. Oh, how strongly I feel about that sister of yours who is at the Doncellas! She doesn't realize that she would be happier here than she is there, so she is losing what would be best for her.

My brother Lorenzo is taking this letter: he is going to Madrid, and from there, I think on to Seville. Will your Paternity be good enough to authorize him to enter the convent so that he can see a little stove which the Prioress has had put in there for cooking purposes? They are saying wonderful things about it, and if it comes up to their reports, it would be a godsend for both friars and nuns; until he has seen it, however, we cannot put one like it in here. I am writing to the Prioress asking her to let him enter the convent for that purpose. If your Paternity thinks this is not a good reason, let me know, as he will be in Madrid for some days. But if you were to read what they write about that stove, you would not be surprised at our wanting one like it here.

They say it is better than Soto's mule and they could hardly say more than that! I think the Prioress is writing, so no more, except to pray God to watch over your Paternity for me.

The Prioress at Alba is very ill indeed. Commend her to God, for, whatever people may say about her, she would be a very great loss. She is very obedient, and, when a nun is that, and is told of her faults, she always improves. Oh, what a bad time the Malagon nuns are having without Brianda! But I ridiculed the idea of her going back there.

Dona Luisa de la Cerda has lost her youngest daughter. I am most deeply distressed at the trials God is sending that lady. She has no daughters left now but the widow. I think it would be suitable if your Paternity wrote her a letter of condolence, for you owe a great deal to her.

Think over this matter of your sisters remaining here. I shall not stand in the way if it seems to you best, or if Senora Dona Juana wants her nearer her. As she herself has decided on Valladolid, I am afraid that, if she stays here, she may be tempted to change her mind later, for she will hear about things they have in that convent which we have not here—their garden alone is much better than ours, for the soil here is wretched.

May God watch over you for me, my Father, and make you as holy as I implore of Him. Amen, Amen. My arm is getting better.

Today is the fifteenth of April

Your Paternity's unworthy servant and daughter,

Teresa of Jesus

Dona Guiomar is still here, and is better; she is most anxious to see your Paternity. She is bewailing the loss of her Fray John of the Cross, and so are all the nuns. It has been a dreadful business. The Incarnation is beginning to return to normal.

Letter 233. To M. Maria de San Jose, Seville; from Avila, June 4, 1578.

May the Holy Spirit be with your Reverence, my daughter. I have had two letters from you: one of them came by way of Madrid and the other was delivered this week by the muleteer here, who takes so long over his deliveries that I get annoyed with him. All the things your Reverence sent me arrived quite safely, and so did the (orange-flower) water, which is splendid, but we have enough of it now and do not need any more. I am delighted with the little jars you have been sending me: I have enough of those too. As I am better now, I do not need so many attentions—I must be mortified sometimes.

The arm is getting better, though it is not yet well enough for me to dress myself; now the weather is getting warmer, they say, it will soon be all right. The box was very nice and so were the other things. Don't think I eat all these sweet things—as a matter of fact, I do not care for them; and, however long I live, I shall never lose the habit of giving. As we always have business affairs on hand, and everyone is not exactly aflame with the charity toward us which the Prior of Las Cuevas and Father Garcialvarez show you, we need all we can get.

We quite understood about the little stove and I don't think it will be possible for us to go wrong. Ours is being made now. All the nuns were amazed to find how clever you are, and are very, very grateful to you, and so am I, for it is quite clear how much you love me from the way you give me pleasure in everything. I have known that all the time—and I can assure you that the love on my side is even greater, for I am amazed at my affection for you. You must not imagine I love anyone more than you, for not all the nuns appeal so much to my nature. The worst of it is I am so wicked that I can be of little use to you, though I am most particular about commending you to God.

I was sorry to hear of that heart trouble you say you are having: it is very distressing; but I am not at all surprised to hear of it, for your trials have been terrible and you have been very much alone. Though the Lord has been good to us in giving you strength and courage to bear such things, you cannot help feeling them physically. You can be glad about this, however, it has been very, very good for your soul. And believe me, I am not saying that to console you, but because I know it is true; and the good of the soul, my daughter, is something we can never purchase, except at great cost.

It distressed me very, very much to hear of the worrying time you are all having just now: you will find it most unsettling. It is a great thing to hear there is some improvement. I hope in Our Lord she will get better [one of the Seville nuns who had severe mental illness], for many whom He afflicts in this way do get better. It is a good thing she is amenable to treatment. God will cure her: it may be that He is being pleased to give your community this cross to bear for a little while, and that you will derive much good from it. That is what I earnestly beseech Him.

And now, with regard to this, pay attention to what I am going to say. Your Reverence should see as little of this sister as possible, for it is very bad for your heart, and might do you a great deal of harm. Remember, that is a command from me. Choose two of the stoutest-hearted nuns, and let them attend to her, and then there will very seldom be any need for the others to see her at all. They must not be any less cheerful or get upset, but must treat her just as they would anyone else who was ill. Indeed, in one way, they can be less sorry for her, for persons in her condition do not feel it as much as those who have other complaints.

We have been reading here recently about the convent of our Order in which St. Euphrasia was a nun: they had a sister with the same affliction as this sister of yours has, and no one but the Saint could do anything with her—in the end, she cured her.

Perhaps you have someone she is afraid of who could do the same. If there were no ill health in our convents to cause us trouble, life would be like a heaven on earth and we should have no opportunity of gaining merit. Perhaps if you were to whip her she would stop crying out like that: it would do her no harm. You are right to keep her apart from the others. I have been wondering if she is suffering from an excess of blood: that, I believe, would account for her pains in the back. May God put things right.

You know, although one is sorry about these things, the distress they cause me is not comparable with what I should suffer if I thought there were imperfections, or restless souls among you. As you have no such trouble as that, I am not going to let myself worry unduly about physical ailments. As you know, if we are to enjoy the (bliss of the) Crucified, we must bear the Cross, and there is no need for us to ask Him for that—though my Father Fray Gregorio thinks it well one should do so—for His Majesty treats those He loves as He treated His own Son.

I wrote the other day to my Father Prior of Las Cuevas, so just give him my kind regards for now. Read the enclosed letter which I have written to Father Garcialvarez, and give it him if you think it will do. I love them both very much, but I do not write to them every time because of my head: it is a little better now, but I still get these dreadful noises. Always give them my kind remembrances.

I was extremely glad to hear that our Father is telling those two nuns who are so much given to prayer that they must eat meat. You know, my daughter, I have been worried about them: they would not have had such a whirl of experiences if they had been with me. The very fact that they have so many of these experiences makes me suspicious about them, and, though some of them may be genuine, I am sure it will be best if they regard them as of little importance, and if your Reverence and our Father do the same, or indeed treat them as of no account at all, for nothing will be lost by that even if they are genuine. By making no account of them I mean you should say that God leads some souls by one road and some by another, and that this particular road is not one that leads to the greatest sanctity, which is quite true.

I was glad to hear what you say about Acosta, and to know that he has so high an opinion of her. I should be sorry if she were to tell him about many of her revelations, in case some of them do not turn out as she says, for he might then go down in his opinion, as she did in mine. I do not mean that she has destroyed all my faith in her, for I know very well that these revelations may often come from God and yet occasionally they may not—but may be produced by the imagination. I have forgotten when it was that what that other nun told you was about to take place; let me know if it turns out to be true or false: letters come quite safely by this messenger. It has just occurred to me that it will be better if I do not answer Garcialvarez's letter until you have told me if he knows anything about these matters, so that I may write accordingly. So give him my kind regards and tell him I was glad to get his letter and will answer it.

With regard to those two postulants, be very careful indeed what you do. It is very much in their favor that Father Nicolao thinks well of them. God willing, our Father will be coming to you in September, or perhaps earlier—he has already been ordered to do so, as you will know—and you must do as he tells you. I get dreadfully worried when I see him going among those people. He is in great need of our prayers. All the sisters send you their warm remembrances.

Oh, and Teresa, how she jumped for joy when she saw what you had sent her! It is extraordinary how she loves you. I think she would forsake her own father to go anywhere with you. The older she grows, the more virtuous and sensible she gets. She has already begun to receive Holy Communion and show no little devotion.

And now my head is getting tired, so I will say no more than "God preserve you to me, as I beseech Him to." Give my kind remembrances to all the nuns, and to the Portuguese sister and her mother. Try not to worry, and tell me how your heart trouble is. The oil of orange flower is very nice. My heart is better than it was a few days ago: evidently the Lord does not want to send me all my trials at once.

Today is the fourth of June.

Think over what I have begged of you—or, rather, have asked you to do—on this sheet of paper. For love of the Lord, you must take the very strictest precautions about it, for it is a thing which has been entrusted to me by someone to whom I am under the deepest obligation, and I have told him that, if your Reverence cannot get it done, no one else will, for I consider you very clever and very lucky in the things you attempt; so you must go about it with the greatest caution, and that will give me very real pleasure. Perhaps the Father Prior of Las Cuevas will be able to do something, though the person I am relying on is Father Garcialvarez. It seems difficult, but, when God wills a thing, everything becomes easy. It would be the very greatest comfort to me, and I even think, too, it would be a great service to Our Lord, as it is for the profit of souls and can do no one any harm.

What is wanted is a collection of sermons, covering a whole year, by Father Salucio—he belongs to the Order of St. Dominic—and they should be the best ones obtainable. If they cannot all be had, get as many as you can, provided they are really good ones. A year's sermons include the following: Lent, Advent, the feasts of Our Lord and of Our Lady and of all the Saints in the year, and the Sundays from Epiphany till Lent and from Pentecost till Advent.

I have been asked for these confidentially, so I do not want the matter to be mentioned except to anyone who can help with it. May it please the Lord to give you good fortune in it. If you send me the sermons, do so by this messenger, and be generous in your payment of him. Send letters here, to St. Joseph's, as long as I remain here: that is the safest plan—better than sending them to my brother, even if there should be some for him (with them), as he may not be at home. And get as many of the sermons as you can, if you can't get them all.

It is very encouraging to me to know how well Father Garcial-varez and Father Fray Gregorio speak of your Reverence and your daughters—though how could they do otherwise, being your confessors? Please God it may all be true!

Your Reverence's servant,

Teresa of Jesus

Letter 252. To P. Pablo Hernandez, from Avila; October 4, 1578.

May the grace of the Holy Spirit be with you, my Father. It must be a week since I received a letter from the Prioress of Toledo, Ana de los Angeles, in which she said you were in Madrid. The news was a great comfort to me, as I thought God must have sent you there to bring me some relief from my trials. I assure you, since last August twelvemonth, they have been so varied and so severe that I should find it a real relief if I could see you and tell you about a few of them: to enumerate them all would be impossible. To crown everything, we are now in a position which the bearer of this letter will describe to you; he himself has had to suffer a great deal through his affection for us and he is a person whom we can trust.

The devil cannot endure seeing how faithfully these Discalced friars and nuns are serving Our Lord: I assure you it would be a great encouragement to you if you could witness the perfection of their behaviour. There are now nine Discalced priories, containing many good friars. As we have not been made into a separate province, we have to endure so many worries and troubles brought upon us by the Fathers of the Cloth that it is impossible to set them down in writing.

At the present moment, our whole future, good or bad, is, under God, in the hands of the Nuncio; and for our sins the Fathers of the Cloth have told him such tales about us, and he has given the tales such credence, that I do not know where everything will end. They talk to him about me and say I am a restless gadabout, and that I have been founding convents without licenses from the Pope or from the General. Can you imagine what more damning or unchristian thing they could have thought of?

There are many other things, not fit to relate, which these blessed Fathers are saying about me; and as for our Father Gracian, who was their visitor, the intolerable false witness they are bearing against him is shameful. I will answer for him that he is one of the greatest servants of God with whom I have had to do, and one of the most honourable and purest of conscience. Do believe that I am speaking the truth. And moreover, he has had all his education from the Company, as you may know.

It has been reported from Alcala that for certain reasons the Nuncio is extremely displeased with him (Father Gracian). If they would listen to him (they would discover that) he is very little to blame, if at all. The same is true of me: I have never in any way opposed the Nuncio's authority; I obeyed a Brief which he sent here with perfectly good grace; and I wrote him a letter with the greatest humility at my command.

I think all this is being sent us from above: it must be the Lord's will that we shall suffer, for there is no one who will defend the truth or say a good word for me. I can sincerely assure you that, as far as I am concerned, this neither perturbs nor troubles me—in fact, it makes me remarkably happy. But it seems to me, if it were proved that what these Fathers say about me is not true, the things they say about our Father Gracian might not be believed either, and that is what matters to us most. So I am sending you copies of the patents, from which I derive my authority to make foundations, as the Nuncio says, we are in a false position for having made them without licenses. I am sure the devil is doing everything he can to discredit these houses, so I wish there were servants of God who would defend them. Oh, my Father, how few are the friends we have in times of need!

They tell me the President [of the council of Castile] is greatly attached to you, and you are in Madrid on his business. I believe he has been given certain information by the Nuncio about all this, and about other things, too. It would be very useful to us if you would undeceive him, as you can from the witness of your own eyes, for you can see into my very soul. I believe in this way you will be doing Our Lord a great service; and you can tell the President how important it is that the recently begun reform of our sacred Order should make progress; for, as you know, the Order had fallen into a bad way.

People say this is a new Order and accuse us of inventing new things. Let them read our Primitive rule, for what we follow is simply that rule without mitigation, with the rigour originally prescribed for it by the Pope. They should not believe anything about our life, and about the life of the Calced, beyond what they see and know. People should not listen to the Calced; I cannot think where the Calced discover so many things which are not true, and which they use for making war upon us.

I also beseech you to speak on my behalf to the Nuncio's confessor: give him my kind regards and tell him the whole truth. Then he can lay it upon the Nuncio's conscience whether he must not spread such harmful things without ascertaining that they are correct. Tell him, too, that, although I am very wicked, I am not so bad that I would dare to do the things they say. Tell him this, I mean, if you think it advisable to do so—not otherwise.

If you think well, you can show him the patents by virtue of which I have made my foundations, one of which contains an injunction that I am not to cease making them. And then, in a letter which our Father General wrote me, after I had written asking him not to order me to found any more houses, he said he wanted me to make as many foundations as I had hairs on my head. It is not right that so many of God's handmaidens should be discredited by reports like these; and since, as you say, I have been formed and trained by the Company, it seems to me it would be right for you to publish the truth, so that a serious person like the Nuncio—who is not a Spaniard and has come here to reform the Orders—may find out who are the people he has to reform, and who it is that need help, and may punish those who come to him with such falsehoods. You will know what ought to be done.

What I beseech you, for love of Our Lord and of His precious Mother, is that, as you have been our helper for as long as you have known us, you will help us now in this time of our need. You will be richly rewarded, and you owe it to the goodwill I have for you to stand up for the truth, in whatever way you think most fitting. I also beg you to keep me informed about everything, especially about your own health. My own has been very poor, for the Lord has been trying me this year in every way, but as far as I am concerned it distresses me but little; what troubles me is to see these servants of God suffering for my sins. May His Majesty be with you and protect you. Let me know if you will be making a long stay in Madrid, as I have been told is the case.

Today is St. Francis' day.

Your unworthy servant and true daughter,

Teresa of Jesus, Carmelite

Letter 253. To P. Jeronimo Gracian; from Avila, October 15, 1578.

May the Holy Spirit be with your Reverence, my Father. Now that I know you are free from that turmoil, I feel free from worry about everything else, come what may. I was intensely grieved at the news which I received about our Father General. I feel deeply moved by it. On the day I heard it I wept and wept—I could do nothing else—and I felt very much distressed at all the trouble we have caused him, which he certainly did not deserve; if we had gone to him about the matter everything would have been smoothed out. God forgive the person who has continually put obstacles in the way; for, though you had little confidence in my suggestion, I could have come to an understanding with your Paternity. The Lord will bring it all right; but I am sorry about the things I have described, and also about your Paternity's sufferings, for really to read what you wrote me in your first letter—I have had two from you since your interview with the Nuncio—was as bitter a draught as death.

I must tell you, my Father, I was dreadfully upset at your not having shown him those papers at once: you must have been advised by someone who cares little for your Paternity's sufferings. I am very glad to think you will now have learned by experience to guide your affairs along the road which they will have to take, instead of going against the current, which I have always warned you about. There have really been obstacles in our way the whole time, so we must say no more about it, for God orders things so that His servants may suffer.

I should like to write at greater length, but the letters are to be collected to-night, and it is almost night now. I have been writing a long letter to the Bishop of Osma, asking him to discuss the matter I wrote to you about with the President and Father Mariano. I told him to send your Paternity the letter. I have just been talking to my brother and he sends you his kind remembrances.

We are all agreed here that our friars must not go to Rome, especially now that our Father General is dead, for these reasons. First, it cannot be done secretly; the Calced friars may seize them before they leave here and that would be as good as putting them to death. Secondly, in that case, they will lose both the documents and the money. Thirdly, they have no experience of negotiations at Rome. Fourthly, when they get there, now that our Father General has gone, they will be arrested as if they were fugitives, for after all, as I have been saying to Father Mariano, they will be wandering through the streets with no one to come to their aid. If with all the influence at our disposal here we could do nothing for Fray John, what could we possibly do (for them) there? Everyone here thinks it will be a mistake to send the friars, especially my brother—and he feels very keenly about the way the Discalced are being treated. We think here that someone should go who knows how to present our case; and my brother, who is well informed about the Calced Fathers, agrees with this, and says it is most important, and the whole thing should be entrusted to the person I mentioned to you [perhaps R. Pablo Hernandez]. Doctor Rueda has such confidence in him that he thinks (in that event) there would not be the least need (to worry).

Your Paternity should consider all this very carefully; and, if you and Father Mariano think well, you can send a messenger to Almodovar, telling them not to arrange for the friars to start (for Rome), and let me have word about this as soon as possible. The friar who would be going from here is extremely good, but would be more expensive; still, if some ready money can be provided now, each convent will make a contribution later on. Something might be borrowed from that money that was left to the community at Alcala; it could be paid back later. If the money has to be found quickly, I have certainly no means of getting it from here. I am writing in that sense to Father Mariano, as your Paternity will see.

Keep well, for my sake, my Father and God will bring everything right. May He grant us sometimes to agree about things and may He allow nothing to be done which will subject the friars to further martyrdom.

May God preserve you. Amen.

Your Paternity's unworthy servant,

Teresa of Jesus

It is dreadful to see the things that are happening now: these (Calced) Fathers are being helped by the devil! I assure you he did a good thing for himself when he took the Great Angel away from us and gave us the slowcoach we have now. I don't know how such a foolish thing could have been done, though I believe if Ardapilla had been here still worse things would have happened. I can see, my Father, what a martyr your Paternity has been since things have started to go in the wrong direction; if they had only left you alone, it would have been clear that God was guiding you. All your daughters here send you their kind remembrances.

I am very glad you have said they are not to talk to anybody about this. Let us proceed slowly and attend to the Rome affair, for time will straighten things out, so, as your Paternity says, we must just wait till they come right. The only thing I wish is that you were nearer, so that we could see each other more often—that would be a great comfort to my soul. I don't deserve that, but only one cross after another. So long as your Paternity has none, let them come and welcome.

I am reasonably well, though this head of mine is dreadfully troublesome. May God be ever with your Paternity. Please don't tire yourself by writing a great deal. I was extremely glad to hear they are not electing a provincial: to judge from what your Paternity says, that is very wise; though, when Fray Antonio told me he could not do other (than accept) without committing a sin, I did not contradict him. I thought everything was being done here; but, if they have to go to Rome to get an election confirmed, they can also negotiate about the province. If they have to come this way, send me full particulars of everything that is going to be done.

Today is the fifteenth of October.

I am your Paternity's subject and daughter,

Teresa of Jesus

Letter 264.
To the Discalced Carmelite nuns of Seville; from Avila, January 31, 1579.

May the grace of the Holy Spirit be with your Charities, my sisters and daughters. I assure you I have never loved you as much as I do now and you have never been bound to serve Our Lord as much as you are now, when He is granting you the great blessing of being able to taste something of the meaning of His Cross and to realize something of the keen sense of desolation which His Majesty felt as He hung upon it. It was a happy day for you when you entered your house, since He was preparing you a period of such good fortune. I envy you tremendously. Truth to tell, when I learned all the ups and downs you had suffered—and they took the greatest trouble to explain it all to me—and of how attempts were made to turn you out of your house, and various other details, there came to me the deepest inward joy, for I saw that, without your having crossed the sea, Our Lord has been pleased to open up for you mines of eternal treasures. I trust in His Majesty you will grow very rich, and share your wealth with those of us who are here. For I have great confidence in His mercy that He will grant you the grace to bear everything and to offend Him in nothing. So, if you feel it all deeply, do not be distressed: it is the Lord Who is being pleased to make you realize that you are not capable of as much as you thought you were when you longed so much to suffer.

Courage, courage, my daughters. Remember, God gives no one more troubles than he is able to bear, and He is with those who are in tribulation. That being so, you have no reason to fear: you must trust in His mercy that He will reveal the whole truth, and it will be realized how the devil has been laying hidden snares to entrap you, which has grieved me more than what is happening now. Prayer, prayer, my sisters; let your humility and obedience shine forth now and let there be none more obedient than your Charities, especially the former Mother Prioress, to the Vicaress who has been set over you.

Oh, what a good time this is for you to harvest the fruits of the resolutions you have made to serve Our Lord! Remember, it is often His pleasure to test our actions and see if they match our resolutions and our words. Let the Virgin's daughters, your own sisters, see you coming honourably out of this great persecution. If you help yourselves, the good Jesus will help you; for, though He is asleep on the sea, when the storm rises He will still the winds. His pleasure is that we should ask Him for what we need, and so much does He love us that He is always seeking ways to help us. Blessed be His name forever. Amen, Amen, Amen.

In all our houses, the nuns are continually commending you to God, so I trust that, in His goodness, He will soon put things right. Try to be cheerful, and reflect that, when all is said, it is very little that you are suffering for so good a God, Who endured so much for us: you have not even shed any of your blood for Him yet. You are among your sisters, not in Algiers. Let your Spouse do His will, and you will see how, before long, the sea will swallow up those who are making war upon us, as it did King

Pharaoh, and God will free His people, and give them all the desire to undergo further sufferings, because they have gained so much from (what they have suffered in) the past.

I received your letter and wish you had not burned what you had written previously, as it would have been very useful to me. According to learned men here, you need not have given up the letters I had written you, but it is no great matter. Would it were His Divine Majesty's will that all the blame should fall on me, though the distress of those who have suffered innocently has fallen on me heavily.

What distressed me very much was to see that the statement of facts drawn up by the Father Provincial of Andalusia contained a number of allegations which I know to be completely false, as I was there at the time they refer to. For love of Our Lord, think carefully if any one of you made them through fear or perturbation, for nothing matters if no offense is committed against God. Still, I have been very sorry about these falsehoods and the harm they will do. I simply cannot believe them, for everyone knows how good and how single-minded Father-Master Gracian has been in his dealings with us and how much he has helped us to make progress in Our Lord's service. That being so, it was very wrong to accuse him of such things, even if they are not very serious. Please tell this to the sisters concerned, and abide with the Most Holy Trinity. May God watch over you. Amen.

All the sisters here send you warm greetings. They are hoping that, when these clouds have lifted, Sister San Francisco will be able to narrate the whole story. I send remembrances to good Gabriela, and beg her to be very happy, for I am well aware how it will have grieved her to see the way Mother San Jose has been treated. For Sister San Jeronimo, if her desires (to suffer) are genuine, I am not sorry at all; otherwise I should be sorrier for her than for anyone else.

Tomorrow is the eve of Our Lady of the Candles.

To Señor Garcialvarez I should very much rather talk than write; so, as I cannot say what I should like to him in writing, I am not writing to him at all. Give my kind regards to any other sisters to whom you dare to mention this letter.

Your Charities' unworthy servant,

Teresa of Jesus

Letter 274.
To MM. Isabel de San Jeronimo and Maria de San Jose, Seville; from Avila, May 3, 1579.

May the grace of the Holy Spirit be with your Reverence, my daughter, I got your letter and my sisters' letters yesterday. Oh, Jesus, what a comfort it would be to me if I could be in your house now! And it would have been just as great a one if I could have been with you earlier so as to share in the wealth of treasures which Our Lord has been giving you. May He be blessed forever. Amen.

I loved you all dearly as it was, but I love you twice as much now, especially your Reverence, who has been the chief sufferer. But you may be quite sure that, when I heard they had deprived you of your voice and seat (in Chapter), and of your office, it gave me special comfort; for, although I know my daughter Josefa is very wicked, I know, too, that she fears God, and would never have committed any sin against His Majesty which could merit such a punishment.

I sent you all a letter by my Father, the Prior of Las Cuevas, and asked him to arrange how it was to be given you. I am anxious to know if his Paternity received it, and one which I wrote him too, and also to whom he entrusted the letter for you, even if it means your having to write again. When Father Nicolao heard what had happened to his brother's letter, he tore it up. Your Reverence owes him a great deal; he thinks very much more of you than Father Garcialvarez does.

I am sorry Garcialvarez is not saying Mass for you now, though it is only the community which suffers—for him it means the saving of a great deal of trouble. We are certainly most indebted to him, but I cannot think of any means we can employ (to get the decision revoked). For if the most Reverend Archbishop would not alter it for the Father Prior of Las Cuevas and for Father Mariano, I know of no one for whom he would.

I was rather annoyed about those notes of Father Mariano's. To think it could ever have entered his head to try to have such a thing done in your community, let alone to put it into practice! The fact is, the devil has been getting so angry with us that he is attempting to oppress us in every way he can, especially as regards what is being done for us ... greatest torment of all. But apparently Our Lord is not going to give him so much freedom and I hope His Majesty will ordain that, little by little, the truth shall be revealed.

Little truth has been spoken lately in your convent and it grieved me deeply to hear the things that were said when they brought those charges against you. Some of them, I knew, were completely false, as I was with you when they were supposed to have happened. Now that I have seen what those nuns have been doing I have given our Lord hearty thanks that He did not allow them to bring up anything worse.

Those two souls have filled me with dismay: we must all offer very special prayers that God will give them light. I have been apprehensive of what has now happened ever since Father Garcialvarez began to behave in that way, and, if your Reverence remembers, I told you in two of my letters that I believed there was trouble brewing inside the community. I even named one of the nuns—I never realized that Margarita was in it—and warned you to be on your guard; for, as a matter of fact, I was always dissatisfied with her spiritual condition, though sometimes I thought that was because I was so wicked myself and was yielding to temptation. I even discussed it with Father-Master Gracian, who had a great deal to do with her, in order that he could be on the lookout. So it has been no great surprise to me— not that I thought she was bad, merely a weak-minded person who had been led astray: she was just ripe to be tricked by the devil, as she has been, for he is very good at taking advantage of temperamental and unintelligent people. So we must not blame her so much as be very sorry for her. And your Reverence and all of you must do me the kindness of not departing from what I am about to say to you: believe me, I really think what I suggest will be best. You must also give the Lord heartfelt praise for not having allowed the devil to send any of you such a severe temptation: let us reflect, as St. Augustine says, that if we had been tempted in such a way, we should have behaved still worse. See that you do not lose what you have gained in this time (of trial), my daughters. Remember how St. Catherine of Siena behaved to the woman who had accused her of wrongdoing. Let us fear, my sisters, let us fear; for if God withdraws His hand from us, what wicked things are there that we shall not do? Believe me, that sister has neither the wit nor the skill to have invented all those things she said, and that was why the devil decided to give her a companion, who must certainly have been instructed by him. May God be with her.

The first thing I want to say is that you must commend her to His Majesty very earnestly in all your prayers—pray for her every moment of the day, if you can: that is what we shall do here, so that He may grant us the favour of giving her light and the devil may release her from the spell under which he is at present holding her. In some ways I look upon her as a person out of her mind. You see, I know of certain persons, though not in any of our houses, whose imagination is so unstable that they think they really see everything that comes into their minds. The devil must be at the back of this. What I am afraid is that he must have made her think she saw what he wanted her to, with the object of bringing about the ruin of your community. So perhaps she is not so much to blame as we thought she was, just as no blame attaches to a madman who really gets it into his head that he is God the Father so that nothing will drive the idea out again. Your love for God, my sisters, must show itself in your pity for her, which must be as great as though she were as much the daughter of your own father as she is of this our true Father, to Whom we owe so much and Whom the poor creature has wanted to serve all her life. Pray, sisters, pray for her, for many of the saints have fallen and then become saints again. Perhaps she needed this experience to humble her, for if God, of His goodness to us, grants her to realize what she has done and to retract it, we shall all have gained through suffering, and she may gain too, for the Lord knows how to bring good out of evil.

Secondly, you must not even consider letting her leave your convent for the present: that would be a foolish thing to allow and there is no point in it at all. Far from banishing all danger you would simply be rushing into it. Let some time elapse first; this is not the moment for such a change, as I could bring many reasons to show, and I am astonished that your Reverence should not have thought of them. Reflect on the matter and God will reveal them to you. Trust in His Majesty and in those of us who are giving mature consideration to your community's good. And be very careful not to talk about the thing just now; do not even think of it if you can avoid doing so.

The third thing is that you must not show the two sisters any sort of enmity. In fact you should treat the chief culprit more kindly than before, and you must all be kind and sisterly to her, and to the other nun as well. Try to forget what has happened, and think, each of you how you would like to be treated if it had happened to you. No one may realize it, but, believe me, she will be suffering agonies in her soul; the devil will see to that, as he could achieve nothing further. He might make her do herself some harm which would end in the destruction of her reason and soul; it would probably not take much to affect her reason. We must all bear that in mind and not think of what she did. The devil may possibly have made her believe she was winning merit for her soul and rendering great service to God. You must not say a word of this in front of her mother, whom I have been very sorry for. Why has no one told me how she has been bearing all these things and what she has said to Beatriz? I have been wanting to know about that and if she has realized what a schemer she has been.

I am afraid the devil will be subjecting these sisters to fresh temptations now, and telling them they are disliked and being ill-treated. I should be extremely annoyed if they were given any excuse for thinking that. I have already had a letter which says that the Fathers of the Company think it wrong of the nuns to be ill-treating that sister. Be very much on the lookout for this.

The fourth thing is that she must not be allowed to talk to anyone except in the presence of a third person, and this third person must be on her guard. Nor must she—or any of the other nuns—make confessions to anyone but a Discalced friar. She may choose which of these she likes, as the Father Vicar-General has authorized any of them to hear the nuns' confessions. Be very careful not to let the two nuns have a lot of private conversation together. But do not put any strain upon them—for we women are weak till the Lord begins to do His work in us. It would not be a bad idea to keep Beatriz occupied by giving her some duty to perform, provided it is not one which brings her into any kind of contact with people from outside; she must mix only with the community. If she is alone, and allowed to think all the time, it will be very bad for her, so if any of the nuns see they can do her good, let them sometimes spend some time with her.

I expect I shall be seeing Father Nicolao before he goes to Seville. I wish it might be soon. We shall then be able to discuss everything in detail. For the present, please do just what I ask you. In any case, those who have a real desire to suffer never bear rancour against those who do them wrong—they only love them the more. You will be able to tell by this if you have all profited by your period of trial. I hope in Our Lord that He will soon put everything right and that the house will be just as it was before, or even better, for His Majesty always gives a hundredfold.

Now mind, I ask you once again very earnestly not on any account to talk among yourselves about the past: it can do you no good and may do a great deal of harm. As regards the future, we must walk very warily, for, as I have said, I am afraid the devil may work upon that poor silly Beatriz and lead her to do some harm to herself or tempt her to run away. I am less apprehensive about the other one: she has more sense. Be very much on the lookout, especially at night; for the devil is trying to bring discredit upon our convents, and he sometimes turns a thing that has seemed impossible into a possibility.

If these two sisters ceased to be friendly, and something arose to make them displeased with each other, we might get nearer to the root of things and find a way of undeceiving them. Your Reverence will bear this in mind. The closer friends they are, the more likely they will be to plot together. But a great deal can be done by our prayer, so I trust the Lord will give them light. I am extremely worried about them.

If it would be a help to the community to have a written account of all that has happened, it would not be a bad idea to have one drawn up. It would enable us to take warning from experience—a warning in this case, not from the follies of our neighbours, but, for my sins, from our own. If the historian should be Sister San Francisco, however, she must not exaggerate, but give a perfectly straightforward description. The actual writing should be done by my daughter Gabriela.

I should like to write to all the sisters, but my head is not fit for it. I wish you all many blessings. May the blessings of Our Lady, the Virgin, and of the Most Holy Trinity, be showered upon you.

Your community has laid the entire Order under an obligation to it, especially those of its members who are not yet professed. You have given clear proof that you are its true daughters. Beg them, from me, to remain steadfastly so. Let those who have written to me consider this letter as addressed to them. Though it is going to Mother Maria de San Jose and the Mother Vicaress, my intention has been to write to each of you individually.

I should have liked to write to my sister Jeronimo. Tell her she will do better to regret the harm done to the community's reputation through its no longer having Father Garcialvarez than to be sorry for that Father himself, for he is well known in Seville. It is on the poor nuns who are "foreigners" that the brunt of the trouble will fall. Obviously, even if it were thought that he was at fault, the nuns would not be exempt from criticism; but of one thing I am sure, and that is, as I say, that he is well known to be a man of virtue. Apart from that, he is getting out of a good deal of work. But what he has suffered in Seville on our account, and what we all owe him, cannot be overestimated—only God can repay it.

Give him my best remembrances. If my head had been equal to it I should have written him a long letter, though it would be difficult to put the things I should like to say to him into writing. So I am not doing so: if I were, I might have a few complaints of my own to make, for, as other people had been told about the dreadful things which those blessed women said were being done in the house, it would not have been much trouble to have kept me informed about them occasionally, as I was the person most affected. As it was, I had to wait until the thing was taken in hand by people who have little love for us, as the whole world knows. However, when all is said, truth suffers, but never dies, so I hope the Lord will yet reveal things more clearly.

Remember me to good Serrano: I hope the time will come when we can repay our many debts to him. Give a special message from me to my saintly Prior of Las Cuevas. Oh, if I could only spend a whole day with him! May God watch over you all for me and make you as holy as I beseech Him to. Amen. The sisters here have wept over your troubles more than I have: they send you their very kind remembrances. I shall write again soon, and, as to the matter of Mother San Jose, which you commend to my prayers, perhaps by the time this reaches you it will be settled. You are getting on well now; do not hurry: there is no need to have the election until we send you instructions from here, and we are not being neglectful about arranging it.

If Father Mariano should be at Seville, send him this letter (to read) and ask him to give it back to you. I am not writing to him now, as I am not sure if a letter will reach him there. Give my greetings to Father Fray Gregorio: I am looking forward to hearing from him. With regard to the Mass, I don't know what to say to you: don't be in a hurry. And don't fret if there is no one to say it for you. Till the Lord provides for you, you must be content with having it on Sundays: that will give you no lack of opportunity for gaining merit.

I am reasonably well.

Father Julian de Avila has felt for you very much in your troubles. If he had thought he could do anything to relieve them, I think he would have been very glad to come to you. He commends himself earnestly to your prayers. May God give you strength to suffer more and more, for even now you have not shed your blood for Him Who shed all His for you. I can assure you we have not been idle here.

Today is the Day of the Cross.

Your Reverence's unworthy servant,

Teresa of Jesus

Letter 351.
To Jeronimo Gracian, Alcala de Henares; from Palencia, February 21, 1581.

May the Holy Spirit be with your Paternity, my Father. I have received the letter you wrote me from Alcala, and am delighted at all you say in it, and most of all to know you are well. Praised be God, Who shows me such great mercy, after all your journeys and labours. I, too, am well.

I have written your Paternity a letter and sent it in duplicate and have dispatched my memoranda so that my views may look authoritative. I had forgotten to tell you about what I have written to the Father Commissary in the letter which I enclose in this. I should like your Paternity to read it, so I am sending it to you open in order not to tire myself by copying it all out again. Please seal it with the seal you have which is like mine and give it him.

The Prioress of Segovia remarked to me on this question of being free to have preachers from outside (the Order): I thought it all right as it stood and left it as it was. But we must not only consider those who are living now, my Father: we must remember that some day there may come superiors who will be opposed to this form of freedom, and to others. So it will be very kind of your Paternity if you will help us by seeing that both this matter and the one I wrote you about the other day are put to the Father Commissary very simply and clearly. If he were not to leave us free in this respect, we should have to see about getting sanction from Rome, for I realize the great importance of such freedom to the sisters' happiness, as well as the dreadful unhappiness that arises in other convents where there are too many restrictions in spiritual things. A soul restricted in such a way cannot render effective service to God, which enables the devil to tempt it. When religious are allowed freedom, on the other hand, they often care nothing about it and have no desire to use it.

If the Father Commissary has authority to amend the constitutions, and after due consideration to put fresh articles in those which are about to be drawn up, I should like omissions or additions to be made, as we are now asking. But no one will do anything about this unless your Paternity and Father Nicolao make a great point of it; and, as your Paternity says, and as I think I wrote to you in my letter, there is no need to discuss the nuns' concerns with the friars—Fray Pedro Fernandez never did so. He and I had an arrangement about the rules he made that he should never do anything without consulting me. I owe it to him to say this.

If the Constitutions can be recast, or anything can be deleted from them, will your Paternity see that nothing is laid down as to whether stockings are to be of hempen thread or coarse woolen cloth? It should merely be said that the nuns be permitted to wear stockings, or they will never quiet their scruples. And where it is specified that coifs are to be of *sedena* the word "linen" should be used. If you think well, will you delete Father Fray Pedro Fernandez's rule that the nuns are not to eat eggs or take bread at collation? He *would* make the rule and I could never prevail upon him to omit it. It is sufficient if the obligations of the Church are fulfilled, without any others being added to them, for nuns get very scrupulous, which is bad for them, and some who really need these things think they do not.

We have been told that the General Chapter has just made a great many ordinances about the recital of the Office and laid down that the ferial Office is to be recited twice every week. If you think well, will you put in that we are not bound to observe all these changes but may say the Office as we do now? Your Paternity must also remember how very inconvenient it has been for the Discalced to have had to stay in houses of the Order (observing the Mitigated Rule) wherever there have been such houses. If it were possible, one might say that they need not do this where there are other houses in which they can stay with due edification.

Our Constitutions say that our houses must be founded in poverty and may not have an income. As I can see that they are now all on the way to having one, you might consider wise to delete this clause, and everything else to be found on the subject in the Constitutions. Otherwise, anyone who reads them will think we have not been long in becoming relaxed again. Alternatively the Father Commissary might say that, as the Council (of Trent) allows convents to have incomes, they are permitted to do so.

I should like these Constitutions to be printed, as there are different versions of them, and there are prioresses who have them copied out and add or omit what they like without thinking they are doing anything in particular. A definite rule must be laid down that nothing is to be added to them, or subtracted from them, so that this may become quite clear. In all these trifling matters, your Paternity will do as you think best: I mean I want you just to consider these points which concern us. Father Nicolao should also have a say in the matter, or it will be thought that (I am consulting) no one but your Paternity. Father Fray Juan de Jesus, too, I think, will look on our affairs kindly. I should like to write more, but it is almost night, and they will be collecting the letters, and I am also writing to some friends.

I was touched by your Paternity's asking what will become of the Discalced nuns. At least, you will be their true Father, and they are under a great obligation to you for this. If your Paternity could live forever, and they would not have to deal with anyone else, it would be unnecessary for us to ask for some of these things. How they long for you to be Provincial. Nothing else, I think will satisfy them. May God watch over you for us. All the nuns send you their remembrances.

Today is the twenty-first of February.

I am your Paternity's true daughter.

Teresa of Jesus

The enclosed are the memoranda I have received; when I get the others, I will send them on. I am not sure if they are all right: it was highly necessary for your Paternity to say they should be sent through me. God protect you. The only memorandum which was in proper form when it reached me was your friend Isabel de Santo Dominto's: I send it just as it came.

Questions and Activities

1. Compare and contrast Teresa's account of her early life in chapters 1-8 of *The Life of Teresa of Jesus* with that given by Ignatius of Loyola in his *Autobiography*. Note similarities and differences in these two works, both written by mystics who were also reformers in approximately the same time and place. Can any of the differences which you note be accounted for by Teresa's specifically feminine experience?

2. Read Martin Luther's statement on Christian spirituality entitled "The Freedom of the Christian." Write an essay in which you judge Teresa of Avila by Luther's standards.

3. How do the ideals and style of Teresa differ from those of Heloise who was also a religious superior whose commitment to spiritual development came later in life? Imagine a dialogue between them on the nature of holiness and the difficulties they encountered in their lives.

4. Look out on the world of today with Teresa's eyes. Where might her reforming zeal take her today? To what task might she address herself and how would she undertake the task?

Selected Additional Reading

Allen, Christine. "Self-creation and the Loss of Self: Mary Daly and St. Teresa of Avila." *Studies in Religion* 6:1 (1976-77) 67-72.

Auclair, Marcelle. *Teresa of Avila*. Garden City, New York: Doubleday Image Books, 1959.

Chorpenning, Joseph F. "The Monastery, Paradise, and the Castle: Literary Images and Spiritual Development in St. Teresa." *Bulletin of Hispanic Studies* 62:3 (July, 1985) 245-57.

The Autobiography of St. Ignatius Loyola, trans. by Joseph F. O'Callaghan and ed. by John C. Olin. New York: Harper and Row, 1974.

Lincoln, Victoria. *Teresa: A Woman.* Ed. by Elias Rivers and Antonion T. deNicolas. Albany: SUNY Press, 1984.

Luther, Martin. "The Freedom of a Christian," trans. by W.A. Lambert. *Three Treatises.* Philadelphia: Fortress Press, 1970.

Fittipaldi, Silvio E. "Human Consciousness and the Christian Mystic." *Journal of the Academy of Religion and Psychology* 3 (April, 1980) 94-104.

Palacios, Miguel. "Saint Teresa and Islam: A Study of the Simile of the Castle." *Bulletin of the Christian Institutes of Islamic Studies* 6:1-2 (Jan.-June, 1983) 12-27.

Paul, Irven. "St. Theresa of Jesus of Avila." *Journal of Religious and Psychological Research* 4 (July-Oct., 1981) 179-81.

Porcile-Santiso, Maria Teresa. "Solitude and Solidarity." *Ecumenical Review* 38:1 (Jan., 1986) 35-47.

Slade, Carol. "Saint Teresa's *Meditaciones sobre los Cantares:* The Hermeneutics of Humility and Enjoyment." *Religion and Literature* 18:1 (Spring, 1986) 27-44.

The Letters of Saint Teresa of Jesus, Trans. and ed. by E. Allison Peers. Westminster, Maryland: The Newman Press, 1950.

The Complete Works of Saint Teresa of Jesus, Trans. and ed. by E. Allison Peers. New York: Sheed & Ward, 1946.

Notes

1. Though somewhat dated, Marcelle Auclair's *Teresa of Avila,* tran. by Kathleen Pond (Garden City, NY: Doubleday Image, 1959) is still an excellent biography. A more recent one by Victoria Lincoln, *Teresa: A Woman,* eds. Elias Rivers and Antonio T. deNicolas, (Albany: SUNY Press, c1984) contains a helpful chronology and list of people and places. It is particularly clear on the legal troubles that beset the reform of Carmel.

2. *The Life of Teresa of Jesus,* trans. and ed. by E. Allison Peers (Garden City, New York: Doubleday Image Books, 1960) 65.

3. *Life* 84.

4. The Complete Works of Saint Teresa of Jesus (in 3 volumes), trans. and ed. by E Allison Peers (New York: Sheed & Ward, 1946). Two volumes of her letters also give some idea of the vast correspondence in which she engaged while keeping the demanding schedule of Carmelite life and providing for the numerous new foundations. See *The Letters of Saint Teresa of Jesus,* tran. and ed. by E. Allison Peers (Westminster, Md: The Newman Press, 1950). A new edition and translation of all of Teresa's works, including the letters, has been published by ICS, Washington, D.C.

5. Carol Slade, "Saint Teresa's *Meditaciones sobre los Cantares:* The Hermeneutics of Humility and Enjoyment," *Religion and Literature* 18:1 (Spring, 1986) 29.

6. *Life* 66.

7. *The Way of Perfection*, trans. and ed. by E. Allison Peers (Garden City, New York: Doubleday Image Books, 1964) 95.

8. *Life* 114.

9. An instructive essay on this theme, which echoes and explicates Teresa's understanding is "Wholeheartedness" by Robert O. Johann, *Building the Human* (New York: Herder and Herder, 1968) 145-147.

10. *Life* 347.

11. *Life* 348.

12. See Christine J. Allen, "Self-creation and the Loss of Self: Mary Daly and St. Teresa of Avila," *Studies in Religion* 6:1 (1976-77) 67-72, for a discussion of the difficulties encountered by someone living within the Christian tradition of 'death to self' who discovers the importance of personal autonomy in the search for liberation.

13. An apostolic visitor is one who visits individual convents, usually on behalf of the local Bishop or even the Pope. His purpose is to ascertain whether, on the one hand, individuals are being treated with the care and dignity called for by their Rule and Canon Law and, on the other hand, whether they are observing those Rules and Canons to the best of their ability.

14. Auclair 341.

15. All are taken from *The Letters of Saint Teresa of Jesus,* Vol II, trans. and ed. by E. Allison Peers (Westminster, Md: The Newman Press, 1950). They are identified by their numbers in that collection and used with the permission of Sheed & Ward.

16. Maria Teresa Porcile-Santiso calls her a "privileged [exponent] of the conjunction of mysticism and prophecy which has been pointed out by Henri Bergson, and which we so easily tend to dichotomize...," "Solitude and Solidarity," *Ecumenical Review* 38:1 (Spring, 1986) 45.

6.

"The Rays of Her Candle": Sarah Grimke

The experience of women in the churches of the New World did not, at first, differ substantially from that of their sisters in Europe. Women continued to be indicted as morally weak and incapable of leadership, learning or public speaking. The virtues of submission and domesticity continued to be recommended to women by American pastors.[1] But the social and religious situation in the colonies and the new Republic contained new opportunities as well. Women performed critical economic service on both farms and plantations and their practical importance to the community allowed them possibilities for power and influence in many colonial congregations. The positive puritan theology of marriage as a spiritual relationship mitigated, to some extent, the more traditional theology of woman as temptress. The Great Awakening, with its emphasis on narratives of conversion and public testimony, encouraged women in the application of biblical texts to personal life, in the use of their experience as a commentary on the scriptures and in public speaking. In Quaker communities, women were theoretically equal to men in all religious matters, public and private. In practice, there was separation by gender, but Quaker women had a great opportunity for religious leadership.[2] Within this climate, various women rose to some prominence in religion.[3]

156

Anne Hutchinson in the seventeenth century, Anne Dutton and Sarah Edwards during the eighteenth century revival, along with others, were part of a pattern of feminine initiative that set the stage for women's enlarged participation in public religious activity during the nineteenth century.[4] As American churches organized for both reform and missionary purposes, women began to claim their full membership and exercise leadership in church life. The rise of the abolition movement first provided women with both a vision of universal human dignity and some expertise in strategies for change. Out of the debates and activities designed to challenge slavery came a direct confrontation with the question of the oppression of women. The issue quickly became a debate on biblical teaching and interpretation. Organizers in the abolition movement had concentrated on the Pauline text, Galatians 3:28, in their attempt to arouse the consciences of Americans. It was a text that they could use to balance or to interpret others that seemed more tolerant of the institution of slavery. It was not long before women, who found their work on behalf of abolition restricted because they were women, began to point out the parallels between their experience and that of the slaves, parallels found within the criticial Galatian text itself. Gradually these women gained confidence in their own exegetical abilities; they

> had learned the techniques of biblical exegesis and had absolute faith in their own interpretation in numerous debates over the biblical basis of slavery. They met the clergy on their own ground, skillfully refuting them quote for quote.[5]

Recent scholarship has focused on the person of Elizabeth Cady Stanton as an early feminist biblical critic.[6] Her ongoing battle with churchmen who tried to restrict her public advocacy of the cause of abolition led her to denounce the Bible as an irretrievably sexist text. Eventually, she wrote her own version of Christian revelation in *The Woman's Bible*.[7] The Grimke sisters also found themselves obliged to confront the sexist traditions in the Christian gospel in order to justify their activity on behalf of freedom for the slaves.

Sarah (1792-1873) and Angelina (1805-1879) Grimke were born and raised within a context unlikely to produce reformers. They were members of exclusive South Carolina society. Their father, a veteran of the Revolutionary War and a published authority on the laws of South Carolina, had inherited both wealth and status; he increased both even while serving his state in significant magisterial and legislative posts. He was also a published authority on the laws of South Carolina. Sarah and Angelina grew up on the family plantation and in a gracious Charleston town house, surrounded by privilege, comfort and the services of black slaves. Sarah later described her discontent with the frivolous nature of that society; having once witnessed a slave being whipped, she became an immediate opponent of slavery. She noted a serious contradiction in the daily home life of Southern whites: the Bible was read and prayers were said with meticulous piety, but the treatment of slaves, even in some of the best families, lacked all human compassion.[8]

The Grimke sisters received an education deemed appropriate for their sex and class: reading, writing, some arithmetic and French, drawing, singing and, especially, good manners. Sarah had a quick and inquisitive intelligence and for a time studied with her brother Thomas; when he began the study of Latin, the first stage of serious academic preparation, she tried to continue with him but was prevented from doing so by her father.[9] Sarah would feel handicapped all her life long by her lack of education, and when she and Angelina finally discontinued their career as public speakers, it was to devote themselves to conducting progressive schools.

In 1819, Sarah accompanied her father to Philadelphia to consult an eminent physician, Dr. Phillip Synge Physick. Dr. Physick was a Quaker, and through his help she lodged in a Quaker household. After her father's death and burial in

Philadelphia, Sarah remained there for two more months and when she finally returned to Charleston, it was to discover that she was no longer at home there. Sarah was 27 and a spinster by the standards of the day. She spent a little over a year in South Carolina, investigating different religious denominations for help in her own spiritual difficulties. She grew gradually closer to the Society of Friends, returned to Philadelphia, and was finally accepted as a member there in May, 1823.[10] Eventually she was joined by Angelina who was accepted for membership in 1831.

The Quaker community at first provided a liberating environment for the anti-slavery mission of the Grimke sisters, but eventually they grew dissatisfied with the moderation of that religious tradition and with the discrimination still evident within some of its activities. Angelina never spoke during the four years that she attended Friends' Meetings in Philadelphia[11] and Sarah found the orthodoxy imposed in the movement so painful that she prayed for sickness to release her from her obligations to the Meeting. Later she described the Quaker restraints as the "bonds which almost destroyed my mind."[12] They began to be involved with more radical abolitionist groups and, finally, a letter which Angelina wrote to William Lloyd Garrison (and which he published without permission) committed her, and subsequently, Sarah to the Garrison cause. By 1836, they were invited to participate in the Agents' Convention of the American Anti-Slavery Society in New York. They were the only women among forty people being trained by "experienced agitators, writers, and organizers" to spread the message of abolition.[13] This training would lead ultimately to a new level of feminism.

By contrast with the moral reform movement, Garrisonian abolitionism provided women with a political framework that assisted the development of a feminist movement. As Garrisonians, women learned a new way to view the world and a theory and practice of social change that they found most useful in elaborating their protofeminist insights. In addition, the anti-slavery movement provided them with a constituency and a political alliance on which they were able to rely until the Civil War. Thus, American feminism developed within the context of abolitionism less because abolitionism taught women that they were oppressed than because abolitionists taught women what to do with that perception, how to develop it into a social movement.[14]

Throughout 1836 and 1837, the Grimke sisters devoted themselves to the lecture circuit in New England. Their correspondence during this time demonstrates that they were becoming ever more comfortable in public speaking, even before what were then called "promiscuous" audiences, *i.e.*, men and women together.[15] They had also begun to publish in the reform press. Soon the furor over the issue of abolition gave rise to intense controversy over the activity of women in the public forum. In July of 1837, Sarah began to publish her *Letters on the Equality of the Sexes* in the *New England Spectator,* provoking an immediate response from the ministers of the Congregational Church. On July 28, the ministers issued their condemnation under the title, "Pastoral Letter of the General Association of Massachusetts to the Congregational Churches under their Care."[16] Sarah responded almost immediately and her answer became the third letter in the *Equality* collection.[17]

In 1838, Angelina Grimke married Theodore Weld, an ardent participant in the abolition movement, and, though she and Sarah continued some public activity for the first several years after the marriage, by 1840 they were fully occupied in domestic activities. Thereafter, their professional work would focus on progressive schooling though they continued to take an active interest in the woman's movement and participated, from time to time, in the various conventions through letter and an occasional appearance. Sarah separated herself from the Held household for a period of about six months in the early 1850s during which time she did some further writing on the women's movement.[18] But her public life was virtually over and her genuinely innovative work was done. Sarah Grimke died in 1873.

Unlike her contemporary and fellow-abolitionist, Elizabeth Cady Stanton, Sarah Grimke did not believe that the Bible was intrinsically anti-feminine. In her letter to the Congregational Ministers she argues theologically that the Bible could be proved to affirm the equality of all people. Her letter, the third of the *Equality* collection, is a remarkable piece of theological writing for one of Sarah's limited education and experience. It demonstrates her ability in exegesis as well as a firm confidence in that ability. She debates with the Association of Congregational Ministers in language and a method that was easily equal to their own. She confronts the problem of biblical hermeneutics at its root and formulates an exegetical principle remarkably like those offered in our own day by feminist hermeneutics: it was "false translations" and perverted interpretations, perpetuated by the male dominance of the clergy and religious teachers that wrung a suppressive doctrine from the scriptural text. She believed that once women had the scholarly tools necessary for scripture study (she cites specifically knowledge of biblical languages), "we shall produce some various readings of the Bible a little different from those we now have" (#3). Recent history certainly vindicates her judgment.[19] She offers some specific examples of what she considers misreadings of the text based on male bias. She then reflects on the central premises of those who argued against women in public life. In these reflections, she weaves together biblical evidence, her own personal experience and some insights culled, it would seem, from the American constitutional tradition.

Sarah Grimke finds evidence for the equality of women in the preaching of Jesus, specifically the Sermon on the Mount. She notes that in the moral challenge of that sermon, Jesus makes no reference whatever to any distinctions between the sexes, "giving," as she says, "the same directions to women as to men..." (#4). She points out that the attempt of pastors to require submission of women contradicts the gospel injunction that all should become a light shining before the world. For Sarah, the desire of the Congregational ministers to keep women passive denies a central truth of Christian faith: that woman is a fully responsible moral being whose exercise of duties and privileges is necessary for the well-being of society. Indeed, she implies that the suppression of women is one of the main causes of social disorder.

The Pastoral Letter had, as its primary purpose, the prohibition of woman's public preaching, even in so worthy a cause as the freeing of the slaves. The ministers argued that such public activism was "ostentation" and therefore inappropriate to the special condition of women. Sarah cites specific New Testament examples (*e.g.*, Anna the prophetess) to demonstrate that the ministers have allowed their preconceived notions of women's differences to distort their understanding of the text. But she goes beyond merely citing one textual example to refute another; rather she confronts the sexist premises on which the ministers argued. She refutes the idea that woman is, by nature, "different" from men in ways that seriously affect her moral and Christian responsibilities. She argues that all the moral prescriptions of the New Testament, those that require public as well as private virtue, are addressed to everyone without sexual distinction. Unequivocally she concludes, "In that book [the Bible] I find nothing like the softness of woman, nor the sternness of man; both are equally commanded to bring forth the fruits of the Spirit, love, meekness, gentleness, etc." (#5).

She reinforces biblical evidence with empirical reflections: she will accept that men may be physically stronger than women but affirms that any intellectual or moral weakness presently found in women comes from lack of education and opportunity:

male domination has crushed women's minds and male interpretation of women's duties has impaired their sense of morality
(#6). She details the specific ways in which woman has learned
from man the lesson of her dependence. She has been brain-
washed to accept as privilege some small measure of what are
her natural rights; she has been taught to be content with the
power to manipulate from her hiddenness and has thus been
drawn into consummate hypocrisy while men exercise the
"reality" of power. Finally, woman has allowed her vanity to be
over-developed so that she might win some influence over men
by her willingness to gratify them (#5). For Sarah Grimke, this
is not the natural state of woman but a male-contrived state that
has resulted from perverting nature and is "utterly at variance
with the doctrine of the Bible" (#5).

Sarah Grimke not only speaks in the language and categories
of the biblical tradition, but also argues from a liberal philosophy
of nature that she finds in the early Federal documents, according to Rosemary Ruether. She assumes that the rights of women,
as those of slaves, are self-evident and "need only be examined to
be understood and asserted..." (#2). In paragraph after
paragraph, she links a reference to creation by God with the call
for equal rights for women. Further, she subscribes to the idea
that the full harmony in which nature was created and which
must be regained is dependent upon the accession of women to
the rights with which they were created. The Pastors have asserted that the proper order of the universe requires that women
keep their place (a foundational belief of male supremacy).
Sarah agrees with the principle but affirms that woman's rightful place is one of absolute equality with men. "...I believe her
having been displaced from that sphere has introduced confusion
into the world. It is, therefore, of vast importance to herself and
to all the rational creation, that she should ascertain what are
her duties and her privileges as a responsible and immortal
being" (#3). In Ruether's words, Grimke was the heir of a new
way of thinking about nature, historical society and eschatology

that was to be found in the original documents of the American republic.[20] In this, Sarah Grimke is part of an ongoing attempt to do theology from the perspective of American experience.

It is thus that Sarah confronts the religious patriarchy of the Massachusetts Pastors, the idea that the subjection of women was founded on divine authority. She rejects that idea outright and demonstrates instead that the subjection of women is against the will of God as revealed in both natural creation and biblical text. The authority of those who name the dependence of women a doctrine, she calls a "usurped authority" (#2), and thus identifies the issue of patriarchy as substantially a question of the distribution of power.[21] Her remarks are particularly biting when she discusses the way in which the doctrine of dependence has affected the exercise of teaching in the church. Her response is both biblical and existential. She gathers a chain of quotes which assert the primacy of God as teacher and leader; from these she concludes that women must obey only what God teaches and ignore the instructions of the men who interpreted that teaching. Her own experience shows her the wisdom of this: "I have suffered too keenly from the teaching of a man, to lead anyone to him for instruction" (#8). For Sarah, the essence of religious teaching is to "rouse a sinner to his lost and helpless condition...." and to lead him to the springs of living water (#8). For this task, no particularly masculine quality is needed.[22]

This letter of Sarah Grimke's is a feminist piece in a way that no earlier text in this volume is. In it she not only brings a critical habit of mind to the institutionalized status of women but she locates the causes of the oppression of women in the ill will of men. As Lerner says,

> her contribution to feminist theory was considerable and, in two substantial respects, far ahead of that of her contemporaries. Sarah Grimke always showed an awareness of what we would today call sex-role indoctrination and of its pernicious influence on the self-confidence and self-

respect of women. She also repeatedly and vigorously stressed the need for female autonomy and self-definition. While developing her argument in the tradition of the American Revolution, claiming for women their natural rights and demanding justice and equality, she was far in advance of her contemporaries in placing the source of women's oppression and 'slavery' on 'the will and selfishness and passions of man.'[23]

At the same time, she brings to the biblical text principles of interpretation that anticipate the work of feminist criticism being done today. Only now have a significant number of women acquired the "Greek and Hebrew" skills of which Sarah saw the need in 1837.

The Pastoral Letter of the General Association of Congregational Ministers of Massachusetts.

Haverhill, 7th Mo. 1837.

1. Dear Friend,—When I last addressed thee, I had not seen the Pastoral Letter of the General Association. It has since fallen into my hands, and I must digress from my intention of exhibiting the condition of women in different parts of the world, in order to make some remarks on this extraordinary document. I am persuaded that when the minds of men and women become emancipated from the thralldom of superstition and 'traditions of men,' the sentiments contained in the Pastoral Letter will be recurred to with as much astonishment as the opinions of Cotton Mather and other distinguished men of this day, on the subject of witchcraft; nor will it be deemed less wonderful, that a body of divines should gravely assemble and endeavor to prove that woman has no right to 'open her mouth for the dumb,' than it now is that judges should have sat on the trials of witches, and solemnly condemned nineteen persons and one dog to death for witchcraft.

2. But to the Letter. It says, 'We invite your attention to the dangers which at present seem to threaten the FEMALE CHARACTER with widespread and permanent injury.' I rejoice that they have called the attention of my sex to this subject, because I believe if woman investigates it, she will soon discover that danger is impending, though from a totally different source from that which the Association apprehends—danger from those who, having long held the reins of usurped authority, are unwilling to permit us to fill that sphere which God created us to move in, and who have entered into league to crush the immortal mind of woman. I rejoice, because I am persuaded that the rights of woman, like the rights of slaves, need only be examined to be understood and asserted, even by some of those, who are now endeavoring to smother the irrepressible desire for mental and spiritual freedom which glows in the breast of many, who hardly dare to speak their sentiments.

3. 'The appropriate duties and influences of women are clearly stated in the New Testament. Those duties are unobtrusive and private, but the sources of mighty power. When the mild, dependent, softening influence of woman upon the sternness of man's opinions is fully exercised, society feels the effects of it in a thousand ways.' No one can desire more earnestly than I do, that woman may move exactly in the sphere that her Creator has assigned her; and I believe her having been displaced from that sphere has introduced confusion into the world. It is, therefore, of vast importance to herself and to all the rational creation, that she should ascertain what are her duties and her privileges as a responsible and immortal being. The New Testament has been referred to, and I am writing to abide by its decisions, but must enter my protest against the false translation of some passages by the MEN who did that work, and against the perverted interpretation by the MEN who undertook to write commentaries thereon. I am inclined to think, when we are admitted to the honor of studying Greek and Hebrew, we shall produce some

various readings of the Bible a little different from those we now have.

4. The Lord Jesus defines the duties of his followers in his Sermon on the Mount. He lays down grand principles by which they should be governed, without any reference to sex or condition: 'Ye are the light of the world. A city that is set on a hill cannot be hid. Neither do men light a candle and put it under a bushel, but on a candlestick, and it giveth light unto all that are in the house. Let your light so shine before men, that they may see your good works, and glorify your Father which is in Heaven.' I follow him through all his precepts, and find him giving the same directions to women as to men, never even referring to the distinction now so strenuously insisted upon between masculine and feminine virtues: this is one of the anti-Christian 'traditions of men' which are taught instead of the 'commandments of God.' Men and women were CREATED EQUAL; they are both moral and accountable beings, and whatever is right for man to do, is right for woman.

5. But the influence of woman, says the Association, is to be private and unobtrusive; her light is not to shine before man like that of her brethren; but she is passively to let the lords of the creation, as they call themselves, put the bushel over it, lest peradventure it might appear that the world has been benefitted by the rays of her candle. So that her quenched light, according to their judgment, will be of more use than if it were set on a candlestick. 'Her influence is the source of mighty power.' This has ever been the flattering language of man since he laid aside the whip as a means to keep woman in subjection. He spares her body; but the war he has waged against her mind, her heart, and her soul, has been no less destructive to her as a moral being. How monstrous, how anti-Christian, is the doctrine that woman is to be dependent on man! Where, in all the sacred Scriptures, is this taught? Alas! she has too well learned the lesson which MAN has labored to teach her. She has surrendered her dearest

RIGHTS, and been satisfied with the privileges which man has assumed to grant her; she has been amused with the show of power, whilst man has absorbed all the reality into himself. He has adorned the creature whom God gave him as a companion, with baubles and gewgaws, turned her attention to personal attractions, offered incense to her vanity, and made her the instrument of his selfish gratification, a plaything to please his eye and amuse his hours of leisure. 'Rule by obedience and by submission sway,' or in other words, study to be a hypocrite, pretend to submit, but gain your point, has been the code of household morality which woman has been taught. The poet has sung, in sickly strains, the loveliness of woman's dependence upon man, and now we find it reechoed by those who profess to teach the religion of the Bible. God says, 'Cease ye from man whose breath is in his nostrils, for wherein is he to be accounted of? Man says, depend upon me. God says, 'HE will teach us of his ways.' Man says, believe it not, I am to be your teacher. This doctrine of dependence upon man is utterly at variance with the doctrine of the Bible. In that book I find nothing like the softness of woman, nor the sternness of man: both are equally commanded to bring forth the fruits of the Spirit, love, meekness, gentleness, etc.

6. But we are told, 'the power of woman is in her dependence, flowing from a consciousness of that weakness which God has given her for her protection.' If physical weakness is alluded to, I cheerfully concede the superiority; if brute force is what my brethren are claiming, I am willing to let them have all the honor they desire; but if they mean to intimate that mental or moral weakness belongs to woman more than to man, I utterly disclaim the charge. Our powers of mind have been crushed, as far as man could do it, our sense of morality has been impaired by his interpretation of our duties; but no where does God say that he made any distinction between us, as moral and intelligent beings.

7. 'We appreciate,' say the Association, 'the unostentatious prayers and efforts of woman in advancing the cause of religion at home and abroad, in leading religious inquirers TO THE PASTOR for instruction.' Several points here demand attention. If public prayers and public efforts are necessarily ostentatious, then 'Anna the prophetess (or preacher), who departed not from the temple, but served God with fastings and prayers night and day, . . . and spake of Christ to all them that looked for redemption in Israel,' was ostentatious in her efforts. Then, the apostle Paul encourages women to be ostentatious in their efforts to spread the gospel, when he gives them directions on how they should appear, when engaged in praying, or preaching in the public assemblies. Then, the whole Association of Congregational ministers are ostentatious, in the efforts they are making in preaching and praying to convert souls.

8. But woman may be permitted to lead religious inquirers to the PASTORS for instruction. Now this is assuming that all pastors are better qualified to give instruction than a woman. This I utterly deny. I have suffered too keenly from the teaching of a man to lead anyone to him for instruction. The Lord Jesus says, 'Come unto me and learn of me.' He points his followers to no man; and when woman is made the favorite instrument of rousing a sinner to his lost and helpless condition, she has no right to substitute any teacher for Christ; all she has to do is, to turn the contrite inquirer to the 'Lamb of God which taketh away the sins of the world.' More souls have probably been lost by going down to Egypt for help, and by trusting in man in the early stages of religious experience, than by any other error. Instead of the petition being offered to God,—'Lead me in thy truth, and TEACH me, for thou art the God of my salvation,'—instead of relying on the precious promises—'What man is he that feareth the Lord? Him shall HE TEACH in the way that he shall choose'—'I will instruct thee and TEACH thee in the way which thou shalt go—I will guide thee with mine eye'—the young convert is directed to go to man, as if he were in the place of God,

and his instructions essential to an advancement in the path of righteousness. That woman can have but a poor conception of the privilege of being taught of God, what he alone can teach, who would turn the 'religious inquirer aside' from the fountain of living waters, where he might slake his thirst for spiritual instruction, to those broken cisterns which can hold no water, and therefore cannot satisfy the panting spirit. The business of men and women, who are ORDAINED of God to preach the unsearchable riches of Christ to a lost and perishing world, is to lead souls to Christ, and not to Pastors for instruction.

9. The General Association say, that 'when woman assumes the place and tone of man as a public reformer, our care and protection of her seem unnecessary; we put ourselves in self-defense against her, and her character becomes unnatural.' Here again the unscriptural notion is held up, that there is a distinction between the duties of men and women as moral beings; that what is virtue in man, is vice in woman; and women who dare to obey the command of Jehovah 'Cry aloud, spare not, lift up thy voice like a trumpet, and show my people their transgression,' are threatened with having the protection of the brethren withdrawn. If this is all they do, we shall not even know the time when our chastisement is inflicted; our trust is in the Lord Jehovah, and in him is everlasting strength. The motto of woman, when she is engaged in the great work of public reformation should be,—'The Lord is my light and my salvation; whom shall I fear? The Lord is the strength of my life; of whom shall I be afraid?' She must feel, if she feels rightly, that she is fulfilling one of the important duties laid upon her as an accountable being, and that her character, instead of being 'unnatural,' is in exact accordance with the will of Him to whom, and to no other, she is responsible for the talents and the gifts confined to her. As to the pretty simile, introduced into the 'Pastoral Letter,' 'If the vine whose strength and beauty is to lean upon the trellis work, and half conceal its clusters, thinks to assume the independence overshadowing nature of the elm,' etc. I shall only

remark that it might well suit the poet's fancy, who sings of spar-
kling eyes and coral lips, and knights in armor clad; but it seems
to me utterly inconsistent with the dignity of a Christian body, to
endeavor to draw such an anti-scriptual distinction between men
and women. Ah! how many of my sex feel in the dominion, thus
unrighteously exercised over them, under the gentle appellation
of protection, that what they have leaned upon has proved a
broken reed at best, and oft a spear.

10. Thine in the bonds of womanhood,

Sarah M. Grimke

Activities and Assignments

1. The selected reading list points to other nineteenth century
American reforming feminists. Read as much as you can on one
of these other women and write a short essay on her contributions to early feminism, making such comparisons and contrasts
with Sarah Grimke as are appropriate.

2. The work of Sarah Grimke shows us the intimate link between formulating strategies for social action and theological
reflection. We have seen the same dynamic at work in liberation
theology which has itself been a source of insight for Christian
feminism. Do some reading in the connection between social action and biblical reflection and write up your own thoughts on
why this connection is both necessary and helpful. A limited
number of books in this area can be found in the "Selected Additional Reading."

3. Interview three or four women whom you know who are involved in various kinds of social action. Make the focus of your
interviews the role biblical reflection and prayer have played in
their active lives. Write up the results of your interviews.

4. Letter-writing is a means too often neglected for involving oneself in public life. Write a letter to your local paper on a current issue of concern to you.

Selected Additional Reading

Dubois, Ellen. "Women's Rights and Abolition: the Nature of the Connection," in *Antislavery Reconsidered: New Perspectives on the Abolitionist*, eds. Perry, Lewis and Michael Fellman, Baton Rouge: Louisiana State Univ. Press, 1979.

Dunn, Mary Maples. "Saints and Sisters: Congregational and Quaker Women in the Early Colonial Period." *Women in American Religion*, ed. by Janet Wilson James. Philadelphia: University of Pennsylvania Press, 1980.

Gifford, Carolyn De Swarte. "Women in Social Reform Movements." *Women and Religion in America*, Vol I: The Nineteenth Century. Rosemary Radford Ruether and Rosemary Skinner Keller, eds. San Francisco: Harper and Row, 1981.

Gold, Ellen Reid. "The Grimke Sisters and the Emergence of the Woman's Rights Movement." *Southern Speech Communication Journal*, 46:4 (1981) 341-360.

Griffith, Elisabeth. *In Her Own Right: The Life of Elizabeth Cady Stanton*. New York: Oxford Universtity Press, 1984.

Grimke, Sarah. *Letters on the Equality of the Sexes and the Condition of Woman*. Boston: Isaac Knapp, 1838.

Lerner, Gerda. *The Grimke Sisters*. New York: 1967.

_____. "Sarah M. Grimke's 'Sisters of Charity,'" *Signs* 1:1 (1975) 246-56.

Ruether, Rosemary Radford. "The Subordination and Liberation of Women in Christian Theology: Saint Paul and Sarah Grimke." *Soundings* 61:2 (1978) 168-81.

_____, and Rosemary Keller, eds. *Women and Religion in America: The Nineteenth Century: A Documentary History.* San Francisco: Harper and Row, 1981.

Stanton, Elizabeth Cady. *The Woman's Bible.* American Women's Series: Images and Realities. Salem, New Hampshire: Ayer Co. Pubs., 1972.

_____, Susan B. Anthony and Matilda Joslyn Gages, eds. *The History of Woman Suffrage.* New York: Source Books Press, 1970.

Ulrich, Laurel Thatcher. "Vertuous Women Found: New England Ministerial Literature, 1668-1735." *Women in American Religion.* ed. by Janet Wilson James. Philadelphia: University of Pennsylvania Press, 1980.

Williams, Richard E. *Called and Chosen: The Story of Mother Rebecca Jackson and the Philadelphia Shakers.* ATLA Monograph Series, No. 17. Metuchen, N.J. & London: The Scarecrow Press, Inc., 1981.

Notes

1. See Laurel Thatcher Ulrich, "Vertuous Women Found: New England Ministerial Literature, 1668-1735," *Women in American Religion,* ed. by Janet Wilson James (Philadelphia: University of Pennsylvania Press, 1980) 67-87.

2. Barbara J. MacHaffie, *Her Story: Women in Christian Tradition* (Philadelphia: Fortress Press, 1986) 75-91.

3. See Mary Maples Dunn, "Saints and Sisters: Congregational and Quaker Women in the Early Colonial Period," *Women in American Religion* 27-46.

4. See Rosemary Radford Ruether and Rosemary Skinner Keller, eds., *Women and Religion in America* 2; *The Colonial and Revolutionary Periods* (San Francisco: Harper and Row, (1983).

5. Ellen Dubois, "Women's Rights and Abolition: The Nature of the Connection," *Antislavery Reconsidered: New Perspectives on the Abolitionist,* ed. by Lewis Perry and Michael Fellman (Baton Rouge, Louisiana: Louisiana State University Press, 1979) 244.

6. See, for example, Elisabeth Griffith, *In Her Own Right: The Life of Elizabeth Cady Stanton* (New York: Oxford University Press, 1984).

7. The 1895 edition has been reproduced in *American Women Series: Images and Realities* (Salem, NH: Ayer Co. Pubs., 1972).

8. Gerda Lerner, *The Grimke Sisters* (Boston: The Schocken Co., 1967) 35-37.

9. Lerner, *Sisters* 17-18.

10. Lerner, *Sisters* 42-59.

11. Ellen Reid Gold, "The Grimke Sisters and the Emergence of the Woman's Rights Movement," *Southern Speech Communication Journal* 46:4 (1981) 345, n. 13.

12. Lerner, *Sisters* 141-2.

13. Lerner, *Sisters* 148.

14. Dubois 241-2.

15. Gold 346.

16. Lerner, *Sisters* 182-92.

17. Sarah Grimke, *Letters on the Equality of the Sexes and the Condition of Woman* (Boston: Isaac Knapp, 1838). This volume has been published again in *Letters on the Equality of the Sexes and Other Essays,* ed. by Elizabeth Ann Bartlett (New Haven: Yale University Press, 1988).

18. Bartlett 19.

19. In Letter XIII, September, 1837, entitled "The relation of Husband and Wife," Sarah Grimke gives another sound principle of hermeneutics which also had bearing on the question of women. She points out that the biblical text must be understood as a whole; isolated quotations cannot be taken out of context.

"Now I must understand the sacred scriptures as harmonizing with themselves or I cannot receive them as the word of God," 96.

20. Rosemary Radford Ruether, "The Subordination and Liberation of Women in Christian Theology: Saint Paul and Sarah Grimke." *Soundings,* 61:2 (1978) 168-181. "Liberalism assumed that the order of Original Nature was one of equality. The present class structure is contrary to Nature. The theology of Original Nature is a critical ideal over against the traditional social order.... Nature, itself, in effect, becomes a futuristic ideal," 177. See also the Introduction by Elizabeth Ann Bartlett to Grimke's *Letters,* 6-15. Bartlett identifies other intellectual traditions as sources for Grimke's thought than American constitutional theory including "romanticism, utopian socialism and radical sectarianism."

21. In a parallel piece of argumentation, she argues in Letter XIV, the "Ministry of Women," that specific Christian ministries became restricted to men as soon as power and its accoutrements became identified with ministry. "... I believe the secret of the exclusion of women from the ministerial office is, that that office has been converted into one of emolument, of honor, and of power," Bartlett 86.

22. In the letter on ministry, she affirms that this is the role of all ministry biblically understood. It is the one form of ministry that is found in the earliest Old Testament books, it antedates the foundation of priesthood in the Old Testament and it, not the Aaronic priesthood, is the prototype of Christian ministry. "The common error that Christian ministers are the successors of the priests is founded in mistake," Bartlett 86. This forms the first step in her argument that women ought to be allowed full participation in the ministry of proclaiming the gospel.

23. Gerda Lerner, "Sarah M. Grimke's 'Sisters of Charity,' " *Signs* 1:1 (1975) 252.

7.

"I got a bucket and supplied a man's place": Sister Blandina Segale

In June of 1876, a Sister of Charity from Cincinnati, Ohio had a plan for building a new school (complete with hall and stage) in the frontier town of Trinidad, Colorado. She climbed up on the roof of the existing delapidated school and, with a crowbar, began to detach the adobe bricks, one by one, and throw them to the ground. A woman who passed by found out what she was doing, asked her for a list of her needs and within the day a group of construction workers was hard at work at her new school. Toward the end of the job, however, only one plasterer remained and, as she records in her journal, "there was not a man to carry the mortar to the plasterer, ... [so] I got a bucket and supplied a man's place."[1] While carrying her hod of plaster, Sister Blandina Segale encountered the visiting bishop of Denver, the Most Rev. Macheboeuf, and amazed him with her activities. Thus did the Catholic sisters in America by their work as teachers, social workers, construction workers, leaders in prayer and in reconciliation serve the Church; their simple faith and their energetic leadership were, like the apostles and mar-

176

tyrs of old, "the foundation on which it was built." Sister Blandina Segale (1850-1941) was only one among thousands, unusual only in that she recorded her own story.[2]

The story of the American Catholic Sisters remains largely untold despite the existence of abundant, though scattered, archival material and primary sources.[3] Some individual communities have recorded the histories of their foundations and individual biographies have been written, but a comprehensive evaluation of the contributions of women religious to the Church and to the social and intellectual development of America remains an unattempted task. One historian writes that in America, "convents and the virgin life continued to function for these women much as they did the early centuries of Christian history—as places of economic security, female autonomy, self-expression, and the nurturing of faith."[4]

While this is true in a general way, certainly the "economic security" of the Sisters was qualitatively different from that experienced in established convents in Europe. Many communities were founded by small groups of sisters—four or five—who landed at a new, often strange, city with less than ten dollars among them. And, on the other hand, "female autonomy and self-expression" seems to have had greater scope in a world where social structures were more fluid and the horizons broader than they had been elsewhere. Certainly Sister Blandina Segale, traveling alone on a train to St. Louis and then by stagecoach to Trinidad, Colorado, had a different experience of "serving the Kingdom of Heaven" than had the cloistered nuns of the Middle Ages or even the active sisterhoods of contemporary Europe. Nineteenth century America was to be the context of a substantially different chapter of the story of women in the Catholic church, indeed the whole Christian movement.

Though Ursuline nuns first came to New Orleans in 1727 and cloistered Carmelites to Maryland in 1791,[5] the real story of women religious in America begins after 1830. As the numbers of Catholics in the United States increased exponentially through massive immigration, religious sisters of a multitude of congregations came with, and for the service of, the immigrants. Once here they took up the traditional tasks of teaching and nursing, but added as well, a variety of social services required by the economic and social problems of a large, usually unskilled urban population. Sisters also followed the frontier, and as Sister Blandina's journal narrates, wherever they went, they taught and healed and brought some of the refinements such as music and drama to small towns. They gradually brought into being the American Catholic parochial school system which helped shape the development of a large percentage of the American Catholic population. "By the mid-1960s, parochial schools were educating 5,800,000 elementary and highschool pupils, or one out of every seven American children."[6]

The tasks which confronted the Sisters demanded that their European traditions of cloister and isolation be relaxed and they soon became one of the most prominent symbols of growing Catholic influence.[7] This made them natural targets of the anti-Catholic bigotry that increased steadily throughout the second half of the nineteenth century and on into the twentieth. Their habits and customs provided a clear focus for the charges of "alien" and "un-American" that grew sharper as the immigrants became an ever more visible presence and perceived threat. Wherever the waves of "nativism" flowed, the nuns were threatened and persecuted. In 1834, the Ursulines in Charlestown, Massachusetts were intimidated by an angry mob and their convent was burned. One of the major genres of anti-Catholic propaganda was the lurid tale of "life inside the walls," the most well-known of which was *The Awful Disclosures of the Hotel Dieu Nunnery in Montreal* by Maria Monk.[8] Though Ms. Monk was denounced as a fraud by many, including her own mother, the book went through regular reprintings, the last in 1960 provoked by the Kennedy Campaign. The quiet persistence and fidelity of the Sisters, however, gradually won them the

respect of the American public. Their heroic service on the bat-
tlefields of the Civil War eventually won public recognition: on
September 20, 1924, a monument was erected across the street
from St. Matthew's Cathedral in Washington, D.C., to com-
memorate their contributions.[9] But the less dramatic examples
of service had their role to play as well; daily encounters between
Americans whose bigotry came more from ignorance than malice
and the Sisters who gave so generously and selflessly to
charitable works were eventually to win the respect and sympathy of the Americans. Sister Blandina records many such
small encounters in her journal.

These Sisters worked not only against the practical difficulties
of their tasks nor against the misunderstandings and antipathy
of those among whom they lived. They also labored under an
ideology which restricted their activity in public life and continued to mandate their submission to a patriarchal hierarchy.
The nineteenth century was, after all, the age of the "cult of true
womanhood," an ideology that praised woman for her superior
virtue and purity but restricted her activity to the domestic
sphere. In the Catholic tradition, that cult was reinforced by the
devotion to the idealized figure of the Blessed Virgin Mary.[10]
This traditional ideology continued to dominate the writing and
preaching of American clerics and bishops long after ideas of
reform began in the latter part of the nineteenth century.
Catholic clerical voices were strident against woman's suffrage
and a public role for women, and this despite the increasingly
public and important work of the Sisters. That same
Macheboeuf who had watched Sister Blandina's hod-carrying
with approval and amazement castigated the suffragists as "old
maids, disappointed in love," while James Cardinal Gibbons, a
forthright proponent of the Knights of Labor who were involved
in organizing women workers, insisted that "the vote would rob
woman of her character..."[11]

Some cracks were inevitable in the concrete solidity of Catholic thinking, however. Some Catholic women did speak out in their own behalf. Rose Hawthorne Lathrop, convert daughter of Nathaniel Hawthorne, addressed the Catholic Congress at Chicago in 1896 with these stirring words:

> Oh, woman, the hour has struck when you are to arise and defend your rights, your abilities for competition with men in intellectual and professional endurance, the hour when you are to prove that purity and generosity are for the nation as well as for the home....[12]

Occasionally, the social teaching which Bishops and clerics began to develop after the turn of the century suggested the possibility of a new direction. In 1919, John A. Ryan put together an integrated and far-reaching plan for the social reconstruction of America after the first World War. Ryan called for sweeping changes, including the abolition of child labor and the inauguration of a graduated income tax. About women's roles, however, Ryan was ambivalent. He wanted women to "disappear as quickly as possible" from those public activities for which, he believed, "conditions of life and their physique render them unfit." But he was adamant on one principle of economic justice: that women should "receive equal pay for equal amounts and qualities of work" when they were "engaged at the same tasks as men."[13]

Ryan's thought was suggestive, but Catholic thinking on women remained substantially unchanged and prohibitive well into the twentieth century. The work of the Catholic Sisters was a living contradiction to that thought, but that contradiction went without serious reflection, even by the Sisters themselves.

For the most part, American Catholic Sisters did little theorizing about their status in the Church or about a theology of women. As Sister Elizabeth Kolmer says:

If they refused to accept a bishop's categorization of them as weak, inexperienced, and ineffective, they worked, so far as we know, on a practical level as individuals or individual congregations to prove him wrong, rather than looking for intellectual or moral support in the broader society.[14]

There is no evidence that they were actively interested in the movement for women's suffrage nor in the earlier movement for women's rights born among the abolitionists like Sarah Grimke or Elizabeth Cady Stanton. They were builders and activists in a foundation period of their congregations and, indeed, of the whole American Church. But they were not without resources for their action; indeed, the Sisters had access to an empowerment that other women often lacked. The tradition of spirituality, that was central to the lives of the Sisters, transmitted an important principle: that holiness and genuine spiritual discipline allows one to transcend cultural and gender limitations. They had vibrant role models of such transcendence: in the panoply of Catholic saints, they could find autonomous women who had assumed significant public roles in the Church, women such as Joan of Arc and Catherine of Siena. By seeing their own lives as a fulfillment of the will of God, the Sisters could feel empowered by God and self-confident about their own actions. They thereby experienced the freedom to act according to circumstances and out of their own faith, energetically and without undue concern over the expectations of others. Any woman who has tried to put aside social and cultural barriers will not underestimate this freedom.

We must not forget the importance of such action in the life and faith of the whole Church. Action itself is a theological category because in a church that is imbedded in history the action of the community is both a reflection of the faith as already understood and a source of the reflection from which comes new understanding. In the lives and work of the Sisters, we see an anticipation of what Avery Dulles will later identify as the "servant model" of church. Dulles gives credit for the development of this model to the theologians Chardin and Bonhoeffer: he says that the "official statements of the churches simply register and sanction ideas that have been previously developed by theologians."[15]

But Dulles fails to observe that the ideas of theologians are themselves rooted in the lived experience of the Christian community. The experience of a church that is at the service of the human community, that takes human achievements and needs seriously, that makes no distinction between believer and unbeliever when it comes to dispensing the concrete evidence of God's saving love—this experience was alive in the hearts and minds of the American Sisters long before it became matter for conscious theological reflection. It was they who imparted this experience (along with the more traditional teaching) to later generations of Catholics who understood and accepted the changing ecclesiology of the Second Vatican Council.

As the frontier faded, the re-establishment of a more traditional social order imposed renewed restrictions in the activities of Catholic Sisters.[16] Yet, the stories of the religious in a freer past lived on in the imaginations and memories of the Catholics whom they educated and otherwise served. They were celebrated in school pageants and remained a vital force in the Catholic subculture. Catholic women today are drawing on their legacy, though it has taken some time before their experience has been raised to the level of conscious reflection. Such reflection is presently leading Sisters to create bonds of kinship that cut across distinctions between different "states of life" and between different denominations. These bonds enable the Sister to make a significant contribution to the work of opening up the public sphere to women. But the reflection and the kinship are rooted in the stories, the personal narratives of risks taken, of impossible things achieved, of faith acted out in a new environment. It is such a story that Sister Blandina Segale has left us in her journal, *At the End of the Santa Fe Trail.*

Born in Cicagna, Italy, Rosa Maria Segale accompanied her parents and three siblings to Cincinnati when she was four years old. She attended Mount St. Vincent Academy and entered the Sisters of Charity when she was sixteen, pronouncing her vows as Sister Blandina in 1868. Four years later, she was sent to the Southwest; her letter of mission said simply "Trinidad" and at first she thought she was going to an island in the Caribbean. After a rather difficult visit with her family (her father tried to dissuade her, her mother to send her brother as companion), she boarded a train for St. Louis and "the frontier." She traveled by rail to Kansas City, Missouri, where her train was derailed and she was forced to seek accommodation in a local convent. Since she was traveling without papers of any kind, the Sisters did not trust her so they locked her in one of the parlors for the night and posted a nun outside as a guard. The next morning she returned to the railway station where the only train going west was a construction train; she cajoled the conductor into allowing her passage and rode to the end of the line where she boarded a stagecoach for Trinidad. Her first view of Trinidad was unnerving: she saw from the outskirts what she "would have thought were kennels for dogs," but the moment of apprehension passed quickly, she set about reviewing her Spanish and addressing herself to the multitude of tasks that faced her. She taught in the public school and in the academy for girls, she organized a student committee to report any "case of distress in families or individuals," buried dead Indian children, organized musical programs and Christmas relief efforts, tried to prevent the exploitation of Indians and Mexicans and intervened in violent situations that erupted regularly in a frontier town visited only rarely by circuit judges.

In December, 1876, Sister Blandina left for Santa Fe, New Mexico. She reveled in the Catholic heritage of the city and

worked side by side with the legendary Archbishop Lamy there
for the next five years. In Santa Fe she continued and expanded
many of the activities she had engaged in in Trinidad. Her early
editor sums her work up thus:

> In Trinidad she had built a one-story schoolhouse with no
> funds; in Santa Fe she would build a three-story building
> from empty pockets. She begged funds for the hospital
> from the miners and railroad workers. She made caskets
> and buried the dead; wrote letters to the bereaved
> families. She distributed alms, visited Billy the Kid and
> other prisoners in the Santa Fe jail. In December, 1880,
> she saw with satisfaction the Sisters' Hospital lighted
> with gas for the first time. She established an excellent
> school for the orphans and gave them a mother's love.[17]

In addition to all this, she continued to build upon the cultural
heritage of Santa Fe, giving more time and energy to music and
dramatic performances. As Lamy's biographer tells us, Blandina
was "by her own animated account ... for a long time at the center of leading events in the diocese."[18]

In 1881, she went from Santa Fe to Albuquerque where she
remained until her return to Trinidad in 1889. During her last
stay there, she faced the transferral of the public school into
political control with the passing of a new school act. She and
the nuns passed the qualification exam without difficulty,
though they seem to have been intentionally disturbed during
the administration of the exam; however, when told that they
would have to put aside their habits in order to teach, they left
the school permanently and turned all their attention to the
Catholic grammar school. After Trinidad, Sister Blandina
returned to Ohio and from 1897 until her death in 1941 she
worked among the Italian immigrants in Cincinnati, assisted by
her blood-sister, Sister Justina until the latter's death in 1929.

In the selections which follow, we see Blandina at some of her more dramatic moments and we hear, often in a kind of background echo, of her concerns and her faith. The first two journal entries come from the early days in Trinidad in 1875 and 1876. Both open by recording small triumphs for education and then go on to paint dramatic encounters between Blandina and the quasi-legendary characters of the West: the desperado, the vigilante and the lynch mob. As Paul Horgan says, Blandina "always valued overstatement to achieve her effects,"[19] and does not seem entirely immune from the glamor which people like Billy the Kid exuded; yet between the lines of the heightened account, we see a pervasive pattern of her life. Assigned to classroom teaching in a Catholic school, she moves freely outside of it in a daily routine of truly catholic service to a diverse frontier population. Much of this service was directed to the disreputable: she visits the imprisoned, cares for the victims of sin and violence and supports the tentative structures of justice. Through it all, she is committed to mercy and to reconciliation. Acting against her own real fear and even loathing for the criminal element, she none the less perseveres in her unpleasant tasks, noting along the way the atmosphere of religious bigotry and competition in which she worked. Blandina acts out the servant model of the Church.

The third excerpt from the journal is from 1880 in Santa Fe. Here we see Blandina the businesswoman. In spite of the respect which the Sisters generated by their selfless devotion, they remained as vulnerable to fraud and crass thievery as their fellow citizens in the competitive, boomtown atmosphere of Santa Fe. It was not just the affairs of the soul and the well-being of others that required Blandina's courage and imagination. Frequently the survival of the convent and its undertakings required her to be as crafty as the serpents in the desert sands that surrounded her. Even in the attempt to recover stolen property, however, there was her continual effort to remain in a conciliatory rather than a confrontational position.

In the final selection, which dates from 1881 in Albuquerque, Blandina collects some of her own reflections on the region. All of her time in the southwest, she struggled against the stereotypes of the Mexican and Native American that were held and propagated by the Anglo population. On her train trip from St. Louis to Kansas City, en route to Trinidad, Blandina first encountered the use of pejorative epithets for the Mexicans and the condescending attitude out of which they arose. Years later, in Albuquerque, the same attitudes still prevailed, intensified by the desire to defraud the earlier inhabitants of the land which was becoming suddenly so valuable. Her love for the land and its people is evident in her prophecies about its future. If her conviction about the final outcome of all the development seems overly optimistic, we can attribute that optimism, in part at least, to her temperament; it seems to smack as well of the social Darwinism that was so prevalent in the nineteenth century. Blandina had surely seen a good deal of the evidence for original sin; she seems to have risen above it.

Selections from
At the End of the Santa Fe Trail

November 14, 1875

Three of my senior pupils have gone to Albuquerque to be among the first subjects of the Jesuit Novitiate in these parts. The good Fathers are also to publish a Spanish paper—*The Revista Catolica*—Rest assured, I'm working for subscriptions. I have twelve already. The paper, I know, will be a medium of instruction for our native population....

One of my oldest pupils came to ask to have his sister excused from school. He looked so deathly pale that I inquired, "What has happened?" He answered, "Haven't you heard?"

"Nothing that should make you look as you do."

"Sister, dad shot a man! He's in jail. A mob has gathered and placed men about forty feet apart from the jail to Mr. McCaferty's room. The instant he breathes the last, the signal of his death will be given, and the mob will go to the jail and drag dad out and hang him."

"Have you thought of anything that might save him?" I asked.

"Nothing, sister; nothing can be done."

"Is there no hope that the wounded man may recover?"

"No hope whatever; the gun was loaded with tin shot."

"John, go to the jail and ask your father if he will take a chance at not being hanged by a mob."

"What do you propose doing, Sister?"

"First to visit the wounded man and ask if he will receive your father and forgive him, with the understanding that the full force of the law be carried out."

"Sister, the mob would tear him to pieces before he was ten feet from the jail."

"I believe he will not be touched if I accompany him," I said.

"I'm afraid he will not have the courage to do as you propose."

"That is the only thing I can see that will save him from the mob law. Ask your father to decide. This is Friday. I'll visit the sick man after school this afternoon. Let me know if he will consent to go with me to the sick man's room."

Immediately after school, with a companion, I went to see the wounded man. Sister Fidelis had preceded me. She was writing a letter to his mother bidding her goodbye until they would meet where the Judge was just, and their tears would be dried forever.

I looked at the young man, a fine specimen of honesty and manliness. My heart ached for the mother who expected frequent word from her son, then to receive such news! To be shot unjustly, to die in a strange land, among strangers, so young!

As soon as Sister Fidelis and companion took leave of the sick man, the subject of the present visit was broached. The young man was consistent. He said, "I forgive him, as I hope to be forgiven, but I want the law to take its course."

Fully agreeing with him, he was asked: "Will you tell Mr. _____ this if he comes to beg your pardon?"

"Yes, Sister," he answered.

Friday evening the prisoner's son came to say his father was very much afraid to attempt to walk to Mr. McCaferty's room, but if Sister would walk with him, he would take the chance of having the court pronounce sentence on him.

Early Saturday morning we presented ourselves to the Sheriff in his office.

"Good morning, Sister!

"Good morning, Mr. Sheriff. Needless to ask if you know what is taking place on our two principal streets."

"You mean the men ready to lynch the prisoner who so unjustly shot the young Irishman?"

"Yes. What are you going to do to prevent the lynching?"

"Do? What has any sheriff here ever been able to do to prevent a mob from carrying out its intent?"

"Be the first sheriff to make the attempt!"

"How, Sister?" Standing to his full height—he must be six feet four—he reminded me of a person with plenty of reserve strength, and on the *qui vive* to use a portion of it.

"The prisoner was asked if he would be willing to walk between the sheriff and Sister to the victim's sickbed and ask his pardon." The sheriff interrupted—"Sister, have you ever seen the working of a mob?"

"A few, Mr. Sheriff."

"And would you take the chance of having the prisoner snatched from between us and hanged to the nearest cottonwood?"

"In my opinion, there is nothing to fear." He straightened himself and looked at me, shrugged his shoulders and said, "If you are not afraid, neither am I."

We—the sheriff, my companion and myself—started to walk to the jail. All along the main street and leading to the jail were men at about a distance of a rod apart. These were the men who were to signal Mr. McCaferty's death by three taps of our school bell, in order that the mob might proceed to the jail, take the prisoner and hang him. Our group arrived at the jail, where we encountered the greatest discouragement. The prisoner saw us coming. When we got near enough to speak to him he was trembling like an aspen. We saw his courage had failed him. We paused while we assured him he was safe in going with us.

He hesitated, then said: "I'll go with you." All along the road we kept silence, and no one spoke to us. When we got within a block of the sick man's room, we saw a crowd of men outside his door. It was at this juncture that my fears for the prisoner began. Intent upon saving our protégé from mob law, we hastened to the sick man's door. The crowd made way. Intense fear took possession of me. "Will the prisoner be jerked away when he attempts to enter his victim's room?"

The Sheriff and I remained at the foot of the few steps which led into the room. Meanwhile, I quietly said to the prisoner: "Go in," which he did, myself and companion following. The sheriff remained outside. The door was left wide open that those standing outside might hear the conversation taking place within.

The culprit stood before his victim with bowed head. Fearing a prolonged silence, I addressed the prisoner: "Have you nothing to say?"

He looked at the man in bed and said: "My boy, I did not know what I was doing. Forgive me."

The sick man removed the blanket which covered his tin shot leg, revealing a sight to unnerve the stoutest heart. The whole leg was mortified and swollen out of proportion, showing where the poisonous tin had lodged and the mortification creeping toward the heart.

"See what you have done!" said the wounded man.

"I'm sorry, my boy, forgive me."

"I forgive you, as I hope to be forgiven, but the law must take its course."

I added, "Yes, the law must take its course—not mob law." Those outside the door with craned necks distinctly heard the conversation.

We returned to the jail where the prisoner was to remain until the Circuit Court convened.

From the time Judge Hallet became judge of the Circuit Court, he and his court members have regularly made a visit to the Convent.

September 1876

The pupils and myself will have to be introduced daily to our schoolroom. It will take some time to wear off the novelty of entering a well-lighted, well-ventilated room, flowers in blossom on window sills, blackboard built into the walls, modern desks, and a stage for Friday exercises. I think one of my ambitions has been reached, *viz.:* to walk into my schoolroom and feel that it is "up-to-date" and I, "Mistress of all I survey," particularly of the minds to be taught.

My scattered notes on "Billy the Kid's Gang" are condensed, and some day you will be thrilled by their perusal.

The Trinidad Enterprise—the only paper published here—in its last issue gave an exciting description of how a member of "Bill's Gang" painted red the town of Cimarron by mounting his stallion and holding two six-shooters aloft while shouting his commands, which everyone obeyed, not knowing when the trigger on either weapon would be lowered. This event has been the town talk, excluding every other subject, for the past week.

Yesterday members of the Vigilant Committee came to where I was on our grounds—acting as umpire for a future ball game—and said: "Sister, please come to the front yard. I want you to see one of 'Billy's gang,' the one who caused such fright in Cimarron week before last." My informant passed the news to the Nine and their admirers, so that it became my duty to go with the pupils, not knowing what might take place.

When we reached the front yard, the object of our curiosity was still many rods from us. The air here is very rarefied, and we all are eagle-eyed in this atmosphere. We stood in our front yard, everyone trying to look indifferent, while Billy's accomplice headed toward us.

He was mounted on a spirited stallion of unusually large proportions, and was dressed as the *Toreadores* (Bull Fighters) dress in old Mexico. Cowboy's sombrero, fantastically trimmed, red velvet knee breeches, green velvet short coat, long sharp spurs, gold and green saddle cover. A figure of six feet three, on a beautiful animal, made restless by a tight bit—you need not wonder, the rider drew attention. His intention was to impress you with the idea "I belong to the gang." The impression made on me was the one of intense loathing, and I will candidly acknowledge, of fear also.

The figure passed from our sight. I tried to forget it, but it was not to be. Our Vigilant Club, at all times, is on the alert to be of service. William Adamson, a member of the Club, came excitedly, to say—"We have work on hand!"

"What kind of work?" I asked.

"You remember the man who frightened the people in Cimarron, and who passed our schoolhouse some weeks ago?"

"Yes, William."

"Well, he and Happy Jack, his partner, got into a quarrel, and each got the drop on the other. They kept eyeing and following each other for three days, eating at the same table, weapon in right hand, conveying food to their mouth with left hand.

"The tragedy took place when they were eating dinner. Each thought the other off guard, both fired simultaneously. Happy Jack was shot through the breast. He was put in a dugout 3 x 6 into Trinidad, thrown into an unused adobe hut, and left there to die. He has a very poor chance of living."

"Well, William, we shall do all we can for him. Where did this all take place?"

"At Dick Wootton's tollgate—the dividing line between Colorado and New Mexico."

At the noon hour we carried nourishing food, water, castile soap and linens to the sick and neglected man. After placing on a table what we had brought, my two companions, William Adamson and Laura Menger, withdrew. I walked toward the bed and, looking at the sick man, I exclaimed, "I see that nothing but a bullet through your brain will finish you!"

I saw a quivering smile pass over his face, and his tiger eyes gleamed. My word seemed heartless. I had gone to make up for the inhuman treatment given by others, and instead, I had added to the inhumanity by my words.

After a few days of retrospection, I concluded it was not I who had spoken, but Fear, so psychologists say.

At our first visit I offered to dress the wound, but to my great relief the desperado said, "I am glad to get the nourishment and the wherewith to dress my wound, but I shall attend to it myself." Then he asked: "What shall I call you?"

"Sister," I answered.

"Well, Sister, I am very glad you came to see me. Will you come again?"

"Yes, two and three times a day. Good-bye."

We continued these visits for about two months, then one day the sick man asked: "Sister, why is it you never speak to me about your religion or anything else?"

I looked and smiled.

He continued: "I want to tell you something. I allude to the first day you came. Had you spoken to me of repentance, honesty, morals, or anything pertaining to religion, I would have ordered you out. 'I see that nothing but a bullet through your brain will finish you.' Sister, you have no idea what strength and courage those words put into me. I said to myself, 'shamming here, but the right stuff.' "

Dear Sister Justina, imagine what a load was lifted, to know for a certainty I had not added pain to the downtrodden culprit, for so he is at present. The patient seemed to wish to talk. He asked:

"Sister, do you think God would forgive me?"

I repeated the words of Holy Scripture as they then came to my mind. "If your sins were as scarlet, or as numerous as the sands on the seashore, turn to Me, saith the Lord, and I will forgive."

"Sister, I would like to tell you some things I have done—then, I will ask you, if you think God can forgive me."

Seating myself, I waited, as he continued:

"I have done all that a bad man can do. I have been a decoy on the Sante Fe Trail."

He saw I did not grasp his meaning, so he explained:

"I dressed in my best when I expected to see horsemen or private conveyance take to the Trail. Addressing them politely I would ask, 'Do you know the road to where you are going?' If they hesitated, I knew they were greenies. I would offer to escort them, as the Trail was familiar to me, and I was on my way to visit a friend. We would travel together, talking pleasantly, but all the while my aim was to find out if the company had enough in its possession to warrant me carrying out my purpose.

"If I discovered they did not have money or valuables I would direct the travelers how to reach the next fort. If they possessed money or jewelry, I managed to lose the trail at sunset and make for a camping place. When they slept, I murdered them and took all valuables. The fact of being off the Trail made it next to impossible for the deed to be discovered.

"Another thing I took pleasure in doing was to shoot cows and steer for their hides. I remember one time I shot several cows that belonged to a man from Kansas. I left the carcasses for the coyotes. The old man had a great deal of spunk in him, so he and his herders trailed and caught me with the hides.

"They had a rope with them which they threw over the limb of a tree and placed me under the rope. Before going any farther the old man said to me, 'Say your prayers, young man; you know the law of the plains, a thief is hanged.' I said, 'I'm not a thief, I shot at random. When I saw my shots had taken effect, I took the hides of the animals I had shot. What would you have done?'

" 'I would not have shot at random into a bunch of cows,' he answered. I saw some of the fellows felt sorry for me, and I added: 'Did none of you ever make a mistake? I acknowledged I did wrong.' All but the old man said, 'Let the fellow go,' and waited for the old man to speak. 'Well, if you all think he ought to be let go, I don't say anything against it,' he said. So they let me go. As soon as I got where my pals were, I told them how near I came to being strung up. They all laughed and said I had the young ones to thank that I was able to tell the tale. I added, 'I'll wager ten cents I'll scalp the man and throw the scalp on this counter.' They laughed and took up my wager.

"The next day I went to find in what direction the cattle I had fired into had gone. I soon discovered the herd trail and followed it, and at noon I saw the cattle. The old man was sitting on a stump with his back to me. I slipped up quietly behind him, passed my sharp knife round his head while holding his hair and carried his scalp on a double run to where I had left my bronco; then, whirled to where my pals were. They each had told some of the deeds he had done, and Happy Jack had just finished telling an act which I will not tell you, but I added: 'Here is my last achievement. Scalped a man on a wager of ten cents.' While saying this I threw the scalp on the counter. 'Give me my dime.'

"Sister, now do you think God can forgive me?"

I answered: "Turn to Me in sorrow of heart and I will forgive, saith the Lord."

"Sister, I do not doubt that you believe that God will forgive me: I'm going to tell you what I think God would do. Through you, God is leading me to ask pardon for my many devilish acts."

"He is enticing me, as I enticed those who had valuables; then, when he gets me, He will hurl me into hell, more swiftly than I sent my victims to Eternity. Now what do you think about that, Sister?"

"I will answer you by asking a question. Who was the sinner who asked Christ to remember him when He came into His kingdom?"

"I don't know, Sister."

"It was the malefactor dying at the side of Christ on the cross who called for mercy at the last moment. He was told by the very Christ-God—'This day, thou shalt be with Me in Paradise.'"

"That sounds fine, Sister; but what will my pals think of me? Me, to show a yellow streak! I would rather go to the burning flames. Anyhow, when I get there, I will have to stay chained."

"Experience is a great teacher."

"You bet it is, Sister."

"I'm going to give you an experience." I got the fire shovel and placing two burning coals on it, brought it to the bedside of the patient. "Now place one finger over these coals, or let me tie your hand, so that one finger will burn for ten seconds, then tell me if, in either case, the pain will be diminished."

"Say, Sister, let me think this thing over."

At our next visit the patient did not allude to our last conversation. I do not speak on religious subjects to him unless questioned. This routine work of taking him nourishment, linens, *etc.*, continues. We had been doing it for about four months when this particular incident took place.

On a Saturday morning we arrived at our patient's adobe house when, for the first time, we heard voices in his room. Rapping at the door, the patient in a loud irritated voice called out: "Come in, Sister, and look at these hypocrites and whited sepulchres. Do you know what brought them here? Shame! You shamed them, you, a Catholic Sister, who has been visiting me for over four months and bringing wherewith to keep me alive. You never once asked me whether I was a Jew, Indian, or devil. You shamed them into coming. They say I belong to their church!"

Not noticing the aggressive language, I remarked: "I'm so glad your friends have found you. Should you need us in the future, we will be at your service."

Then one of the ladies of the company said. "It was only yesterday that a member of our Methodist congregation was told that the sick man was a Methodist. She went at once to our minister and he appointed this committee, and we are here, ready and willing, to attend to the sick man."

I told her that it made me happy to know the patient will have his own visiting him.

With a pleasant good-bye, we took our leave. On returning to the Convent, while making our program for sick calls, I remarked: "Billy the Kid's partner has found friends. Rather they have found him, and they intend to give him all the aid he needs. So we will withdraw, but be on the alert, in case we should have to continue our visits." This was said to a member of the Vigilant Club, who always accompanied my companion and myself to this particular patient.

Two weeks had elapsed when our protector of the Vigilant Committee came to the schoolhouse to say: "Sister, Billy's pal needs us again. I visited him several times during the past two days. He told me that no one has been to see him for a week."

So this noon we visited the desperado, the same as we had done at first. His being neglected by those who had promised to attend to him made me think that the ladies we met in his room are perhaps mothers of families, and cannot spare the time from their homes. Again, some of the ladies maybe were as much afraid of him, as I had been, so it is easy to see why they could not keep their promise, but it would have been more just to let me know they were going to discontinue aiding him. Perhaps their husbands did not approve of their visiting a bandit. The general sentiment is, "Let the desperado die."

To-day when we got to the adobe, everything was deathly quiet and the door was ajar. I noiselessly walked in. This is the scene that met me. The patient stretched full length, his eyes glazed and focused on the ceiling; his six-shooter in his right hand with the muzzle pointing to his temple. Quick as a flash I took in the situation and as quickly reached the bedside. Placing my hand on the revolver and lowering the trigger while putting the weapon out of his reach, I remarked: "The bed is not a good place from which to practice target shooting."

He said, "Just in the nick of time, Sister," as though we had not been absent a day. I named the different edibles we had brought him. The subject of the act he was about to commit was never mentioned. By intuition he understood he was not to speak against those who had promised to attend him and did not do so.

Another month passed by and the patient was visibly losing strength. I managed to get his mother's address. She lives in California.

After a week we resumed our visits. At the noon call our patient was quite hilarious. I surmised something unusual had taken place. He lost no time in telling me that Billy and the "gang" are to be here, Saturday at 2 p.m., and I am going to tell you why they are coming.

"Do you know the four physicians who live here in Trinidad?"

"I know three of them," I answered.

"Well, the 'gang' is going to scalp the four of them" (and his tiger eyes gleamed with satisfaction) "because not one of them would extract the bullet from my thigh."

Can you imagine, Sister Justina, the feeling that came over me? One of the gentlemen is our Convent physician!

I looked at the sick man for a few seconds, then said: "Do you believe that with this knowledge I'm going to keep still?"

"What are you going to do about it?"

"Meet your gang at 2 p.m. next Saturday."

He laughed as heartily as a sick man could laugh and said, "Why, Sister, Billy and the gang will be pleased to meet you. I've told them about you and the others, too, who call themselves my church people," but seeing the conversation did not please, he said no more.

In the interval between this visit and the Saturday 2 p.m., which was to be such a memorable day for me, I wrote to his mother not in an alarming strain, but enough to give her to understand he might not recover. Fourteen days later, she arrived. That was quick time, for she depended on mules and horses for conveyance. I cannot give you any idea of the anxiety of the days previous to the coming ordeal of meeting the gang.

Saturday, 2 p.m., came, and I went to meet Billy and his gang. When I got to the patient's room, the men were around his bed. The introductions were given. I can only remember, "Billy, our Captain, and Chism."

I was not prepared to see the men that met me, which must account for my not being able to recall their names.

The leader, Billy, has steel blue eyes, peach complexion, is young, one would take him to be seventeen—innocent-looking, save for the corners of his eyes, which tell a set purpose, good or bad. Mr. Chism—of course this is not his real name—has a most bashful appearance. I judge he has sisters. The others, all fine-looking young men. My glance took this description in while "Billy" was saying: "We are all glad to see you, Sister, and I want to say, it would give me pleasure to be able to do you any favor."

I answered, "Yes, there is a favor you can grant me." He reached his hand toward me with the words: "The favor is granted."

I took the hand, saying: "I understand you have come to scalp our Trinidad physicians, which act I ask you to cancel." Billy looked down at the sick man who remarked: "She is game."

What he meant by that I am yet at a loss to understand. Billy then said: "I granted the favor before I knew what it was, and it stands. Not only that, Sister, but at any time my pals and I can serve you, you will find us ready."

I thanked him and left the room. How much of this conversation was heard by my companion who waited in the corridor, I do not know. Here are the names of the physicians who were doomed to be scalped:

Dr. Michael Beshoar, our Convent and Academy physician; the two Menger brothers. The elder has a large family, the younger is a bachelor. The fourth is Dr. Palmer, whom I know only by reputation. They will never know from me what might have happened.

Life is a mystery. What of the human heart? A compound of goodness and wickedness. Who has ever solved the secret of its working? I thought: One moment diabolical, the next angelical.

April 10, 1860

Dear Sister Justina:

We have just returned from St. Louis with a workman who is an expert and will lay the slate on the Industrial School. Mr. Burke comes with the intention of doing prospecting work. This will exempt us from paying his expenses to return to St. Louis. Our roof will be the first slate roof in the territory.

April 12.—This morning I made a survey of the premises and missed the ten boxes of corrugated iron. Sister Louise was in charge of affairs while we were in St. Louis. I asked Sister Louise what she had done with the corrugated iron.

"Did you not order it to be sold and taken away?"

"Who took it?" I asked.

"Really, Sister, I did not ask his name. He said you told him to sell it, which he succeeded in doing."

I saw we had been over-reached.

The point was to find out who took the iron.

Before we left for St. Louis some gentlemen spoke of forming a gas company. With this in mind I went to the only hardware store in town and asked if anything came of the proposed gas company.

"No, Sister, not yet."

I went to the station agent who asked many questions about our trip. This gave me a chance to ask questions and this was the first:

"Have you had any heavy freighting lately?"

"The heaviest from Santa Fe," he replied, "was your corrugated iron consigned to Colonel Carpenter at Los Cerrillos. I hope Mr. _____ paid you a good price for it, because it was just what the Colonel wanted for his smelter."

So now I know who shipped the iron.

This party has a planingmill and is soliciting orders. I gave him one for some doors and sashes. The order was delivered quickly and in good condition. I gave a second order which likewise was filled promptly and satisfactorily. For the first order I mailed a check by return mail. After the second order was filled, this notice was mailed him:

"Mr. ___, there are forty dollars due you; this being the difference between your bill and the price of the corrugated iron, which you sold. Shall we mail you a check for the amount, or will you be in town soon?"

The next train brought Mr. ___ to Santa Fe.

"Sister, what am I to understand by your letter to me stating you owe me $40?"

"Forty dollars is the difference between the last order we gave you, and the price of the corrugated iron which you sold."

He asked: "What has corrugated iron to do with your order to my mill?"

I told him: "Only this. When you pay for the iron which belonged to us, we shall pay your bill."

He answered: "I see, Sister, you compel me to resort to law to have you pay me what you owe me."

I said: "Suit yourself, Mr. ___."

Thirty-six hours after this interview his wife came to see me.

"Are you Sister Blandina?"

"I am."

"I'm Mrs. ___. Is it possible you are trying to ruin my husband and family by claiming money not owed you?"

"I trust not, Mrs. ___."

"My husband tells me you claim money for a sale of which he knows nothing. Sister, I cannot imagine a Sister of Charity trying to financially ruin a family. My husband put forth every effort to establish a mill for the benefit of this Territory. Now that he is established, you claim money not owed you."

I replied: "Mrs. ___, suppose you let your husband and myself settle this business. I would suggest that you do not make this public—unless your husband tells you to."

"I will make it public. I will not see my husband and family ruined because you claim money not due you. I am going now to your own lawyer and expose you."

"Let me beg of you to permit this affair to be settled between us without any publicity," I entreated. "This I ask for the sake of yourself and family."

Impetuously she answered: "Your plausibility has no effect on me. I go straight to Mr. Catron." With this last answer, she turned toward the door.

I spoke again. "Mrs. ___."

She turned and gave me an indignant look.

I continued: "I will speak more clearly if you will calm yourself."

She retorted: "I am as calm as a wife can be when she sees her husband and children on the brink of ruin and that by a Sister of Charity."

Then I added: "Will you return to your home and deliver to your husband a message from me which I believe will settle our differences?"

Mrs. ___ cheerfully responded, "I will be glad to deliver your message."

This was the message I wrote him:

"Mr. ____ I had hoped this affair would be settled without anyone's intervention.

"You are the consignee of our corrugated iron to Colonel Carpenter at Los Cerrillos. Mr. Conant, the freight agent, has your signature. I did my best to save your reputation and have you retain the love and respect of your wife and children; which to hold or lose is in your hands.

Yours to rehabilitate and not to destroy.

Sister Blandina."

September 21, 1881

We open school to-day. To shelter ourselves from the sandstorms, which are of daily occurrence, we, or rather the Mexican workers, have put up a sort of windshield at the corner of our residence—the corner has collapsed three different times. Father Gasparri has said to me, "For God's sake, Sister, please take it in hand." Mother Josephine thinks I am self-conceited to agree to attend to the constantly collapsing adobe wall.

I went to Santa Fe, engaged an Italian stonecutter, had him lay a stone foundation and carry the stonework halfway above the first story. Naturally, there was no more collapsing. The visitors, Rev. Father Sebastian Byrne, Mother Josephine and Sister Mary Agnes, are desirous to visit the Isleta Indian Pueblo. We are to go there to-morrow.

I predict this Old Town Albuquerque will not long remain the metropolis. Two years ago when Sister Augustine, Sister Dolores and myself came in a private conveyance to Albuquerque there was not a house where the railroad station is now, but the houses are springing up like mushrooms. I foresee that both the Mexicans and Americans here will combine to remove the capital from Santa Fe and have this the capital city. I will continue predicting. The capital will never be removed from Santa Fe while Mr. Thomas B. Catron lives. By the time Mr. Catron disappears, other interests will have taken hold of the minds of the inhabitants outside of Santa Fe, and many will realize that the capital cities in the United States are not usually located in the largest populated towns.

I am going to make a further prediction. The "land-grabbers" will do tremendous havoc among our native population, both spiritually and financially. When you read this, dear Sister Justina, you may be inclined to think I am suffering from indigestion. I wish it were that, and not the clearness of vision which makes me apprehensive for our natives.

Progress will come, I do not doubt, but spiritual death will also come. And "what doth it profit a man if he gain the whole world and lose his own soul?"

You may not know that the Sisters of Loretto had a school in Albuquerque, but withdrew some years ago. The house on the site they occupied is in ruins.

We have taken over the day school taught by the Jesuits. The natives have fallen in line as though we had been here since the place was founded and named after the Duke of Albuquerque, but more particularly with the Territory. For the past fifty years no geographer could map the territory with any certainty, because by the time the map was completed, names and boundaries had been changed. The situation would strongly remind one of some of Europe's wars for certain possessions—Alsace-Lorraine, for instance. The Civil War played havoc with Albuquerque property—not so much by legal confiscation as by illegal contrivance. The territory was a "play ball" for many years. The Navajo and Apache tribes of Indians kept the natives in constant turmoil. So in the end, the "Gringo" was a welcome intruder. This is the information I gathered from the oldest inhabitants, many of who belong to the old school of Spanish aristocracy. No one can deny the refinement of the Spanish race.

Excerpts from a speech made in the House of Representatives, Washington, D.C., taken from records in Santa Fe:

Mr. Richard H. Weightman, Representative cf the Territory of New Mexico, 1852-1853, has this to say:

Should I close my remarks without speaking in their behalf (the natives of New Mexico), I would be unmindful of the courtesies and kindness and hospitality I have invariably received in every part of New Mexico, and be unworthy to represent people who, with frankness and confidence, have trusted me to represent their true condition and promote their interests and happiness. ... I have never met in any part of the United Sates people more hospitable, more law-abiding, more kind, more generous, more desirous of improvement, more desirous that a general system of education should be established among them—more desirous that the many and not the few, should govern, more apprehensive of the tendency of power to steal from the many for the few, more desirous of seeing in their own idiom the Declaration of Independence, the Constitution of the United States, the history and words of the Father of his Country, the messages of presidents and state papers illustrative of the spirit and genius of our government. Among them I have met men of incorruptible integrity, of honor, refinement, intelligence and information.

Some biologists stress the idea that the most refined can become the most cruel. My contact with the Spaniards, natives and mistos, has been most pleasing since my residence in New Mexico. I find a natural culture among the native inhabitants. So much has this impressed me that I lose myself studying the different castes and in each discover an innate refinement never noticed elsewhere. When this village (town now) was founded in 1706, it consisted of thirty families. It requires only an ordinary foresight to picture this sand-stormed place of fifty years hence.

The advent of the A[tchison] T[opeka] and Santa Fe road marks the first stage of progress. Already the rumor has got abroad that a connecting link between the Atlantic and Pacific oceans will be made by a new road whose terminus will be Albuquerque. We are told by the natives that there are gold and turquoise mines not far distant. There is no doubt of coal fields between Lamy Junction and Albuquerque. Granite can be had for the quarrying; good stone abounds throughout the Territory. With "Yankee Pluck," "Land-Grabbers" and "Get-rich-quick" people, what are now sand banks and adobe houses will have been transformed into green fields and stone buildings. The transition period will cause many to forget the end of man's creation.

When the sane period comes, there will be a clearing up of mad-house activities. The conscientious and level headed will emerge serene. The dishonest will fear exposure, the unsophisticated will be submerged, and the Catholic missionary apprehensive and on the alert to prevent wolves in sheep's clothing from entering the flock.

Many former pages back in this journal will have told you I went through this mill-grinding experience. It might more correctly be called an imbecile period. Trinidad did adjust itself, so will Albuquerque. The want of any moral standards is much to be feared. There is an influx of undesirables mixed with those who have thrown their lot with sincere intent to make good lawfully. No hospital, no place to care for abandoned children, no committees to care for the needy. So imagine my work after my teaching period.

Our first attention will be given to the inmates of the jail. As soon as we can get possession of the first house we were to occupy, we will use it for emergency cases. The house has eighteen rooms and a large plaza. I need not mention the want of time to practice on any musical instrument, so will rest on my oars until headquarters sends us reinforcements.

I enjoy many silent laughs at the daintiness of some of our Sisters. Coming home yesterday, we met a Mexican sitting in the public high road. From exhaustion he waited for Providence to assist him. One foot had been cut off some months ago. The stump was festering and bleeding. I became his second crutch until we reached the convent, where the stump was disinfected and dressed. Our dear Sister Mary Alacoque suffered torture, only to hand the dressing bands. I acknowledge the sight was not a bed of white lilies. The man's hair had not felt the teeth of a comb for months. No one could surmise the last time he had dropped into the river for a bath. His clothes shone with ground-in grease. But what of that? You ought to see how Sister Mary Josephine meets every incident with charming serenity!

December 10, 1881.

We are preparing for a Christmas Tree. None of our native children have any knowledge of Santa Claus. Our academic department is attended by American young ladies of all denominations.

We are already securing land where eventually New Albuquerque will be. The railroad station is fully one mile from adobe Albuquerque. Ere long, progress will build adjacent to the railroad station. The Jesuits are planning to put up a church in the same direction. While fortune hunters are making mad rushes to find Aladdin's Lamp, the servants of God work strenuously to land subjects into His court. ...

Most Rev. J. B. Lamy has been in the Territory since 1851. The Sisters of Loretto came in 1852; the Christian Brothers in 1859; and the Sisters of Charity in 1865. From these dates you can see His Grace lost no time in supplying the needs of our native population.

I looked up some old records while in Santa Fe. The facts they contain throw Don Quixote's imaginary occurrences into the shade.

May, 1882.

Preparing a programme for the closing of our schools. Besides our academic departments we teach in the district public school. I am going to tell you my latest on some of our "Want-to-get-rich-quick" people.

A middle-aged lady came to see me. She began by saying "My sons do not know I came to see you! I want to give them a surprise. I heard them say to each other that if they could interest Sister Blandina in their scheme it would be a success. My sons are working to get the right of a ranch, and all they need is a sign like this -X- on paper, and the ranch will be theirs."

I asked: "Is anyone living on the ranch?"

"Only some kangaroos," she answered.

"My sons tell me those who live there are like kangaroos or like coyotes."

I began to understand.

She continued. "My sons thought of shooting them, but my Jim said the road is not clear enough."

I saw the mother was being deceived, and asked:

"Do you realize what your sons mean by a kangaroo, or a coyote?"

She replied, "Animals that cannot talk, I take it."

This conversation took place in our front music room facing the street. I led her to the window, hoping that some of the natives would be passing. To my great satisfaction, Don Perfecto Armijo, with a group of his friends, was standing in earnest conversation. I drew her attention to the gentlemen and asked: "Do they look like dumb animals?"

"Bless my soul, lady, those are nice people!"

"And these people your sons call 'kangaroos or coyotes.' My dear friend, I am going to give you the true facts. Your sons are trying to steal land and call it lawful. You may tell them for me that there is a Vigilant Committee which would be highly pleased to meet them. The committee always carries a rope for just such emergencies as your sons are trying to create."

The dear innocent woman looked at me in surprise, not understanding my meaning. I only repeated, "Tell your sons the Vigilant Committee is active. They will understand."

Questions and Activities

1. Do some searching for Sisters like Blandina in your local church. Consult histories of your parish, its school or a nearby Catholic hospital. Institutions often have anniversary volumes with significant information. Or, perhaps the order which teaches in a nearby school has a biography of its founder. Write up the narrative of one or more of the early Sisters.

2. Turn one of your own nun-memories into a personal essay or short story. Try to highlight the way in which this sister was an incipient feminist or influenced other women (yourself ?) to become a more autonomous woman.

3. Consult the bibliographical essay by Sister Elizabeth Kolmer in *Women in American Religion,* ed. by Janet Wilson James (Philadelphia: University of Pennsylvania Press, 1980), pp. 127-140. Choose another American sister from the nineteenth century whose accomplishments you describe and evaluate in an essay.

4. Interview a selection of Catholics, of various ages, on the role nuns have played in the American Church and in their own lives. Write up the results of your interviews, paying special attention to what may account for the differences in the points of view of your interviewees.

Selected Additional Reading

Burton, Katherine. *Faith is the Substance: The Life of Mother Theodore Guerin.* St. Louis: Herder and Herder, 1959.

Ewen, Mary, O.P. "The Leadership of Nuns in Immigrant Catholicism," *Women and Religion in America* Vol I: The Nineteenth Century, ed. by Rosemary Radford Ruether and Rosemary Skinner Keller. San Franciso: Harper and Row, 1981.

_____. "Removing the Veil: The Liberated Nun of the Nineteenth Century." *Women of Spirit.* New York: Simon and Schuster, 1987.

_____. *The Role of the Nun in Nineteenth-Century America.* New York: Arno Press, 1979.

Horgan, Paul. *Lamy of Santa Fe, His Life and Times.* New York: Farrar, Straus and Girous, 1975.

Kenneally, James J. "Eve, Mary, and the Historians: American Catholicism and Women." *Women in American Religion*, ed. by Janet Wilson James. Philadelphia: University of Pennsylvania Press, 1980.

Melville, Annabelle M. *Elizabeth Bayley Seton.* New York: Scribners, 1951.

Newcomb, Covelle. *Running Waters.* New York: Dodd, Mead and Co., 1947.

Segale, Sister Blandina. *At the End of the Santa Fe Trail.* Milwaukee: Bruce Publishing Co., 1948.

Notes

1. Segale, S.C. Blandina, *At the End of the Santa Fe Trail,* (Milwaukee, Bruce Publishing Co., 1948) 65.

2. Other comparable writings by pioneering nuns in the nineteenth century are *Journals and Letters of Mother Theodore Guerin,* ed. by Sister Mary Theodosia Mug (St. Mary of the Woods, Ind.: Providence Press, 1942) and *The North American Foundations Letters of Mother M. Theresa Gerhardinger,* ed. S.M. Hester Valentine, SSND (Winona, Minn.: St. Mary's College Press, 1977).

3. For documentation of this paragraph and for a more complete evaluation of the state of the question, see the fine bibliographical essay by Sister Elizabeth Kolmer, A.S.C. entitled "Catholic Women Religious and Women's History: A Survey of the Literature," *Women in American Religion,* ed. by Janet Wilson James (Philadelphia: University of Pennsylvania Press, 1980) 127-139.

4. MacHaffie, Barbara J., *Her Story: Women in Christian Tradition* (Philadelphia: Fortress Press, 1986) 120.

5. See Hennesey, James, S.J., *American Catholics* (New York and Oxford: Oxford University Press, 1981) 32 and 86-7.

6. Cogley, John, *Catholic America,* expanded and updated by Rodger Van Allen (Kansas City, MO: Sheed & Ward, 1986). See the entire chapter, "The Schools," 154-172.

7. This relaxation did not come without tension and controversy. Many of the sisters were under the direction of Superiors in Europe who did not understand the new context and saw the requested changes as threatening the holiness of the American sisters. See Ewens, "Removing the Veil: The Liberated American Nun," in *Women of Spirit,* edited by Rosemary Radford Ruether and Eleanor McLoughlin (New York: Simon and Schuster, 1979) 268-9.

8. Hennesey 121.

9. See John Tracy Ellis (ed), *Documents of American Catholic History,* Vol II (Chicago: Henry Regnery Co., 1966) 368.

10. See MacHaffie 93-96 and 118-120.

11. Kenneally, James J., "Eve, Mary, and the Historians: American Catholicism and Women," *Women in American Religion,* 193. Kenneally's entire article is helpful.

12. Quoted in Hennesey 191.

15. Dulles, Avery, S.J., *Models of the Church* (New York: Doubleday and Co., Inc., 1974) 87.

16. For Catholic sisters, the codification of Canon Law in 1919 reinforced these restrictions. A uniform procedure for approving the rules of individual congregations and the imposition of uniform regulations for all religious women, irrespective of history or circumstance brought about a new period of repression. See Ewens, 272f.

17. *At the End of the Santa Fe Trail* 82.

18. Paul Horgan, *Lamy of Santa Fe, His Life and Times* (New York: Farrar, Straus and Giroux, 1975) 321.

19. *Lamy* 322.

8.

"The Crystal in the Rock:" Caryll Houselander

Caryll Houselander was born on October 29, 1901 in Bath, England. Her relationship with the Church was difficult from the beginning and she tells the story of its ups and downs in her religious autobiography, *Rocking-horse Catholic.*[1] She was baptized at the age of six, the result of a sudden conversion on the part of her mother and left the Church at the age of sixteen when she was asked for a penny pew-rent she didn't have at a Sunday service she had struggled to attend. She returned fully to participation in the Church only in 1925, sometime after she had already been engaged in a spiritual journey that was marked by a number of intense religious experiences.

Her childhood was not a happy one.[2] Her family was a network of very difficult personal relationships, fractured by the divorce of her parents when Caryll was eight. Caryll became ill at the time of the divorce, a sign of the added stress the new situation added to her life. The divorce left her in the care of her mother, Gertrude Provis Houselander, a well-meaning and hearty woman whose lack of understanding of her delicately-balanced daughter left permanent scars. The financial situation of the mother's household was precarious; practical considerations as well as a love of company led Gertrude to open a boarding-house. But she was not suited to the situation. She often invited non-paying guests, people down on their luck who touched her overly-generous heart; she wasn't much good at the day to day running of the enterprise, either, and Caryll spent much of her time in her early teens in the arduous and awkward position of general maid, factotum and erstwhile hostess. The physical tasks were beyond her and she was too reserved to enjoy the company. She knew poverty and hard work throughout her life, but rarely was she to be as deprived as she was in her early years of the solitude so necessary to her. Perhaps because of her own difficult childhood, Caryll always had a special sensitivity to children and their needs. She considered her writing for the *Children's Messenger* among her most important tasks and, after the war, she was asked by Dr. Eric Strauss, later to be named President of the Psychiatry Section of the Royal Society of Medicine, to collaborate with him in the treatment of young boys. For some time thereafter, Caryll spent one day a week doing what will come to be called art therapy at a school for disturbed boys. She was also to write perceptively on the topic.

She had some education at convent schools between 1912 and 1917, but it was a scholarship to St. John's Wood Art School that opened the door into the kind of life she would find satisfying. She enjoyed her art studies and she quickly made friends with the somewhat "bohemian" people she met at St. John's. With some of them, she set up a kind of hutch-studio at the foot of her mother's garden, nicknamed the Spooky. Then suddenly, in the midst of this happy time, Caryll became engaged to a rich young man, who employed an Italian countess to teach her deportment.[3] The engagement didn't last long and ended amicably, but it points to an ongoing set of tensions in Caryll's life—between respectability and eccentricity, between particular loves and an all-consuming love, between a love for poverty and a struggle against it.

On the surface, Caryll's life was essentially respectable. When asked how she became engaged, her response was that "it seemed so awfully rude to refuse."[4] Her family background and her convent schooling fitted her to move easily among the cultured middleclass and Catholic intellectuals. Indeed, her early spirituality was quite conventional; she participated in the "spirituality of numbers" so popular in the late nineteenth and early twentieth centuries, counting up rosaries, acts of self-denial and "aspirations" as a sign of spiritual progress. Yet she had an early and enduring affection for people on the social fringe. While still a teenager, she walked the streets of London at night as an escape from the stress in her family home. So comfortable was she among the prostitutes of London that one of them once mistook her for a colleague, advising her to improve her looks if she wanted to get any "customers." Similarly, her affection for artists who paid little heed to the social niceties was not superficial; she found in them a magnanimity of spirit and a joyousness that she was disturbed not to find among more conventionally "spiritual" people. As she said:

> You never hear unkind talk or see unkind deeds among artists, and with them poverty is still honoured, still beautiful. How gladly would I give my life to infuse this gay bohemian spirit into [spiritual] people. Why does spite, envy and cruelty thrive in the porches of churches when love and good will and content go hand-in-hand in so many studios?[5]

Eventually Caryll's love for less-than-respectable people would be integrated into her deep sense of personal vocation, her desire to be a life-force for unity, for the building up of the Mystical Body of Christ. This Catholic doctrine, which became Caryll's own through a process, not of study, but of lived spiritual experience, was to be the integrating reality of her life. More than most, Caryll Houselander's life became *whole,* with one clear focus through which all reality was perceived and understood.

The series of religious experiences through which Caryll appropriated the reality of the Mystical Body began very early. Some of these experiences were clearly mystical and out of the ordinary; others were more ordinary but intensified by Caryll's own particular sensitivity. She was only a child, in her first convent boarding school, when she "saw" the suffering Christ in the person of a Bavarian nun polishing shoes. It was early in the first World War and Sister Mary Benedicta was the single Bavarian sister in a convent of primarily French nuns; she was a lay sister in an educated community, devoted to menial tasks while most of the others were involved in the education of the children. Lonely and alienated, she was discovered by Caryll one day polishing the boarders' shoes and weeping. The young Caryll was abashed by the sight and sat down to help her; when she looked up she saw the nun crowned with thorns.[6] It is significant that the nationality of the nun played some part in the vision. Caryll grew to adulthood in a world intensely aware of national identities and allegiances. In her awareness of the unity of all people in Christ, she struggled to understand the role of nationality as a basis for unity rather than division.

Her second "vision" was even more nationalistic. Hurrying along a London street to buy potatoes, she suddenly saw stretched out against the sky a massive Russian icon of the Crucified Christ the King. Shortly thereafter, she saw a newspaper photograph of the assassinated Czar and recognized his face as that of the Christ of her vision.[7] From this moment on, Caryll was dedicated to the conversion of Russia—a not uncommon Catholic concern at the time—and this commitment led her to her own great love affair. She began to associate with the Russian émigrés in London and there she met Sidney Reilly, a glamorous and worldly man who was one of the earliest members of British Intelligence. Their affair seems to have lasted several years, then Reilly fell in love with someone else and moved out of Caryll's life. But their love had made a permanent impact on her; much later she wrote that "*because* I loved that man I have loved many other people, animals and things"[8] and, when Reilly went back on a mission to Russia from which he never returned, Caryll had yet another experience which she describes as traveling a great distance to a small cell where she suffered greatly with him.

But before that, she was to have a third vision which she describes as "an unimaginably vaster experience than on either of the other occasions." It began on the underground and lasted for several days: everywhere she went, each passer-by and strap-hanger became Christ before her eyes. In everyone, she saw Christ, "living, dying, rejoicing, sorrowing."[9] This vision gave her her deepest understanding of sin, of the reverence which one must have for the sinner as well as an appreciation of what hope means in a sinful world. It was a kind of culmination of her spiritual journey; though she would not return to the Church for some time, the outlines of her personal vocation were clear in the vision and needed only to be filled in with the insight and wisdom gleaned through daily living and the practise of what she had begun to understand. For Caryll, all reality was interpersonal. Though she used the abstract language of "the mystical body" and "the church," these terms had very specific content for her. She thought always in terms of individual and unique persons and was committed to every human being she met as an irreplaceable embodiment of the Risen Christ. She would ever distrust an organized spirituality or a bureaucracy of good works: "We find that it is not the social reformer or the economist or even the church leader who has done tremendous things for the human race," she would affirm, "but the silly saints in their rags and tatters, with their empty pockets and their impossible dreams."[10]

The asceticism of such a love is demanding in the extreme; it involved what was probably the most difficult tension in Caryll's life, that between her artistic work and the ever increasing demands which others placed upon her in the day-to-day exist-

ence. Work was both livelihood and life for Caryll Houselander.[11] She lived always on the brink of real poverty and had
to struggle continuously to pay for the necessities of life, especially during the Second World War and immediately after, when
all of England suffered great deprivation. At the same time, her
writing was as the breath of life to her. But as she became more
and more committed to responding to the needs of everyone who
came to her, she found herself distracted from her work and
drained by the demands of others.[12] Part of that was her
temperament; Maisie Ward describes her mode of action as a
kind of prodigality. "Indeed there was about Caryll in action an
element for which the best word I can find is exorbitance. She
not only did all she had undertaken but she seemed always to
think up ways of adding to her own burden."[13] When her life-
long friend Iris Wyndham took on the care of her grandchild,
Caryll agreed to take care of the child at night in her bed-sitter.
This meant that she had to relegate her writing—probably of
The Comforting of Christ and *Guilt*—to the hours of 10:00 p.m. to
3:00 a.m. in her tiny bathroom.[14] The drain on her physical and
psychic energy was enormous, but her love for the tiny Clare illuminated those endlessly long days. Caryll continually over-
worked in the service of others even while she yearned for
solitude. Her health was poor all of her life, and yet she sometimes welcomed her recurrent bouts of illness as a chance for
peace and quiet, as she did when hospitalized for pneumonia in
1950. She wrote to her friend Henry Tayler showing quite clearly that her tension over the artistic work which was part of her
very being and her loving devotion to others was never fully
resolved. She writes:

> One thing this illness has taught to me; it has made me
> realize that though God has given me gifts, I have never
> in all my life, for one single week, been free to *enjoy* them.
> They have always been violated, scamped, hurried, fitted
> into other people's convenience, and never allowed to
> grow. They might never have come to much in the way of

art, and now they certainly won't, for I am too old, and, in spite of this little resurgence of life, too broken to develop talents now, even *if* I ever could have. But one thing I am sure, they could come to great personal happiness, and they should do—that alone is a real thanksgiving to God, and now I am going to achieve that. What remains to me of life, I am going to live happily. . . .[15]

Her vision of the mystical body, so eloquent when she described it, was an endless source of suffering and of joy in the concrete experience. It created a continual tension in her striving to be faithful to her own gifts and unique personality.

At first reading, the life and work of Caryll Houselander does not fit easily into feminist categories. She lived in a Catholic context in which fixed feminine roles were not disputed and she began no debate on the subject. She does not give any evidence that the restrictions placed on women by church or society in any way constrained her. Much of her writing was about children; if read quickly she may seem to imply that women's reality is somehow determined by the maternal role. But, in fact, she believes that motherhood is a universal vocation. All are called to give birth to the Christ within; every person is the mother of her own soul (#3). There are other elements of Caryll's life which challenge the stereotypes, and her central passion for unity among all people in the body of Christ, illustrates a concern of Christian women in every century.

At a time when the norms for "respectable women" were very clearly laid out, Caryll Houselander refused to accept the limitations that those norms implied. She eschewed the two choices open to conventional Catholic women of her day. She neither married nor entered a convent; the vocation to "single life" was not much encouraged in the rhetoric of the time and, though Maisie Ward suggests that Caryll "would very much have liked to be married,"[16] it is because Ward seems otherwise unable to account for her passion for Sidney Reilly.[17] Caryll slowly evolved her sense of her own particular vocation by paying serious attention to her own temperament and gifts. When she speaks of finding her own vocation, she is not at all talking about "state in life" as vocation was most often understood then. She is speaking instead of her own deepest conviction of the unique and irreplaceable reality of every person; she was determined to live that reality as it unfolded day to day. In her own life, she ignored the distinctions between sinners and conventional persons and allowed her love to embrace prostitutes, the national enemy, and the neurotic. She even seems to have attempted to "dress the part" of the eccentric, the unconventional. Somewhere in her late twenties or early thirties, she began to wear a kind of opaque, white face powder. No one knew exactly why she did this; she herself said it was because her face was too pink. But it had the effect of making her odd and she continued to do it, even after she saw the uncomfortable reaction of others.[18] Free of social and ecclesiastical stereotypes, she chose her own life and many of the details in it. It is a freedom that still eludes many on all sides of the feminist debate who insist on talking in terms of gender.

Caryll Houselander's vision of Christ among the masses of London was the passion she lived by; like Blandina Segale, she anticipated the public teaching of the Catholic Church in her lived understanding of what the Church was. Pius XII published his encyclical on the mystical body, *Mystici Corporis*, on June 29, 1943. This document had significant impact on ecclesiology in the decades which followed because it was a significant step away from the impersonal image of the Church as institution to a more interpersonal understanding of Church. This was the notion of church that Caryll lived by long before the encyclical was written and, unlike Pius XII, she thought of the Mystical Body not as composed of actual baptized Christians alone but of all those whom Christ loved and for whom He died. Perhaps this is even more significant in light of the sensitivity to national distinctions in her day. As we have seen above, her sense of mystical communion with the whole world did not ignore nor abrogate her awareness of nationality; rather it was shaped by that awareness. This is dramatically evident in her encounter with a German woman soon after the first World War. At first she finds the woman "full of bitterness" and "offensive," but she prays for her and begins to see how her love for her country had torn her apart. Caryll says: "... I saw her with Germany in the form of a child, trying to hide the child's faults with one hand and to bind up his wounds with the other."[19] When she worked in the British Censorship office in 1942, it was the hate propaganda leveled at Germany that she found most disturbing; this in spite of the fact that, like everyone else, she lived in a state of almost continual terror because of the Blitz. In this, she seems to anticipate some of the themes of the feminist social activists of our own day (Dorothy Day, Mother Teresa and Dorothee Sölle come to mind) in their insistence that the human family is one and that to hate the enemy is the ultimate self-destruction. This is a prominent theme in the Christian feminist tradition.

The piece which follows, entitled "Justice," is taken from *The Passion of the Infant Christ,* published in 1949.[20] It was written when she was involved in caring for the infant Clare, mentioned above, and reflects her work with emotionally and mentally disturbed boys in the school at Frensham. It is an extended meditation which begins with a contemplation of the actual children displaced and disoriented by the war which has just ended. It leads, then, by a process of association to a consideration of others whose situation of dispossession and unwilling dependence confers on them the status of children: the elderly, emotionally disturbed, those alienated and dispossessed because of race, expatriates, the incarcerated. Finally it moves in an ever-widening vision to a reflection on the condition of nations, also like children because they have been conquered, dominated and exploited by others. Throughout the piece, Caryll sees a single norm of justice that must be applied to all, individuals and nations alike.

That norm is the biblical understanding of "justice." Caryll arrived at this understanding of justice, not through the study of ethics, but through prayer, scriptures and liturgy. Her two models of justice are God, whose divine justice is central to the scriptures, and St. Joseph, who is called 'the just one' in those same scriptures. Caryll's understanding of divine justice is very faithful to the entire sweep of the Old Testament where God's justice is identical with His saving love and mercy. As she explains, the justice of God encompasses mercy and love because God acts, not according to the laws of human behavior, however noble, but according to his own inner reality. It is the inner reality of God—the ultimate "law" of which human law is but a pale reflection—that mandates mercy as the very fulfillment of justice. Justice in God is, as Caryll says, "the extreme logic of love" (#15). When translated into human terms, God's justice gets subdivided, as it were, into various human virtues (mercy, forgiveness, justice) which seem, if not at odds with each other, at least in painful tension. But in God, the entire plan for creation and redemption is both just and merciful. In Caryll's meditation, divine justice is most perfectly mirrored in the act of parenting—not the biological bearing of children but the ongoing nurturing of fragile life that transforms justice into "...the defense of the defenseless. It protects the weak, and restores to little ones those things of which they have been robbed by force" (#13).

For Caryll, St. Joseph is the biblical human model of this justice. St. Joseph, called the "just one" in Matthew because he fulfills "the whole law and the prophets," subsumes all the details of the law into the greater reality of holiness, in which love and mercy, as they do in God, are fused again. Caryll is not sentimental about this; she lives, after all, in a world where violence and exploitation are all around her and she does not advocate passivity. She describes justice as a kind of two-edged sword. On the one hand, it requires, as she says, "forgiving the injury done to ourselves" (#13). Christian justice cannot countenance retaliation. It cannot be used as a mask for "the relief of hurting as I have been hurt ..." (#11). Justice equally requires that we protect the little and the weak. We cannot ask the powerless to forgive injustices done against them (#13). We must speak up for them and Caryll is aware that this involves keen personal renunciation, even danger. Nowhere is this more true than when the individual Christian speaks up in a politically antagonistic environment for defeated and exploited countries. Caryll knows what is required if Christian peace is to be more than a personal privilege or a passive acquiescence to historical determinism.

> Justice constrains us to insist openly on the rights of the little nations, to make penance for the sins against them, in our own lives, to give all that we can for their relief, and to be ready, if it is expedient to do so, to give our lives for the restoring of the freedom of the Divine Child in their midst (#18).

Though Caryll Houselander lived before the great social encyclicals of John XXIII and Paul VI, she anticipated their thinking (as she had anticipated the thought of Pius XII); she expressed herself in mystical language, however, and her appeal is to individual conscience rather than to government.

This is Christian social teaching at its best: social justice informed by personal holiness and the Christian vision of life, built on self-sacrifice and requiring personal action and commitment. In its own way, hers is a call to action, but not to an action born of anger. She does not minimize the sufferings of others; she does not lay responsibility for that suffering on the system or on vague generalities such as sin or society. She recognizes "the network of interdependence which spreads the responsibility for every sin not only among countless people but over many generations ..." (#12). She also refuses to deny the redemptive value of any suffering. No matter how pointless any person's death may seem to be, "it is Christ on the Cross who dies in all their deaths"

(#15). All suffering is to be understood as potentially redemptive; no one's suffering is without meaning if it is accepted and offered. But all exploitation and violence is to be fought against, whether by the redemptive forgiveness of the injury done to the self or by protecting others—especially the weak—from the injuries done by the powerful. Caryll's gentle voice is essentially a voice of protest.

Along the way in this little piece, she voices protest against some prevailing attitudes of her time, including some specifically Catholic distortions. She speaks of attitudes—both social and religious—that affirm value only to the married woman and the nun. Here we get some small insight into Caryll's own sense of her single vocation. She describes the negative criticisms she undoubtedly heard: that celibacy was "either a disease or a disgrace and, in either case, a disaster," especially if such an "empty" life were not filled up with making money (#8). She also paints a positive picture of those who live singly, but with genuine love for others. Sensitive and humble, they have special access to the lowly; they fan the spark of life "with the warm breath of their humanity" and "reverence the solitude of other people's souls" (#10).

People like this are very different from the kind of "reformers" for whom Caryll had such distaste, even scorn. She believed, as she explains here, that they were motivated by "an unrecognized sense of power or vanity" (#9) and always felt that they were more likely to do harm than good. Caryll had great difficulty with organized welfare groups. An early attraction to the Grail movement gradually gave way to a desire to keep her distance. She wrote to Lucille Hasley a rather scathing description of what she called the "Catholic Worker" type of spirituality[21] and when she decided, with friends, to do some kind of concrete, organized "charity" work, it was of the most loose and secret sort. They organized the "Loaves and Fishes" to alleviate the needs of individuals whom they encountered. They engaged in no money-making schemes; like the gospel story from which they took their name, they merely shared what little they had. They invented elaborate stratagems to protect their own anonymity as well as the dignity of the recipients (non-existent contests and lotteries being particularly favored). The group was organized in the economic depression of the twenties and Caryll was active in it until her death. Maisie Ward, conscripted into the work after she met Caryll, describes how "a visit to a theater or cinema, a 'slap-up meal' or a bottle of wine given to the depressed and discouraged ..."[22] was part of the plan of action in the forties. In those hard days, people were as hungry for joy and beauty as they were for the necessities of life; such things, which some may term luxuries, had a large place in the view of justice by which Caryll lived.

But if Caryll protested against the organized social worker type of spirituality, she is equally harsh here in her indictment of those bookkeepers of the spiritual life who keep a "double entry account of their kindness and have a balance sheet of 'merit' " (#10). This was a very common Catholic distortion of spirituality in Caryll's day (and even, of course, much later). Caryll herself had passed through an early stage of counting— both good deeds and sins—as a form of spiritual life. But once she grew out of it, she recognized this as another form of vanity. One might complain that Caryll Houselander had critical words for every form of spirituality except her own. To the end of her life, she descried her own two vices, an addiction to cigarettes and to an overly critical habit of mind. But she was rigorous in her demands for reality in Christian life and, for her, the most all-encompassing reality was the organic unity of all people in the redeeming Christ. Unless Christian life was a manifestation of this reality, Caryll had little use for it. Her passion for reality gives her writing an astringency which only sharpens the compassion that permeates her thought.

Justice and mercy, astringency and compassion, cigarettes and visions—perhaps Caryll's Houselander's importance and charm lie in her refusal to separate what others seem to see as incompatible. Her vocation was to become herself; in being true to that vocation, she liberated herself to become both a "divine eccentric" and a woman of justice.

"Justice," from
The Passion of the Infant Christ

1. Abroad the Infant Christ is hunted and persecuted. In England He has become a foundling. He who has said to us with such tenderness: "I will not leave you orphans," has been left an orphan in countless souls where He lives, but is forgotten, neglected and even unknown.

There are many of whom this tragic indictment is true and who yet are not culpable for it. The vast number of English people, whose baptism was regarded by their parents as a social occasion, not as a Sacrament; whose godparents were chosen not for their Faith, but for the material advantages which might result from the compliment paid to them; who have been brought up "free to choose their own religion," which is to say without any definite teaching about any religion at all, in an atmosphere of shifting prejudice, doubt and materialism, with no example of Christian practice in their homes, and instead of it a general understanding that any outward adherence to God is in bad taste and the whole subject of Faith sufficiently embarrassing to be taboo in polite conversation.

2. Moreover, they grow up in an environment of materialism, by which they are necessarily submitted to the daily suggestion that the only really unimportant things are the things of spirit.

Attendance at church is mainly confined to weddings and funerals and occasional national days of prayer; but with the increase of Registry Office weddings and the lack of immediate danger of invasion, funerals take the lead, so that, to the very people who most fear death, and who avoid facing its inevitability, the thought of God becomes associated with the thought of death, and from this it follows naturally that they shrink from the very idea of the personal love of God, as a form of morbidity.

3. What has happened to the little flame of Christ-life that illuminated these souls on the day of their baptism?

If they have not killed their supernatural life by deliberate sin, Christ remains in their lives, but is orphaned in them. They do not know the wonder of the Motherhood that they have forfeited; if they have any culpability, it is in that their souls are too noisy, with the clamour of the fears and desires and pleasures and grievances that they continually entertain, to hear the weeping of the tiny child in their house.

There is in this one more note in the unity of the Passion and the Infancy. The Divine Child takes upon Himself the characteristic sorrows of the race in which He abides. In His infancy in us, He is identified with the suffering that our sins have inflicted on our children.

4. Divorce, arrogance and thoughtlessness have given us a nation of spiritually starved children. Over a thousand of them between six and twelve years old, evacuated from London during the war, were questioned concerning their knowledge of God by a group of people temporarily responsible for them; out of them all, one only was familiar with Christ's Holy Name—as a swearword; not one knew that Christ was God, or even who God is.

The Christ-Child in the soul of the average English man or woman is a forgotten, unwanted child, waiting for adoption in a children's "home" that is not a home, for it is without beauty and without love.

5. "The sins of the fathers are visited upon the children." How true that is and how baffling! It seems the limit of injustice. But, because the sins of the whole race are visited upon the *Christ Child in us,* whose sorrow redeems, we see that here is the mysterious justice of God which is the logic of extreme love.

Our sins are visited upon our children; but the sorrows of our children are carried in the Divine little hands which, though they have been folded in death, have unfolded and lived to open the buds of two thousand springs with their touch.

6. Besides those who do not know the mystery of their own being there are others in whom the Christ-Child needs fostering; people who through circumstances share some essential characteristic of childhood: dependence, poverty, the necessity to obey, and so on. Very old people and invalids, the nervously unstable, "borderline cases" who are avoided instinctively by happier people. Prisoners, the inmates of workhouses, institutions and asylums. Coloured people segregated by soulless conventions, psychosthenics, workers who are subject to the authority of others, conscripts to the Services, sinners who have lost their way like bewildered children lost in a city. And children who are really children in years, but in whom the Divine Child is neglected: spoilt children, nurse-bound children, delinquent children, children without homes.

Besides all these, and many more, there are those who share the outward circumstances of the Infant Christ in Bethlehem, in the desert, in Egypt.

Foreigners, strangers here, who have fled from their own countries, where they are not strangers but of the family and at home. Jews, who have perceived the prophecies in the storm of suffering scattering their race, and by becoming Christians have given birth to the Messiah in Israel. Converts, in whom the

Faith is still a newborn, naked Child, blinded by the blaze of the light of glory, and even by the flicker of the votive candles!

7) The Divine Foundling has His fosterparents in the world.

Every mother may contemplate the Infant Christ in her own children. But there is also a vocation of motherhood for the childless. Listen to these mysterious words of Our Lord: "Whosoever doeth the will of My Father who is in Heaven, is My brother, My sister *and My Mother*" (Mt 7:50).

There are nuns who mother Christ in orphans and in schoolchildren; but it not of these that I am speaking, but of those celibates who seem to have no place or *raison d'être* at all in the eyes of the world, but who, nevertheless, know well the truth of those words, "many are the children of the barren, more than of her who has a husband."

8. To be a fostermother or father of the orphaned Christ is a sublime vocation; it exacts a profound humility from those who are called to it and confers a unique majesty upon them. Very often, the worldly pass such people by with a vaguely uncomfortable contempt; they regard celibacy itself as either a disease or a disgrace and, in either case, a disaster. Lives that are neither those of married people nor of vowed religious, which are not breathless with social success or obsessed with making money; lives so "empty" that there is time in them to "go about doing good," as Christ did on earth; lives which are, in fact, spent largely with the lowly and the outcasts and the insignificant seem, to the vast masses of mediocracy, to be deserts of arid waste, stony, uncultivated wilderness. But in the eyes of God, they are the wilderness that flowers. If they are in a wilderness, these fosterparents of the Child Jesus, they are there with the angel who comforted Christ after the forty days of fasting, and with their prototype St. Joseph with the Infant Christ in the desert.

9. "Thus saith the Lord: the land that was desolate and impassable shall be glad, and the wilderness shall rejoice and shall

flourish like the lily. It shall bud forth and blossom, and shall rejoice with joy and praise: the glory of Libanus is given to it; the beauty of Carmel and Sharon; they shall see the glory of the Lord, and the beauty of our God."

These fosterparents of Christ are not those terrible reformers of individual lives who, urged and driven by an unrecognized sense of power or vanity, interfere with people's lives, fumbling at the locked doors of their souls with clumsy fingers, and bruising when they touch to heal.

They are, on the contrary, sensitive people who approach others not with exhortation, but with sympathy. Not with self-satisfaction but with humility.

10. They give and they listen, they see the spark of life wherever it is and fan it by the warm breath of their humanity; they reverence the solitude of other people's souls; they bear other people's burdens and rejoice in their joy, without imposing upon them. Not only do they tread delicately not to crush the broken reed, but they go down on to their knees to bind it up. They take the neglected Christ Child to their own hearts instinctively and comfort Him.

They are those people who will be amazed when Christ calls them on the day of judgment and greets them by telling them that they gave Him food and shelter and clothed Him and came to Him in prison. For it is certainly not those who make a double entry account of their kindness and have a balance sheet of "merit" prepared against the day of wrath who will receive this lovely recognition and be astonished by it.

"Then shall the just answer Him, saying: Lord, when did we see Thee hungry and fed Thee, thirsty and gave Thee drink? And when did we see Thee a stranger and took Thee in? or naked and covered Thee?" And the King answering, shall say to them: "Amen, I say to you, as long as you did it to one of these, My least brethren, you did it to Me."

11. They are "the just"; and of St. Joseph, Christ's earthly fosterfather, the Evangelists tell us this one thing without elaboration: he was "a just man."

Justice and just people are the world's present crying need. Justice is a word that is on many lips and in few hearts, for it is little understood.

When we say, "I must have justice!" we usually mean, "I must have the relief of hurting as I have been hurt, of despoiling as I have been despoiled."

"Blessed are those who hunger and thirst after justice" does not mean, "Blessed are those who are tormented by a personal grievance against life," or "Blessed are those who, having put themselves in the place of God, have judged others and now itch to see their sentences carried out."

12. Justice is not vengeance, it is love; in it is included forgiveness; yet there are many who think that forgiveness is *in* justice!

If it were, Christ would not have commanded us to forgive as often as we are injured, or have made that, for each one of us, the condition of our own forgiveness in His day of judgment.

If we knew the heart of man as God knows it, and the network of interdependence which spreads the responsibility for every sin not only among countless people but over many generations, we should not attempt to untwist the skeins of right and wrong. For us, justice is to forgive and to make reparation ourselves for all sin.

We must be just not because we are judges, for that we are not; but because we are trustees of God's love to the world, and justice is a supreme expression of His love. Justice belongs to God, it is a tender expression of His tenderness and pity.

13. By this word "pity," I do not mean the contemptuous patronage from which sensitive people shrink. Pity is the gentle-

ness of the strong. It is compassion that identifies the strong with the weak in suffering. It is the skill and gentleness of the strong hand, that lifts without breaking and tends without hurting the open wound. It is the expression of the selfless love that is born of compassion, of the sharing of the sorrow. Love which brings the strong man to his knees to wipe the tears from the face of the tiny child in reverence and awe.

Justice is the defense of the defenseless. It protects the weak, and restores to little ones those things of which they have been robbed by force.

The forgiveness demanded of us by justice means forgiving the injury done to ourselves. We may leave it to others to forgive the injury done to them; this more especially when they are weak and wronged by the strong and powerful; for then the just must come to their defense.

14. St. Joseph, the "just man" who was Christ's foster father, is an example of this. The gray-bearded statues of him that we are used to, and drugged by, quite misrepresent his character. He was one who did violence to himself, who accepted hardship and danger, and renounced self to protect the little and the weak. In that mysterious anguish of misunderstanding of Our Lady, his one thought in the midst of his own terrible grief was how to save the Divine Infant from Herod. He, like all those who cherish the life of an infant, had to give up all that he had in order to give himself. We know nothing of him after Christ's boyhood; all that is recorded of him is that he protected Our Lady in Advent; that he was the first to protect the unknown, unguessed Christ in another; and that he was the defense of the Infant Christ when he was defenseless and threatened by Herod. A just man and a strong man. Love was in him like the crystal in the rock. Justice is both the tenderest and the sternest expression of God's Fatherhood: it is the inflexible logic of Divine Love.

15. It is both the kiss of peace on our mouth and the sword in our hand. It is the sword in the hand of pity.

That which in our eyes seems unjust is often the extreme logic of love which is justice.

It seems unjust to us, when young men in the Maytime of their lives, and often the gentlest of them, must go to war and be slain; when the poet must die with the poem still in his heart, the love with his love still unconsummated.

But it is Christ on the Cross who dies all their deaths. In Him, in the Word of God's love, all poetry is uttered; in Him, incarnate Love, all love is consummated. On the field of Calvary, the battle between love and death is fought, which restores the Kingdom of Heaven to the children whom Satan has despoiled.

Justice is the rich giving to the poor; the strong defending the weak; the injured forgiving the injurer. Calvary was all that. There, Christ was the young man slain, but He was the rich man giving to the poor, innocence forgiving sinners, the hero restoring the Kingdom of Heaven to the lowly.

16. Today justice must restore the Kingdom of Heaven to the little nations. The nations which are little, not in their territory, but in their participation in Childhood.

Sorrowful countries in the power of tyranny, outwardly depersonalized by the pattern of ideology imposed upon them by force, their own characteristics and racial beauty effaced for the time being, stripped of their national dress, as Christ was stripped of His garments. Poor as children; subject as children; helpless as children.

These little countries are Bethlehems. It is certain, because the conditions of the Incarnation are realized in them, that in them the Incarnation is taking place. In many afflicted lives, clothed in the drab uniformity of the tormentor's bleak mind,

Christ is born—"He has not comeliness whereby you shall know Him."

17. God does not change—the Nativity, true to His plan, takes place, as it always has, in secrecy, in humility, in darkness.

In that darkness shines the Star of Bethlehem.

Lift up your eyes and see the star, burning over the martyr countries of the world.

We cannot cast off our responsibility to these Bethlehems. We cannot, unless we wish to identify ourselves with Pilate, wash our hand of Czechoslovakia and Poland.

We cannot, unless we wish to be identified with the crowd that shouts out, "Crucify Him," leave Austria, Germany, Hungary to be torn to pieces by men who hate God.

We cannot delude ourselves that time and distance efface the guilt of unexpiated sin.

What doom awaits us if we, who assented to the choice of Barabbas in Czechoslovakia in 1938, betray the already betrayed Christ again there a second time!

What doom awaits us if we are among those who have said of Hiroshima and Nagasaki: "Their blood be upon us and upon our children!"

What doom awaits us if we are one of those who insult the face of Poland with the kiss of Judas!

18. Justice constrains us to insist openly on the rights of the little nations, to make penance for the sins against them, in our own lives, to give all that we can for their relief, and to be ready, if it is expedient to do so, to give our lives for the restoring of the freedom of the Divine Child in their midst.

For in them Christ will be born again; that lovely truth which haunts Herod down the ages will be realized—any child may be Christ. In any humble, frustrated life, Christ may be born. It may be that in the heart of an old peasant, who has lost all his sons, the Divine Son will be born, and the old man will be made new, and his life will renew the earth. It may be that in the life of some forgotten prisoner, the Incarnation will take place, and there, secretly, in swaddling-bands, the country's life will begin again. It may be that in the soul of a hungry little child, the Light that illuminates the whole world will begin to shine in the darkness.

19. When Christ, born secretly in the little nations, in the martyr countries of the world, is recognized and worshipped openly, those countries will be clothed in their own particular heritage of beauty once more and receive back their own individual character.

Then the meek will inherit the earth, the earth that has nourished them like a mother; that has flowered for them and given them their bread. The earth on which their homes were built; the earth that has been watered with the blood of their sons and in which their sires sleep.

The gentle one, in whose power the meek will inherit the earth, will be the Child Christ, crowned as King.

20. Then the bereaved will see the Child King again; and He will have the face of one of their own sons. In Germany, He will be a fair boy with wide, blue eyes, and suddenly German children will laugh again; in Poland, He will be grave, but with childhood's gravity, and will turn to the people the face of dusky gold and the damson eyes of their little sons. In France, His sceptre will be the crook of the shepherd boys their sons were long ago. In Japan, He will walk among the reeds on naked delicate feet, and to every parent the little Child of ivory will come back. In Russia He will come back again among the peasants,

the oval of His grave and holy face caressed by the flickering of the icon lamps.

When the Christ Child is crowned again in the little nations, then, and only then, there will be Peace on earth.

"And thou Bethlehem Ephrata, art a little one among the thousands of Judah: out of thee shall He come forth unto me that is to be the ruler in Israel: and His going forth is from the beginning, from the days of Eternity ... and this man shall be our Peace."

Questions and Activities

1. Read one of Caryll Houselander's works in its entirety. Write an essay in which you comment on it according to the judgment made in the last paragraph of the introduction, that she refused to separate what others see as incompatible.

2. Reflect on the Beatitudes in Luke 6:20-26 and think about your own network of friends and acquaintances. What contacts do you have with people who are on the fringe of respectability or who are described by Luke as blessed? What keeps you away from people who are very different from you? Do any of the people in your life qualify as "dispossessed children" such as Caryll Houselander describes? Reflect on what you have learned or could learn from "the saints in rags and tatters."

3. Spend a day (or longer) as a volunteer at a Catholic Worker house or in a comparable situation. Reflect on your experience there and write an essay on the inner meaning of that experience, borrowing Caryll Houselander's *genre* but not her thoughts. You might find it helpful to compare both essays after yours is complete.

4. Take a walk along a busy street in your city or town or, alternatively, take a ride in a city bus. Look carefully at all the people you see and imagine that you see them as Caryll once did, with the face of Christ. How difficult or easy is the exercise? Do you think you could sustain this kind of personal vision for any length of time? What effect might it have on your experience of your own life?

Selected Additional Reading

Houselander, Caryll. *The Reed of God.* London: Sheed & Ward, 1944.

_____. *The Dry Wood.* New York: Sheed & Ward, 1947.

_____. *The Flowering Tree.* New York: Sheed & Ward, 1945.

_____. *Guilt.* New York: Sheed & Ward, 1951.

_____. *The Mother of Christ.* London: Sheed & Ward, 1978.

_____. *The Passion of the Infant Christ.* New York: Sheed & Ward, 1949.

_____. *The Risen Christ.* London: Sheed & Ward, 1959.

_____. *Rocking-Horse Catholic.* New York: Sheed & Ward, 1955.

Sölle, Dorothee. *Of War and Love.* New York: Orbis Books, 1983.

Ward, Maisie. *Caryll Houselander: That Divine Eccentric.* New York: Sheed & Ward, 1962.

_____. ed. *The Letters of Caryll Houselander.* New York: Sheed & Ward, 1965.

Notes

1. New York: Sheed & Ward, 1955.

2. The only biography of Caryll Houselander is that by Maisie Ward entitled *Caryll Houselander: That Divine Eccentric* (New York: Sheed & Ward, 1962).

3. Ward, *Eccentric* 600-62.

4. Ward, *Eccentric* 62.

5. Quoted in Ward, *Eccentric* 84.

6. *Rocking-Horse Catholic* 72-74.

7. *Rocking-Horse Catholic* 110-113.

8. Letter to Christine Spender, *The Letters of Caryll Houselander,* ed. by Maisie Ward (New York: Sheed & Ward, 1965) 109.

9. *Rocking-Horse Catholic* 137-139.

10. Quoted in Ward, *Eccentric* 201-2.

11. See, for instance the letter to Archie Campbell, *Letters* 59-60.

12. See, for instance, *Eccentric* 209.

13. *Eccentric* 229.

14. *Eccentric* 230.

15. Ward, *Letters* 95.

16. *Eccentric* 272.

17. *Eccentric* 76. Ward tries to correct the language of Caryll's letter on the subject. Where Caryll sees that her love for Reilly has *caused* her to love more widely, Ward assumes that it is the renunciation of that love which has increased her capacity for loving. Caryll's words do not imply that.

18. *Eccentric* 123-4.

19. Quoted in Ward, *Eccentric* 87.

20. London: Sheed & Ward.

21. Ward, *Letters* 225-6.

22. *Eccentric,* pp. 125-128.